RAISING EMPOWERED DAUGHTERS

A DAD-TO-DAD GUIDE

MIKE ADAMICK

SEAL PRESS

For Emmeline and billions of girls like her.

May we be decent dads so you no longer have to break glass for simple equality.

Until then, may we provide the hammers.

Seal Press
Hachette Book Group
1290 Avenue of the Americas, New York, NY 10104
sealpress.com
@sealpress

Printed in the United States of America

First Edition: June 2019

Published by Seal Press, an imprint of Perseus Books, LLC, a subsidiary of Hachette Book Group, Inc. The Seal Press name and logo is a trademark of the Hachette Book Group.

The Hachette Speakers Bureau provides a wide range of authors for speaking events. To find out more, go to www.hachettespeakersbureau.com or call (866) 376-6591.

The publisher is not responsible for websites (or their content) that are not owned by the publisher.

Print book interior design by Amy Quinn.

Library of Congress Cataloging-in-Publication Data

Names: Adamick, Mike, author.
Title: Raising empowered daughters: a dad-to-dad guide / Mike Adamick.
Description: New York, NY: Seal Press, [2019] | Includes bibliographical
    references.
Identifiers: LCCN 2018041437| ISBN 9781580058650 (pbk.) | ISBN 9781580058643
    (ebook)
Subjects: LCSH: Fathers and daughters. | Parenting. | Feminism.
Classification: LCC HQ755.85 .A327 2019 | DDC 306.874/2—dc23
LC record available at https://lccn.loc.gov/2018041437

ISBNs: 978-1-58005-865-0 (paperback), 978-1-58005-864-3 (ebook)

LSC-C

10 9 8 7 6 5 4 3 2 1

CONTENTS

Introduction

—1—

THE EARLY YEARS

Chapter 1—Clothes Hounds

How simple T-shirts lead to big differences in how we raise our kids.

—21—

Chapter 2—Nature Versus Nurture

*There are real, proven gaps between the sexes, but not as many
as we create in our parenting and societal messages.*

—35—

Chapter 3—The Low Dad Bar

*In expecting very little from dads, society does two things at once: cut
dads out of the everyday lives of our children, and pigeonhole women as
the caretakers. It's a lose-lose paradigm we can shift together.*

—45—

Chapter 4—You Are What You Eat

*We bombard children with horrible messages that appearance is more
important than health, but we can make big gains through subtle shifts
in how we speak to our kids about simple things like food.*

—57—

Chapter 5—Boys Will Be Boys

*We men need to do a better job raising boys to enjoy a full spectrum
of emotion while no longer shrugging off poor behavior. It all adds
up to serious lifetime consequences for boys—and girls.*

—67—

GROWING UP

Chapter 6—Her Best Frenemy

*We do a lot of damage in raising girls to only be "nice," so let's do
a better job in helping our kids express themselves.*
—87—

Chapter 7—Sorry, Not Sorry

*The word sorry carries a lot of baggage: as a simple apology, a social lubricant, and
even an expectation—but it's just one of the many ways we police the language of girls.*
—95—

Chapter 8—Movies and Myths of the "Strong, Powerful Female Character"

*The stories told onscreen—at movie theaters and online—often leave out half the
population or reinforce the sexism and underrepresentation we see in the "real world."*
—111—

Chapter 9—Not Playing Around

*Playtimes should be about fun and exploration, but the toys we buy for our
kids often undercut the equity and opportunity we want for them.*
—125—

Chapter 10—Throw Like a Girl

*Although boys and girls play sports in roughly equal numbers,
culturally, sports are still very much a "man's game."*
—135—

Chapter 11—Online Harassment

*Girls and women are harassed, abused, and belittled online in ways
boys and men can't fathom, and the repercussions are chilling.*
—149—

Chapter 12—Like, Math Is So Hard!

*From Barbie dolls to depictions of scientists in popular movies, we tell boys and
girls early and often just who the "smarter" sex is. Let's stop doing that.*
—159—

Chapter 13—Black Girl Magic

*Lofty goals of raising "color-blind" children do more harm than good.
Instead, experts agree it's important to talk with our kids about
race and obstacles people face because of differences.*
—171—

THE LIFETIME CONSEQUENCES OF OUR EARLY LESSONS

Chapter 14—Pay Day

You know there's a "gender pay gap," but you may not realize how big a role we play in perpetuating it at home by telling our boys to be "leaders" and our girls to be "caretakers." It all adds up to lower pay for women and fewer opportunities for girls—and boys.

—189—

Chapter 15—Waiting for Madam President

It's no surprise women are vastly underrepresented in government positions when many weren't allowed to vote until a couple generations ago and are still denied today, but what example are we setting for our kids when we discuss our leaders?

—205—

Chapter 16—Your Opinion on Abortion Is Invalid

Let's be clear: in our everyday conversations and social media interactions to actual votes cast in legislatures, we put the basic human rights of girls and women on the table as if they warrant male debate, and we need to stop. Now.

—221—

Chapter 17—Daddy's Got a Gun

In seemingly innocuous and "funny" ways, boys and men perpetuate broader societal notions that girls and women are property in need of protecting, but you can help by no longer laughing it off.

—233—

Chapter 18—Having "The Talk"

For many parents, the talk about "the birds and the bees" is a one-time event, but it should be an ongoing conversation—that starts early.

—245—

Resources—You're on the Right Path. Keep Going.

There are many, many great resources to help guide you on your journey as you try to raise empowered children, and I want to leave you with some that have inspired me. As they say, the internet is free.

—257—

INTRODUCTION

THE PROBLEM NEVER lay buried. It was everywhere—a creeping haze, a fog, an atmospheric river atomized into breathable vapor. You couldn't avoid it.

A generation after the question, "Is this all?" it was still interrupting to offer the answer, ghostlike and haunting, a pervasive specter mumbling "Well, actually," in the background for boys to overhear, boys through it all turning into men. We're dads now, raising yet another generation today with the original problem still serving as the template.

It was what stirred us in the morning through boyhood, dream-dazed and groggy, suddenly aware of a new song thrumming from our older brother's room.

"Oh, can't you see," it warbled, "you belong to me."

It glared up at us from the morning paper, a black-and-white parade of dads and grandpas in the news section, all suits and ties, cigarette teeth, and sprayed hair. It popped out of the sports pages with the mullet heroes, and the business pages with the old mustached bores.

It arose in the morning flush of the suburbs, all created from some TV show template of clean-street, picket-fence patriotism. The white moms, with maybe one or two black moms out of a hundred homes—"Progress. See? Things are better now"—wove through streets named for famous men, Founding Fathers, men like Washington, Jefferson, and Lincoln or Lee, some slavers and some actual traitors—literally anyone but a woman. And the moms would all assemble at the school drop-off line, honking and griping, while all the dads went elsewhere, somewhere; they were very busy and important.

It blared out in the soundtrack of the everyday commute, the same pounding anthems that woke us played on the radio for everyone to hear.

1

It resounded in songs about "girls" who "belonged" to someone, someone who watched them or followed them. They couldn't escape: *"Every move you make, every step you take."* It repeated in songs about how these "girls" were actually someone else's, some guy named Jessie—but not if some other man altogether could help it. We'd sing along from the backseat, sweetly, proudly, learning about love. This is how adults did the romance. *"I'll be watching you."* The dads, meanwhile, when we sometimes rode with them, had their own soundtracks on talk radio, all those bloviating, angry men: *"And another thing!"*

It crept into the classrooms, where our teachers, mostly women, called on the "smart" boys and the "good" girls. No one pulled *us* from class, measured the length of our shorts or eyed the cut of our tank tops, but they pulled Penny out one day and sent her home, called her a "distraction," and we got the message—we knew why everyone was there and that Penny, dirty, unclean, was somehow disrupting it all. Even in the hallways it was apparent: the teachers, the secretaries, the school nurse, and the lunch ladies—all women, while the *tough* jobs, the *real* jobs, the physical jobs like janitor, or PE teacher, or principal were all filled by men.

It enveloped us in the schoolyard nomenclature, the slurs, the language passed from schoolboy to schoolboy.

There were boys. Then there were "pussies"—a feminine class, a lower class, the very worst thing a *real* boy could be.

Oh, can't you see?

No men ever followed *us* home after school, slowing their car to a crawl beside the sidewalk, whistling, yelling, gesturing. No men told *us* to smile or called *us* names, threatened us if we didn't, and I'd wager good money that right now, if you thought about it, you probably never considered for a moment wearing a different blazer or tie for fear those slow-crawl, creepy whistlemen might consider your attire an invitation to rape you, knowing you'd probably get blamed for it anyway because, look at the cut of your suit, the polish on your shoe—everyone knew you were asking for it. *Liar.*

No boy ever called you a slut. They asked if you scored with one.

It seeped out of after-school sports: the moms on the sidelines, chatting, and the girls nearby doing cartwheels, perhaps picking flowers or even cheering, while the boys gathered in the dirt with men, communing in sport.

It bellowed from the evening news: images of kindly white grandpas speaking assuredly in voices that belied their horrific mythologies, mythologies that vaporized and then seeped into every home. "America," one of them began, all sunny and warm and white, and then suddenly snarled and warned us about welfare queens. Everyone knew the code, even kids.

It oozed off the screen in the TV shows and the movies, the stories about funny men, about action men, about tough, violent, angry men—the real heroes, the men who fought. They fought aliens. They fought ghosts. They fought each other. Nowadays they fight robots, computers. But back then they just fought other men in fake suits. And, oh, how they fought, cramming down anything they might be feeling in order to "man up" for duty, for country, for all of mankind, by which they meant "everyone," obviously, like the Constitution. And then they'd not only win but they'd somehow also win a "girl" in the process, a real prize. A trophy. No one ever called these men "boys," unless they were not white.

It sloshed out of the cocktail parties and neighborhood picnics, the men drinking beer in stumbly groups and lowering their voices about "the problem with women" when you approached or just holding forth endlessly on anything—anything at all, people, even, and what they "should" be happy for, *let me tell you*—while the women cooked, and then cleaned up, and then packed all the kids off for home.

It came up in the late-night movies, the ones your parents didn't know you watched—the soft-core porn ones a future president would feature in, the ones that hid behind a rainbow scramble on forbidden cable channels, but you could still hear them and make out just enough: an illicit glimpse of men spying on showering "girls" as if ogling some ripe fruit, or men bragging about "fucking" a "passed-out girl," whatever that meant. She probably just belonged to him, like the songs said. Ah, that's it. They were doing the romance again. All the men laughed, and if all the men were laughing, it was good.

There's no rainbow channel scramble nowadays. It's clear as day. It's in your child's pocket.

You belong to me.

Back then, it would all repeat itself the next morning, and if it wasn't a school day, it was during Saturday morning cartoons in which even skunk boys chased and grabbed and kissed cat girls, who didn't seem to like it. But you'd heard from adults that it was okay to hit girls if you liked them, so it was probably all fine because all the men, again, were laughing. Or it was at Sunday church and a gathering of robed men speaking of even higher, holier men, men who would charm you, bless you, save you, and, sometimes, begrudgingly, occasionally, the women, who, if they were *really* lucky, would be "given away," passed from man to man to keep the home—unless, that is, they had sex before men ceremoniously sanctioned it, and then they could burn in hell or perhaps just keep having sex, but this time for money. It was all sort of confusing. Then they let you out for coffee and doughnuts.

Above all, these scattershot and seemingly disconnected fragments atomized and reconnected into a hazy American mythology, making you think all the preceding depictions were a shared experience, a natural, common bond among us all since the beginning—a white suburb, a straight mom, a straight dad, two kids, a commute, and some hijinks along the way—instead of what it really was: a relentless ad campaign, a campaign that played out from the moment you woke up to the moment you went to bed, a campaign that, unsurprisingly, was white and male.

It told all the stories, set the tone, embedded the code words. It never dwelled on segregated cities and neighborhoods; people with two jobs, three jobs, lower pay, and longer hours; people who got stopped on the way home: "Hey, boy, what are you doing here?" It never dwelled on those whose rights were on the table, up for a vote, or those whose love was forbidden, kept hidden out of fear, fear of loss, of violence—they were always "aunts" or "just good friends." No one spoke much about the sidewalks, ramps, rails, lifts, who could access stores, basic needs, society; no one fought over bathrooms, who could use them and which ones, because so, so many were still hiding, terrified, afraid to let even family at long last see their real selves.

This is your inheritance; it repeated relentlessly. All of this. It shaped your views, it made you believe the entire world would be yours to pick apart, discuss, debate, and pass judgment on, just like in the newspapers or on the news or in the songs and movies and in the stumbly, drunken groups of men with very important things to say, while the women cleaned up after you.

No, the problem never lay buried.

It was everywhere, like molecules or cosmic rays landing on every surface.

It was the narrative.

The collective storyline passed down generation to generation across the sweep of Western civilization as if it were all perfectly natural instead of a created thing, an intentional thing, a thing men incubated and passed forward, gifting anew these wretched hierarchies that were as apparent to a 1980s schoolboy as they were to Telemachus when he told Penelope to go knit: speech is the business of men.

Girls and women may have still been asking, "Is this all?"

But boys and men already knew the answer.

We knew the code; we inhaled the vapor of it every waking moment.

We had the narrative at our backs. We had everything.

We still do.

GUYS, MEN, DADS: I'm glad you're here. Welcome. We can do tremendous social good if we band together.

Our kids—our own daughters and sons, and our collective village of them—they need better allies.

They need us, in particular, to do better—not to play savior, mind you, but to finally act like the baseline decent human beings we always told ourselves we were.

> They need us, in particular, to do better—not to play savior, mind you, but to finally act like the baseline decent human beings we always told ourselves we were.

The good news is you can do it right now. Today. At home. With your own family and amid your friend circles. You've already taken the first step, in fact.

Good on you.

"What dads can do to be better allies is to check in with your kids in the first place," says Danica Roem, a Virginia state legislator who made history as one of our country's first transgender representatives, "and just, on the one hand, get to know them, but, second, create an atmosphere and an environment that are inclusive and welcoming."

As a parent, "It's not, 'I'm trying to live my life through you,'" she says. Instead, it's about empowering your kids to be their own independent selves and guiding them in life while at the same time understanding that your role as a parent is to help them be the best version of themselves.

Easy enough, right?

Help our kids be the best versions of themselves?

It's a good start.

We can create an inclusive, welcoming, equitable home life for our daughters and sons, and then we need only widen our circles to create similar environments among our friend groups and our work groups and our broader social networks until, one day, the circles overlap and we stop, as a society, putting basic humanity on the bargaining table. If you take nothing else from this book, take this: we men need to stop debating the worth, dignity, and equality of people as if humanity is a thing that can be voted on, discussed, or decided over coffee or keyboards.

Here's the bottom line: when we learn we're having a child, we do a good job of figuring out the essentials—the feeding, the changing, the burping, the raising, the caring. And yet I'm not sure we do a good job preparing our children for a world that still treats our daughters as second-class citizens and our sons as angry, entitled automatons. I'm not so sure we do a good enough job breaking down our inherited cultural mores and social institutions.

Their lives, quite literally, depend on us to do better—in raising them, yes, but also in calling each other out when one of us slips ever so easily into the comfortable idea that some are lesser because of their gender, race, ability, or any of the thousands of differences among us.

Let's be honest for a moment. Let's not sugarcoat it. America is no less enamored of sexist, racist storylines today than it was when we were children, when we were growing up under the subtle notions that girls and women were lesser and that society was built with *us* in mind.

We didn't somehow, magically, stumble into the one generation liberated of this idea. At some point, we have to stop pretending persistent inequality is not our gross collective inheritance. We have to stop pretending that we were raised under a toxic cloud of sexism and racism but that everything's suddenly fine now, like . . .

Poof.

It all conveniently . . . vanished.

Hard truth here. We have to stop pretending that a nation founded in the genocide of women, a nation founded in the bondage and breeding of women like livestock, a nation that granted some the right to vote in 1920 and the rest forty-five years later, that only a generation ago trusted women with their own credit cards, that allowed marital rape until 1992, that *still* allows child marriage, that considers it normal—righteous, even—for men to gather in gilded rooms to cast votes on women's health care, on trans rights, on gay rights is a nation undamaged at the roots in ways that perpetuate terrible systemic and everyday consequences for our kids today and millions just like them.

Girls and women make up more than 51 percent of the population, and yet they . . .

. . . hold roughly 20 percent of government positions at any level, from the nation's capital to Main Street city hall.

. . . earn, depending on their skin color and number of children, anywhere from three-quarters to half of what a white man makes.

. . . are represented in films and media at fractions of the rate men are, and usually appear as silent eye candy or trophies for those men.

. . . are given just 4 percent of nationwide sports coverage, despite pulling in better ratings and putting up better performances (looking at you, shitty US men's soccer team).

. . . hold roughly 20 percent of top management positions in business— only twenty-four CEO spots out of the top five hundred companies—and roughly 30 percent of tech jobs at major companies like Facebook, Apple, and Google.

. . . are sent home from school for wearing clothes that are "distracting" to boys, and then find fewer college scholarships available to them—even though they outpace boys in earning degrees despite this.

. . . are consistently threatened by men with rape and assault online, at school, at home, at work, and on the sidewalks in ways we men both perpetuate and can't fathom, and then somehow have to deal with the audacity of us *interrogating* them about it, men and women alike asking what they were wearing, or drinking, or doing that made *us* do it.

What. Fresh. Hell.

Don't think for a second these storylines aren't doing a number on our boys as well. We are absolutely crippling the emotional lives of boys, putting them in what one masculinity expert calls the "man box" from infancy. We are telling them over and over, from all corners of society, that the very worst thing they could be is not boys at all . . . but girls.

It's not a zero-sum game between boys and girls. Our struggle is linked, as is our freedom.

We are stopping boys from finding their full selves, and they, in turn, are growing up to face the consequences: fewer jobs, fewer friends, depression, suicide. And when they're not killing themselves, they're killing each other in ridiculous numbers, mind-boggling numbers—numbers that have some absurd veneer of cultural acceptance that starts with the first time they hear they just can't be expected to help it, that "boys will be boys." Make no mistake, when they're not turning their bottled rage on themselves, they're turning it on the people we've told them all along are property, objects, lesser: girls and women.

At some point, dads, we need to examine what role we play in these moral atrocities. Having grown up with these collective biases, we didn't somehow reach adulthood without them.

THAT'S THIS BOOK in a nutshell.

It seeks to connect the atomized dots and to unravel these omnipresent storylines, to expose them so we might yet stamp them out—so that our boys and girls don't have to suffer as we did and still do. As a stay-at-home dad and PTA president who knows full well what happens when men veer outside cultural expectations of what it means to be a "real man," and as a father trying simply to bring up another decent child, I hope you might follow along on this de Tocqueville-esque journey through American parenting in the twenty-first century as we examine all the seemingly disconnected little biases that coalesce to rob boys and men of full emotional lives while robbing girls and women of opportunity, safety, and personal freedom.

Women have been telling us about it forever, like so many Cassandras, and it's high time we had a talk among ourselves about it all instead of one more insipid debate that sidelines what's happening before our very eyes.

Let me quickly break down how I see it play out.

Black babies are twice as likely to die as white babies today, a racial gap wider than it was in 1850—in slave times. On the one hand, there's data we can point to and argue about or deny or whatever. But it's the quieter stories behind the data we need to explore, the underlying, almost invisible cultural forces—in this case, the collision, or intersection, of racism and sexism— that lead to a sort of toxic racial stress that, again, is killing pregnant black women and their babies at rates higher than we saw when white people held them as slaves. (I feel like that needs repeating for the "all lives matter" folks in the back row: the survival rate gap between black and white babies is worse now than it was in slave times.)

"Something about growing up as a black woman in America today is bad for your babies," says Linda Villarosa, the *New York Times* reporter who broke the story (which is featured in depth in the chapter "Black Girl Magic").

So, one part is numbers we can hold in our heads and talk about. It's easy to debate this study or that study, to coolly examine the numbers, perhaps hold someone's life and dignity in the balance for the sake of an intellectual argument. It's more difficult to suss out the narrative, to see how the combined cultural forces of everyday conversations, media depictions, social media arguments, white ladies who call for police interventions over picnics, utensils, and popsicle stands—to see how it all might at first seem disconnected, like frayed bits or separate droplets, but then to understand how it coalesces, becomes our cultural story, something that feels . . . normal. And the consequences of it all are horrific, a rank gruesomeness happening every day while we debate what I believe are largely disingenuous, sexist interpretations of data and research studies.

White men have been told for generations that everyone's dignity, worth, equality are things we can debate, parse, weigh, and that it's all a fun intellectual experiment.

Black women and their babies are dying.

Make no mistake: these things are connected.

The atmospheric dots of it all are key. They surround us. All of them—the sexism, racism, ableism, homophobia, transphobia, you name it—add up and form the cultural forces that quietly inform our opinions, our lifestyles, our career trajectories, our personal safety, and so much more, and they work insidiously under the radar to do the dirty work of perpetual oppression while seeming so disparate as to be innocuous, innocent pieces that form no whole.

"Sometimes when you're raising a child, it's like the universe is in a conspiracy against you," writer Chimamanda Ngozi Adichie said in *Vulture* magazine in 2018 in regard to all the tiny sexisms and how they come from everywhere.

I told my friend Dave I was writing this book, and he threw up his hands in sudden rage. "Oh my god, the sexism is everywhere! It's everywhere!"

Here's the deal: we men don't get to benefit from a sexist, racist society that exalts even the most unqualified among us and somehow also get to think that system, those traditions, don't exist; or that they are lesser than they were a generation ago and therefore everything's fine; or that we can't do anything about it all; or that we all at once have most of the power and yet are powerless.

Like I said, I'm glad you're here. Our children, our own and our village of them, will suffer from the weight of these biases, just as we suffer now, but we can make a change. Together. Right now. A Dad Wave of feminism that holds each other to account to change our circles for the better and to watch them spread: from our homes to our peer groups to our communities and beyond.

LET ME TELL you a few quick stories, lest you think I'm overstating things. I want you to take a step back and consider our current society and how we view women as a historian might in future years.

When top Hollywood moviemaker Harvey Weinstein was finally exposed in the #MeToo movement as a serial abuser and assaulter of women, he argued he came of age in a "different" time. "That was the culture then," he said, as if that explained it all.

But the thing is, he came of age . . . *when we did*.

His culture is *our* culture. Hell, he personally helped write the script, providing us with pop culture entertainment while abusing women along the way.

So, what has changed between "then" and now? There has been no magical moment when Hollywood and America as a whole suddenly stopped being sexist hellscapes for girls and women. In the news, on the silver screen, in politics, in sports, online, and through every other outlet of our culture, we're finding more and more that the guys who have been crafting our cultural realities have also been harassing and assaulting women, churning out copy of their everyday degradation. But we'd be making a mistake in thinking that although nearly all women have personal stories of abuse, somehow it's only a tiny segment of men doing the abusing.

At some point, we need to realize that what was "then" is still very much *now*. And then ask: What role do we play in carrying it forward?

Consider the environment we raise children in today and the messages that creep into their everyday consciousness, just as the atomized messages crept into ours.

In 2017, the Republican Party put its full weight behind a Senate candidate who believed that gay people shouldn't marry and that women shouldn't hold public office and who was accused of sexually harassing and abusing multiple girls. *Children*. Numerous now-grown women accused him of being a child molester.

And people still voted for him. They called the women liars, or said it wasn't so bad, said they just couldn't possibly choose between him . . . and the candidate from the other political party.

Their votes declared a clear pattern of abuse over years was . . . acceptable. There were more important things.

It's nearly impossible to capture this kind of thinking, the consistent ranking of girls and women as things that are less important, in quantifiable data. So, we have to follow the storyline, the stories we tell about each other.

In 2016, as you may recall, sixty-three million Americans voted to elect as president a man who called women pigs, bitches, and nasty, said they should be "treated like shit" and have dinner waiting for him when he gets home from work, assigned women numbers based on his beauty standards, bragged that he could use his celebrity status to sexually assault them, and then, surprise, surprise, had nearly two dozen women from across several decades attest to just that. These voters might not do or say such things themselves. Yet, surely, their votes showed that such things weren't deal breakers.

And why not?

The endless pointillistic dots of sexism work quietly underneath it all to shape our views. He and his enablers excused his behavior as "locker room talk," a phrase that somehow seemed to offer absolution because *where* one speaks of sexually assaulting women somehow makes it socially palatable, just a thing men do.

Consider that for a moment. We collectively consider men rape enthusiasts behind closed doors; it's just a topic men talk about and think about during sports, and then we also publicly call women liars about it all—while *still* giving men unchecked power. In raising our kids in this world that claims it's all perfectly normal, we have failed in a way that's hard to comprehend. It's like a moral rot in our times—which are, of course, no different from all the other times before.

Like I said, what was considered "back then" is still very much now.

So, what could have been so bad about the *other* candidate that this man who has exhibited literally decades of failed ventures, scams, grifts, lying, racism, and sexism was preferable?

When it came right down to it, it was either him or an overly qualified woman—a woman painted endlessly as a ... wait for it ... liar.

This is the environment we're raising children in today. Oh, sure, we may have *reasons* for throwing girls and women under the bus.

But we still do it.

And make no mistake: they *see* us do it. They inhale the code we set anew for them.

SO THOSE ARE the big storylines of our times, the broad culture shapers. Feel free now to go about yelling "Grab 'em by the pussy!" In America, that's a thing half the country is okay with.

Nice job.

But what of the littler pieces? The ones that form our every day?

That's where the other stories come into play and shape entirely different realities for our girls and boys. The major thrust of this book is to shine a light on them for dads so that we might join forces and create waves large enough among ourselves to change the story. Pretty simple. But our task is at once daunting and necessary.

Check it:

Last year, a friend of mine took her daughter and son along with a bevy of their friends to sell brochures at the Sun Bowl football game in Texas to raise money for scouting.

Out of six Girl Scouts, three were sexually harassed by grown men.

Openly. In public.

One girl was called "pushy."

One was called a "bitch."

Two—a nine-year-old and an eleven-year-old—were asked crudely whether they wanted to be the men's "girlfriends."

My friend's son, in his Cub Scout uniform, was patted on the back, offered thanks, given handshakes, and asked whether he would one day become an Eagle Scout.

People said to him, "Thank you, sir." They called him "Mister."

"My six girls got 'sweetie' and 'honey' and 'baby' and 'bitch,'" my friend said. "This is what the world looks like when you are female."

Big question to think about while reading, guys: Should we have to empower our daughters for the "fight," raise them to be strong and powerful for what we know they'll encounter—or do we at long last call each other out and hold each other accountable for being so horrible?

Like I said, you can start today. In your everyday circles. You can be the guy who awkwardly laughs off sexism, ignores it so as not to make waves. Or you can be the guy who tells your friend Bob to shut the fuck up and leave the kids alone, to stop harassing perceived "weaker" groups just for a few yucks from male friends. That's something concrete you can do today to change your world, and your kids' world, for the better. It really is that simple. If our male friends aren't scared to death to be horribly sexist in front of us, we really need to reexamine our life choices, we really need to examine why we find sexualized violence . . . funny.

ANOTHER STORY:

My wife and I applied for that TSA Pre✓ program that allows you to skip the security line at the airport. (You should do it; it's superfast and supereasy.)

We both filled out information online and then headed over to a security agency to give fingerprints and pay. I dropped my wife off at the entrance and then went to find a parking space. By the time I arrived at the office, she was already finished with her appointment.

When I was called not long after, I gave my fingerprints, paid my portion, and we left. (See? Superfast.)

"Wasn't that awesome?" I asked. "Why didn't we do this sooner!"

Dana smirked.

"I bet the guy didn't tell you to smile, did he?" she said. "I bet he didn't say, 'Check you out, Little Mr. Fancy' when you pulled out the credit card?"

For my wife, it wasn't the biggest harassment she had received in her life—far from it. None of these everyday stories will make headlines or the evening news. But if we listen to the girls and women in our lives, or the amplification system social media provides, we learn these instances form the fundamental building blocks of our society, the gross foundations for the horrors that follow.

I see men argue over issues like government representation, women in business, whether dress codes are acceptable, pay gaps, abortion rights—you name it. (All issues explored in this book.) They pull out this study or that, this talking point or that one, but I don't think we men fully account for the things we cannot see and therefore believe do not exist, the baggage we do not have to carry around like dead weight in our lives. Yes, some men do, a lot of men, in fact—largely because of other men.

If we were being honest, we'd admit we live in essentially a different world from women.

No man tells me to smile. No man teases me for having a credit card and using it. No man makes me feel as if it's my responsibility to make him feel good. No man makes me appraise the power dynamics of simply getting something every American is entitled to, with my personal safety, well-being, or dignity in the balance.

"I wanted so bad to tell him just to fuck off," she said. "But I was afraid my application would suddenly 'get lost' in the system. We put up with this every day."

I think of my wife, I think of those kids, carrying around all that emotional baggage of random encounters with random men—men who feel entitled to smiles, to insults, to whispered threats, and to generally creepy bullshit we men generally don't have to deal with.

I think, mostly, of the men who stand by as other men do it, the men who ignore it, perhaps laugh at it. They probably think they are "decent" men. Good guys. But they just stand there, like we all have at some point, laughing as men among them abuse small children or grown women.

It can't be so bad if all the men in our lives are laughing, awkwardly, but still laughing, right?

"YOU WANT TO meet an instant feminist?" asks Michael Kimmel, a sociologist and masculinity expert who wrote *Manhood in America, Angry White Men, The Politics of Manhood, The Gendered Society,* and the best-seller *Guyland: The Perilous World Where Boys Become Men.* "Talk to a man whose daughter hits puberty, and that suddenly makes it very concrete that masculinity is a real issue. . . . We perhaps don't think about it until it affects us personally, but that's maybe a good thing, it's a way in. Fatherhood is very often the way to get men into the conversation about gender and gender inequality."

Indeed.

As we talked, my mind suddenly snapped to an image of a T-shirt. You might have seen one like it online or on a dad. There's a picture of a gun and then the punchline phrase:

Dad's Got a Daughter and a Shotgun.

Dad Will Do to You What You Do to My Daughter.

Rules for Dating My Daughter: You Can't.

The urge to protect—I *get* that.

All dads have that.

As wrongheaded and dangerous as I think those T-shirts are—aren't they just another way of saying girls aren't really in control of themselves? That they're really someone else's property? That boys can be baseline decent only on threat of violence? And that men are violent fucks who threaten children and that's okay? (Seriously, guys, stop)—if I were being honest I'd admit that their intention, at the most fundamental level, is no different from this book's.

We all want to protect our kids. We all want what's best for them.

We just go about it in different ways.

Some dads joke about sitting on the porch holding shotguns or pointing guns at their daughters' dates (ugh, again, stop), and some try to expose the millions of ways society treats girls and women as lesser, as objects, as deserving of low pay, fewer opportunities, and abuse—and then the cruel reality of watching us debate it all as if we didn't create the environment for it, benefit from it, even.

If I were being honest, I'd admit that's a part of this book, deep down: wanting to protect my daughter from a world I inherited . . . and helped create.

But there's something more.

As a stay-at-home dad who as a boy took Calgon soaks and cuddled a favorite doll while also yearning for a girl's affection, who grew up liking show tunes as much as wrestling matches, I've witnessed firsthand what happens when guys stray from what we call masculine norms: teasing, ridicule, abuse, harassment, assault. I've witnessed firsthand—and participated in—the emotional torment we do to our growing boys and then, later, to men—the crippling, emotionally void boxes we try to stuff each other into, laughing all the while.

"The first act of violence that patriarchy demands of males is not violence toward women," bell hooks says. "Instead patriarchy demands of all males that they engage in acts of psychic self-mutilation, that they kill off the emotional parts of themselves."

When I told my friend Chris, a father of two boys, about this book for empowering girls, he said, "Remember the boys."

Indeed, our struggles are linked, and we need to explore the way we raise our girls, for sure, but also how we raise our boys and how it's horrible for them, yes, and how it creates a double bind for girls and women. When we call boys "pussies" or "girly," we snuff out parts of their emotional spectrum, telling them they can't access their full selves, and that does tremendous damage. But statements like these also create a caste system, telling boys, and everyone around them, that we consider girls and women lesser, lower, worthy of ridicule.

Through action, some men cause real, lasting pain to young girls and women, boys and men. Through inaction, some men let it happen.

We need to stop. Stop it all. We even need to consider our *motivations* for stopping it, whether it, too, buys in to hidden biases. Do we want what's best for girls and women, boys and men, because they are somehow ... ours? *Our* daughters. *Our* wives. *Our* women. Or do we simply want to live a decent life, treat people equally, regardless of their relationship to men?

"We don't need you to rescue us, we need you to tell other men their behavior is unacceptable and, man-to-man, you won't stand for it," says my friend Melissa Atkins Wardy, author of *Redefining Girly: How Parents Can Fight the Stereotyping and Sexualizing of Girlhood, from Birth to Tween*. "Put another way—we don't need a knight in shining armor, we need men to insist on higher standards of each other."

Through action, some men cause real, lasting pain to girls and women, boys and men. Through inaction, some men let it happen, quietly nurturing the atmosphere that allows the code words to re-embed themselves, the narrative to continue, generation upon generation.

We are all complicit.

Like I said, I'm glad you're here. We can do great good together. And we can start today, right now. In our everyday lives and in the ways we raise our children and prepare them to help tilt the world a little closer to equity.

You got this, Dad. Let's go.

HOUSEKEEPING NOTES

A few quick things to keep in mind as we move ahead on our journey together.

1. Before I became a stay-at-home dad, I was an investigative reporter, so facts and accurate sourcing are important to me. For this book, when I could, I got in touch directly with experts and parents alike, and you'll see them quoted throughout. Unfortunately, I just could never get in touch with many experts for a variety of reasons. So, you'll also see quotes and references from other interviews these people gave. I made sure to reference these sources so you could go google their works for further reading.

2. Throughout the book, I use the word *sex* to denote a person's biological anatomy and secondary sex characteristics, which are not, please keep in mind, the male-female binary we've been told all along. There are nearly as many intersex folks as there are redheads. When I use the word *gender,* I'm talking about how we all "do gender," or how we display our socially constructed ideas of, for instance, maleness. Think of it this way: imagine an "alpha male" in New York City. What do you imagine? A slick haircut, sharkskin suit, fancy tie, and cool watch? Now what's your version of an alpha male from Texas look like? The Pacific Northwest? Are they the same, or are there myriad ways to express maleness? Think of the buddies in your own groups. We all *express* our gender identities in different ways, and it doesn't always match up with the sex and gender we were assigned at birth. So, let's perhaps stop being assholes to our transgender friends, and let's also stop pretending there is only one way to be a "real man." We'd do some great good together stopping that idea alone.

3. Speaking of dudes. Here's some bullshit, guys, and I want you to keep it in mind as you read and then consider what platforms you might have available to you for serious culture change. Basically, any female feminist writer using even half the curse words or rants you'll see throughout this book would almost immediately be labeled a "bitchy femi-nazi" or some such. I'm sure you've seen it. But white guys like me, let's be honest, can rant and curse and call out some serious garbage from my fellow dudes without being labeled "shrill" or "bitchy." ("I like beer!") Ask yourself why you think that is. All I and basically any female feminist writer are asking for is equality and personal freedom, but why can we male allies win praise for it while

female writers get threats? All to say, it's a shitty paradigm, and I hope it dies soon enough. We don't get cookies for being baseline decent. Until then, guys, I hope you'll join me in using our personal platforms—our male privilege—to call out our male buddies in ways women cannot so easily do, to at long last tilt the world toward a better place, one circle at a time.

Okay, now, really, let's go. Like I said, you got this.

THE EARLY YEARS

—Chapter 1—

CLOTHES HOUNDS

How simple T-shirts lead to big differences in how we raise our kids.

I'M IN THE children's section at H&M, a mall chain of inexpensive high-fashion clothes. It could be any major retailer, really.

I'm looking for a few simple T-shirts for my daughter, but my veins begin to pulse.

My eyes twitch.

My mouth starts and fails at forming words, a fish gasp of incredulity amid the sexist sartorial onslaught.

It happens nearly every time.

Just pick any big store—whether it's Target or Old Navy, JCPenney or Walmart—and I'll tell you about the aneurysm I almost had in the children's section.

The sexism is so obvious and stunning that I've often wondered whether I'd accidentally stumbled into one of those prank TV shows.

"Hey, let's pigeonhole girls as sex symbols from birth and you won't believe what happens next!"

Cue the laugh track.

The children's clothing section seems like a good place to begin this journey through the endless points of sexism our kids face, because it's often the starting point. After all, every baby needs clothes.

But like the rest of our white supremacist patriarchal narratives, it's all at once subtle and stunning, borne forward generation by generation in a culture that actually used to arrest women for wearing "men's" clothes (the fate of the first and, so far, only woman to ever win the Medal of Honor) and that still sends girls home from school for dress code violations, as if the policing of female bodies today is somehow different or better.

It all remains somehow vividly on display and also shockingly invisible, gobbled up and consumed as "normal." Because if it's everywhere and everyone's participating in it, then, why, of course, *wouldn't* it be considered normal?

With a simple onesie or cutesy T-shirt, our kids begin their forays into a society that will seriously mess them up.

And we're all in on it.

ON THE ONE hand, the T-shirts at H&M are inexpensive. It's probably what keeps bringing me back, as the kid seems to outgrow clothes overnight. On the other hand, the children's clothes department is pretty much the easiest place to witness gender bias at work.

Here's how I see it.

In the boy's section, there are roughly thirty different T-shirt and tank top offerings, in blues and greens and yellows and blacks.

There are baseball shirts, soccer shirts, basketball shirts. There are shirts with popular superheroes and cartoon characters. College logo shirts. Angry Birds. Surfboards. Compass symbols with phrases about hiking or exploring or adventure.

In other words, H&M's boys' section basically mirrors selections I have seen from every major retailer—selections that sport slogans such as "Awesome" or "MVP" or "Hero."

One says, "I'm not mad. I'm ANGRY!" It features a popular Angry Bird video game character—the bloated red one with the unibrow.

Take a step back, breathe it all in, and the overall message from this selection of clothes in the boys' section is clear within all of thirty seconds of shopping: boys are awesome adventure heroes on their way to college or the sports stadium, with a perfect mixture of anger and violence thrown in for good measure.

AND THEN . . . THE GIRLS' section.

I navigate the teeming racks and shelves, a veritable sea of pinks and purples, and the very first shirt I encounter in the girls' section has the word *flower* spelled out—wait for it—in flowers.

One shirt says, "Free hugs."

Another features the word *peace*.

There are plenty of hashtags followed by the words *cute* and *beautiful*.

There are puppies and kittens and unicorns. There are ice cream cones and clouds and hearts.

It is like a carnival of cotton candy for your torso. It makes me want to vomit, dizzy from the swirl of sticky sweetness of it all.

I turn to my daughter, a Minecraft lover of epic proportions.

"Can you *believe* it?"

"I know, Dad, I know."

She's heard my rant before.

While I'm still shaking my head and looking for a manager to register a complaint, she moves on to the boys' section to check out the sports T-shirts and shorts—shorts with *pockets,* pockets deep and wide enough to carry everything from phones to frogs.

Is this what girls actually *want*? Or is this all we're selling them?

Look, it's not that peace signs and hashtags are bad. Far from it. What sort of monster attacks a *peace* sign?

It's just that when you step back and view the overall portrait, it's apparent: the sweetness, the obsession with appearance over action, and the obnoxious, daydream puffery of it all are the *only* options.

IS THIS WHAT girls actually *want*?

Or is this all we're selling them?

Are they cutesy, flower-obsessed cupcake tweeters because they just . . . are? Or do we dress them in this sugary muck from day one and they get the message soon enough? What, pray tell, are the ramifications of *that*?

And the boys? Are they "naturally" bouncy and energetic and nonstop sports-obsessed, or do we just tell them they are and, again, they internalize it all soon enough?

What of the kids who fall off this spectrum altogether? The trans kids trying to find themselves, the kids with disabilities, or the little people who can't even wear any of this?

"My money and my existence is as valid as yours," disabled rights activist Sinead Burke told The Business of Fashion, "and yet, I'm not accommodated for."

The embedded codes would have us believe it's all one big either-or, with no one else to consider.

Make no mistake, we may think we're raising boys and girls to be equal. But parents—and kids themselves—are getting a different message with every trip to the clothing store, with each online shopping spree.

LOOK, IT'S EASY to spot and even laugh off *one* silly T-shirt that says, "Too Cute for Homework." But what do you do when it's *not* just one T-shirt? When the messages sent to girls and boys are constant and overwhelming and follow them from the stores to playgrounds to college and far beyond?

How do you counteract a subtle, toxic messaging system that says boys are meant to play hard and go to college while on a violent anger binge and that girls are love-obsessed objects in slim jeans and flower-font hashtags?

Indeed, clothes shopping is probably the first look parents get at the quiet, omnipresent narratives they will have to overcome as they raise strong, confident girls and boys who strive toward equality and any semblance of emotional life beyond crippling anger and entitlement.

MELISSA ATKINS WARDY, author of the book *Redefining Girly,* was so frustrated at the clothes options for kids that she started her own line of clothes called Pigtail Pals and Ballcap Buddies, with each piece designed to offer a more empowering option.

"It's not about bashing one girl's interests over another girl's, or bashing boys in favor of girls—you know, 'Girls rule, and boys drool,'" Wardy says. "It doesn't empower *her* to hurt *him*."

No, it's simply about making sure every gender has more options and doesn't feel constricted by crap roles at even the earliest ages, when exploration and play are so important, Wardy argues. It can't be that girls have nothing but appearance-laden clothes options available, and boys have sports and college wear.

What of the girl who wants a baseball shirt, or the boy who likes hearts or, *gasp,* pink?

In our society, it's much easier for a girl to cross over and become a "tomboy"—ridding herself altogether of the feminine for the stereotypically masculine because she . . . happens to like blue jeans, pockets, and skateboards. We call her strong, powerful, feisty. We literally call her a boy.

But what of the boy who wears a dress or sparkles, even for playtime?

He's no longer a boy at all, in the eyes of many. He's something worse: he's . . . girly.

Come on, dads. That's some bullshit, right?

When we see buds equating something they think is "bad" with "girls," we need to speak up. These stereotypes about girls' and boys' expected roles in society come early and come often. They come at the store and in our friend groups. No more laughing this shit off.

If the social justice of it isn't enough for you, if the emotional well-being of kids isn't your cup of tea, fine. Consider the selfishness of it instead. Your kids are listening, and your boys are going to grow up and believe *you* think women are lesser and act accordingly, and your girls are going to grow up and think you're an asshole.

"It starts with these tiny things that we don't think are that important or that big of a deal but really are," Wardy says.

In other words, they're subtle, and they add up. And they don't just suddenly stop after childhood.

They merely pave the way for more.

A. J. RICHARD, founder of the group Women Belong in Baseball and an avid sports fan, spotted a T-shirt for women last year that looked like a low-cut sports-logo T-shirt with a familiar team script on the front. Only, instead of saying something like "Tigers!" or "Go team!" it said, "Let's touchdown a homerun"—a mix-up of sports phraseology because obviously women don't understand two of America's favorite pastimes. The shirt was only sold in the women's section.

"Clothes and language are part of culture. Clothes and language transmit ideas, stereotypes, and attitudes," Richard says. "If [this shirt] sent a message of negative stereotype of a race, more people might recognize it as harmful. Since it is an entrenched attitude about women, it's somehow okay."

Richard wrote about the shirt in her Facebook group and heard a litany of responses telling her to just chill out, that it's just one shirt, no big deal.

But it's never just one shirt. It's never one stupid joke.

Richard sees shirts like that as one small piece of a cultural system that keeps women out of positions of power, especially in sports. The messages might seem innocuous or even funny, but they don't exist in a vacuum. They coalesce into omnipresent sexist messages—from the T-shirts telling society that women suck at sports to sports TV shows featuring an endless orgy of gasbag dudes to ball fields and coaching positions lacking women. (Keeping an eye on who is speaking on TV or who is featured in the sports pages is an *incredibly* easy way to see the patriarchy at work so you can talk about it with your kids.)

It's difficult to grab a seat at the table, or a position on the field, or a clipboard behind the sidelines when even everyday clothing reinforces the cultural mythology that women don't understand sports, let alone enjoy them or, heavens, aren't equally qualified to play or coach them.

"We can't overcome barriers we don't acknowledge even exist," Richard says.

HERE'S ANOTHER EXAMPLE, one that you can replicate with your own computer.

A few years ago, JCPenney came under fire for selling a girls' T-shirt that said "Too Pretty for Homework."

Okay, that's just silly and stupid. It's easy to laugh off one dumb T-shirt. (But it's never just one shirt.)

But I found something much worse than that while perusing JCPenney's online offerings at the time, something that matches up to the H&M experience and was so achingly obvious that I had to do a quick, not-very-scientific review to make sure I wasn't just seeing things:

The girls' T-shirts section had fourteen options that alluded to appearance, whereas the boys' section had just one.

On the flip side, I found that the boys' section had twenty-six shirts that alluded to action in some way, and the girls' side had just six.

When it came to expectations about education, I found something all at once intriguing and horrible:

Boys had literally *dozens* of college logo shirts available to them.

And the girls?

Zero.

Not one.

College, it seemed, was just not for them.

JCPENNEY WAS BY no means the only offender. Flip open any children's clothes catalog or click around on any online site, and the experience is pretty much the same today. Even the poses are gendered, with boys usually puffing out their chests or actually doing things, while girls are more often shown in the kicky pose you can find on any kindergarten playground: one hand on a hip, one knee bent, one toe daintily poking at the ground.

Is this a natural thing or, again, do we pigeonhole them into these expectations early and often?

"The problem is kids don't grow up in a vacuum," writes Hannah Garcia, a UK design writer, on her website, Blod. "They're constantly creating and recreating their beliefs about themselves and others based on what adults tell them."

Indeed, research shows that gender role stereotypes take hold in children as young as two, thanks to an endless barrage of media and parental messaging, according to a study from Common Sense Media. As those kids age, the study shows, those messages really sink in and they start to form ideas of what they can and can't do for a living simply because of how they do gender.

And no wonder, considering the onslaught they're hit with every day.

Garcia and her husband did something similar to my perusal of the online offerings at JCPenney but turned it up to eleven.

They investigated the online offerings at the top twelve stores in the United Kingdom, and then created a computer program to scan and survey 1,444 pieces of clothing for signs of bias in the animals displayed on, say, T-shirts and sweaters.

What they found was extraordinary. And by *extraordinary*, I mean a whole bunch of sexist bullshit.

I mean, we're even telling kids which *animals* are acceptable to identify with based on gender. Clothes for boys were more likely to have large, dangerous predators, whereas clothes for girls were more likely to depict cute, small prey animals.

Girls, after all, are told from day one that they are ornamental objects, and boys are predatory and angry.

"They are more likely to feature baby animals, too, or add bows and flowers to animals just in case anyone was worried about them being mistaken for boys," Garcia explains.

In other words, girls are cute prey, and boys are wild predators.

One wonders wherever men get the idea it's okay to assault, abuse, rape, or harass women when the idea that men are wild, violent, and angry has been woven into our cultural depictions since childhood—and they're considered heroes for it all. Make no mistake. These are connected. These messages may seem small and innocuous on their own, but they add up.

"Boys will be boys."

Girls will be . . . prey?

IT'S NO BIG stretch to go from an overwhelming display of sexist T-shirts to postpuberty dress codes that force girls to cover up their bodies so as not to "distract" boys from getting an education. Girls, after all, are told from day one that they are ornamental objects, and boys are predatory and angry, destined for university. Every fall, as kids go back to school, I get notes from parents asking how best to combat dress codes that prioritize a boy's education over a girl's.

You may have seen similar disparities as well. On hot days, boys can wear any tank top or shorts they want, but girls are expected to don more modest offerings even at the expense of comfort.

School dress codes target girls for daring to wear the only clothes available to them at popular retailers. And to top it all off, girls are actually sent home or told to change if adults believe their clothes might be distracting to boys. The bottom line and underlying message here is that a boy's education is more important than a girl's personal choices, and really, deep down, the temptress girl shouldn't get in the way of it. Remember how many college T-shirts were available for boys versus girls?

Literally dozens to literally zero.

Now put the absurdity of it all together: women are outpacing men in earning bachelor's degrees, and yet our societal messaging system—from clothing stores to high school dress codes—remind us every day that education is for boys.

And then interlace it all with how we treat sexual assault victims: even seemingly reasonable people point first at her clothes and ask, "What was she wearing?" Well, probably the ornamental bullshit we've been laughing off as harmless since infancy. (Or not. A five-second Google tour turns up heartbreaking art installations showcasing exactly what girls and women were wearing when men raped them.) Though clothes have no apparent link to rape, they do provide an excuse to blame women for the work of their male rapists.

WARDY, A MOTHER of a girl and a boy, points out that the clothes we wear and dress our children in are like miniature billboards that bombard kids with a constant stream of messages about their expected roles in society.

Boys are violent heroes. Girls are sweet and sexy at the same time. It's like that stupid sugar-and-spice-and-everything-nice-puppy-dog-tails-whatever poem has been put on clearance at Walmart.

But something even more insidious is at play in the aisles of nearly every single store. While the boys are told to have adventures and go to college and the girls are told to stand still and look pretty, something else hides among the racks.

The boys' clothes are downright *roomy*, made of breathable fabric, and clearly cut for movement and bouncing around, whereas the majority of girls' clothes are slimming and skinny—to the point of being constricting.

It's a battle women have been fighting since long before the sidesaddle went out of style. Clothes offer a marker for how we perform our gender, and from the beginning we've been using clothes to cloak women in stereotypes.

In *The Amazons: Lives and Legends of Warrior Women Across the Ancient World,* Stanford classics professor Adrienne Mayor explores the real-life Scythian tribes from which the myths about the all-women Amazon clans formed. First, she tells us the horse tribes were basically an egalitarian society, with girls learning to ride and hunt and fight from a young age, and with boys, if they were so inclined, learning to bead. In the harsh climates, people simply did what they were good at to help everyone survive.

In viewing this setup, the Greeks were so appalled that they created entire mythologies about all-women Amazon societies hell-bent on the destruction of men, a myth that endures today whenever you hear a man rail against feminism as the coming apocalypse. Like, come on, guys—all they had was a simple egalitarian meritocracy, the very thing sexist dudes *claim* to want, and yet thousands of years later we are *still* hearing that equality is concomitant with the "downfall" of man.

Next, Mayor points out how these same sexist dudes have always sought to sexualize powerful women, as if to bring them down a peg and make everything about appearance rather than ability. Mayor tells us the badass Scythian tribeswomen created pants to accommodate horse riding. Yet the ancient Greeks, in telling the myths about the Amazons, clad them instead in skirts—a clothing motif that endures in almost any movie about the warriors. Dude, *you* try riding in a short skirt. It's ridiculous.

What of women who stepped outside of these cultural "norms" through the ages? Remember the woman who was arrested for wearing men's clothes? Her name was Mary Walker, and for her work on the battlefields of the Civil War she remains the only woman to have won the Medal of Honor. She hated the skirts and frilly dresses popular in her time because they didn't allow for free movement and activity. So, she took to wearing men's pants and suits instead, and was arrested multiple times for it.

I KNOW WHAT you're thinking. Arrested. How *absurd*.

Is it no less absurd to stop a girl or young woman in the school hallway and then send her home to change? We may not still bring girls and women before judges for official punishments, but surely the rest of us have stepped in to do the judging.

And for what? Freedom of movement? Comfort?

Next time you're at the store, take a shirt in size small for a boy and compare it to a shirt in size small for a girl. You'll see the boy shirt looks like a parachute, while the girl shirt has a narrow waist and shorter sleeves. The boys' shorts are roomy and have ample pockets for rocks or frogs or forgotten snacks; the girls' shorts are generally so short and slim that the wearer would be hard-pressed to carry a phone to call her parents. And don't even get me started on "slim" jeans. Have you tried climbing the steps up to a playground slide in slim jeans? And child heels for everyday wear? Honestly, you might as well just bind her feet.

Bottom line: in the clothes we buy for them and perhaps wear ourselves, we tell boys to move around, play, be adventurous and awesome. And that's great. We should keep doing that while also considering that boys might also enjoy a broader spectrum of choices—rainbow unicorns over angry birds, for instance, because rainbow unicorns are fucking awesome—and then support them because it's all just clothes.

Ponder that for a second: we laugh off sexist clothes for girls, arguing, "Oh, it's just clothes! There are bigger fish to fry." And then we police the shit out of boys for wearing—*gasp*—pink, as if . . . what? Pink will turn him . . . *gay?*

Horrors.

The narrative plays dirty, guys. (In roomy jeans, probably. With pockets.)

We sell girls sexualized clothing and idolize their bodies over their brains in every store and online site, in images on the grocery store magazine racks, at the movies, on TV, in social media, and basically anytime they move around in public—and then we belittle them for it, judge them, send them home from school, and call them tarts intent on distracting boys. This feels more like an adult problem than a girl problem, and as we raise our children we should be more aware of the cultural forces influencing our decisions.

SO, WHAT CAN WE DO?

The internet quickly shut down JCPenney's T-shirt and called out several other stores for similar offerings. It's never one shirt, so let's stop pretending we can just laugh it away. And don't even get me started on the Halloween costumes. What, pray tell, does a toddler crayon need a skirt for anyway?

But what can we parents do about the subtler messages girls' clothing broadcasts?

Don't buy your daughter a wardrobe that consists *only* of fitted clothes with appearance-oriented messages. Some stores, such as Target and Old Navy, have begun offering more empowering shirts and sports clothes for girls. Buy those as well.

That's great. It's a start.

But it's not really a complete fix.

You can't offer roomy sports and college and hero shirts for boys, and then just plant a few "girl power" offerings in a sea of tight jeans and rainbow sparklecorn T-shirts. In some stores, it's literally window dressing—one empowering T-shirt display luring you into inescapable sexism like lotus-eaters of the clearance rack. The handful of good messages don't make up for the never-ending barrage of sexist stupidity that says over and over again that boys are heroes and girls are objects.

AND SO, WHAT happens, in the end?

I admit I still shop at H&M simply because the clothes are inexpensive. It's difficult to pass up cheap clothes for growing bodies. But I'd like my daughter—and awesome girls like her—to have more options and clothes that are made for play, not for appearances.

The good news is that with a simple online search, you can find a wealth of more empowering girls' clothes options outside of the mainstream stores. It's really not that difficult to do, and it'll spare you the horrors of Target's checkout lanes.

When it comes to the mainstream stores, I make a point of buying the empowering T-shirts and clothes options when they're available. I want the store's clothes buyers—the people in charge of actually getting those items on the racks for purchase—to know that such items are selling, that people are, in fact, buying.

My daughter also has no problem "crossing the aisles" for the boys' selections, which, with their superheroes and sports stuff, are simply more appealing to her.

Whereas girls can cross over easily into the supposed realm of boy things, sadly, it's not so easy the other way around. Girls who wear "boy things" are considered awesome and fearless. Boys who don sparkly pink rainbow shirts are, as you can imagine, called some pretty bad names, usually disparaging of feminine qualities. Something easy you can do to change our culture for the better? Don't be that guy who disparages.

But if you downplay the store's signage as you shop with your kids, they'll learn that it's okay to grab something they like no matter which section the store displays it in. In other words, if your girl wants a college logo shirt from the boys' section, don't make a big deal that it's from the boys' section. The same goes for boys who want something from the girls' side.

In the end, as parents, we can change the vocabulary, according to sociologist and masculinity professor Michael Kimmel. There's nothing inherently masculine about sports or inherently feminine about sparkles. If parents stop using words to divide the things kids like or like to wear into binary categories, we might be able to fix this, he says. Instead of pointing out the gender divides in the store, you can treat all of the clothes as available to everyone.

—Chapter 2—

NATURE VERSUS NURTURE

There are real, proven gaps between the sexes, but not as many as we create in our parenting and societal messages.

Y OU'VE BEEN MISLED.
Probably your entire life.
And probably by well-meaning people who are merely passing along what has become an incredibly counterproductive cultural myth, although sometimes, yes, probably also by odious mansplainers who want "science" to back up their crippling sexism, by people who want to put other people's worth on the bargaining table or explain away rampant institutional discrimination as all perfectly "natural"—just innate "differences" between boys and girls, men and women.

Let's stop doing this.

The differences between boys and girls, men and women aren't as wide as the Mars-Venus construct you've probably heard about.

We're more like next-door neighbors.

Or, even more precisely, roommates.

"We have far, far more similarities than differences," says Lise Eliot, professor of neuroscience at the Chicago Medical School and author of *Pink Brain, Blue Brain: How Small Differences Grow into Troublesome Gaps—and What We Can Do About It.*

> **The differences between boys and girls, men and women aren't as wide as the Mars–Venus construct you've probably heard about.**

And here's the upshot of it all: even if differences *were* as wide as some cosmological chasm, would it be right to deny opportunities to girls and women while boxing boys and men into expected roles?

SURE, YES, OF course—there are obvious physical differences between sexes.

Testes and ovaries, average heights and weights. Strengths and hair patterns and rates of growth. Lengths and onset of puberty and development and flushes of hormones sweeping through our bodies. Bones and hips and milk and muscle and fat.

There are, indeed, differences.

No doubt.

No one who studies these things is arguing they don't exist.

Some are large. Some are small. Some are strikingly noticeable, and some are buried deep within.

But here's the thing: when it comes to our brains, the sexes (and let's not forget intersex folks) are not as dissimilar as you've been led to believe.

You've probably heard of left brain, right brain and the popularized Mars-Venus construct—these concepts all sort of bleed together for us lay-people, forming a nebulous cultural notion that men and women are, on many levels, vastly different.

But get this: Do you know what scientists consider a "large" gap in brain differences between the sexes? Do you envision a Mars-Venus gap? Like, I dunno, a 10 percent difference?

Twenty?

Fifty?

It's less than *1 percent*.

A "large" gap between the sexes is considered to be between 0.66 and 1.00 percent different.

A "moderate" gap measures between 0.36 and 0.65 percent.

A "small" gap measures between 0.11 and 0.35 percent.

And a "close to zero" gap, or basically no discernible difference at all, measures between 0.00 and 0.10 percent.

Yes, we know brain difference gaps exist between the sexes. But do these scientific measurements match up with our broader cultural depictions of interplanetary distances?

According to a groundbreaking meta-analysis of all available tests across dozens of fields, 78 percent of brain sex differences are scientifically categorized as small or close to zero.

It's patently absurd, in other words, that these myths of cosmos-spanning differences in "innate" intellectual ability endure.

Nevertheless, here we are.

You may have noticed these tiny differences are often added up, amplified, and used to justify unequal treatment, whether in play, pay, job availabilities, or opportunities by either outright sexist people or those who call themselves "traditional" or "old-fashioned" and don't realize they're being sexist. They don't study differences to *help* people.

They don't say, "Gee, scientists found a difference in how boys and girls think about *X*, so let's explore ways to close that gap if we can!"

No, they say, "Well, this one study says boys like trucks, so therefore girls suck at math and hence discrimination in high-tech fields is perfectly natural. What can we even do?"

shrug

You name an inequity and someone has used "science" and our "natural differences" to justify it.

But remember. Most differences in our brains—which control our abilities—are minutely small. And the tests that discover our "differences" cannot be divorced from the incredibly sexist society that developed them.

> It's slippery and omnipresent, this casual doubting of dignity through science.

I'VE NEVER UNDERSTOOD why people want to point out differences between sexes and genders and then use those differences to . . . I don't know . . . justify fewer rights for some? Sparse opportunities? Less pay? No health care? Scant personal safety?

It's slippery and omnipresent, this casual doubting of dignity through science—arguments, I must confess, that are perpetrated largely by "reasonable" white men in my circles and beyond, white men whose rights and abilities have never been doubted, never been put up for debate.

Think about the discussions we consider socially acceptable.

"Are white men innately dumb?" is not a question you hear passed down generation to generation, but how many times have history books, sociologists—even good friends and family members—asked the same about women, or black people, or Native Americans, or any other population that has rolled under the foot of white men? (Keep in mind, please, that none of this impugns *you*, personally—it's simply the historical record of American experiences, hard truths of our past. Now, if we perpetuate these experiences today, that's on us.)

Before moving on, I want to point out that neuroscientists—people who study this stuff for a living—have indeed pinpointed differences between the sexes when it comes to brain development but also that these differences are not the wide chasms we've been led to believe they are. The narrative asks us to spend far too much time asking whether inequity is somehow scientifically justified.

Not whether it's just.

TAKE THIS ONE myth. It really messes with our boys. You've probably heard it at school or in your friend groups.

A toddler boy is struggling to speak, a skill his girl peers have already mastered. But don't worry, the boy's parents are told. Boys just develop this skill later than girls.

And this is true, Eliot says. They do.

But boys aren't *years* behind girls, or even half a year, or even several months.

On average, boys are just *one month* behind girls in this developmental milestone.

It's not a planetary-wide gap in brain development, in other words.

It's a small one.

With big consequences. We take some kernel of truth—that a very small gap between the sexes exists—and transmogrify it into an enduring cultural story with lasting, damaging consequences.

"That turns out to be a really harmful stereotype," Eliot told me, "because if you have a little boy who is eighteen months and not saying any words yet, and the pediatrician—this really happens—says, 'Oh, don't worry, he's a boy and boys talk later,' that is exactly the wrong response because we know early intervention is the best way to remedy speech and language deficits."

It's not that parents should start fretting immediately. Based on averages, some boys are outliers and naturally do not utter words for several months, or even years, beyond the average age of first speech—or they learn to speak much, much earlier than average boys.

But it also doesn't mean parents should wait long before intervening simply because of cultural expectations, playground legends, and pop science.

Again, the average gap is one month, not several.

Of this myth Eliot says, "It lowers parents' expectations, and we know achievement is so fueled by parental expectations. If anything, he needs a little extra social and verbal interaction."

Eliot encounters misinterpretations like these all the time in her study of the differences between male and female brains.

"They're everywhere."

And they can't be separated from the sexist culture at large.

THE THING ABOUT studies is there always seems to be a new one. And they usually filter down to us regular folk in shiny, breaking news articles— stories that are shared and that form the basis of our culture, and then our expectations.

"News! Wide gap in how men and women taste potatoes!"

Or something like that. You've seen it.

And while some of us are left wondering, "Who actually studies crap like that for a living?" some others among us are filing the conclusions away, preparing to use it as ammunition in the war of the sexes. More innocently, perhaps, we toss one more piece of evidence that boys and girls, men and women are inherently different onto the quiet, mountainous pile of "evidence" that reconfirms all the old biases we consume in media messages, old wives' tales, and playground banter.

If laypeople are confused by the latest research, regurgitating this result or that one from whatever new "groundbreaking" study happens to hit the newspaper or glossy grocery store aisle magazine, just imagine being a neuroscientist. As we regular folks pick through the latest essay to hit the internet and then amplify it in ways that cement our cultural myths about dissimilarities, scientists pore over endless, eye-crushing studies that never seem to stop.

Guess which ones receive the most recognition and review—the few that reveal large gaps or the many more that reveal little to no gaps at all?

It's a quirk in the field, Eliot argues, and helps explain why we are constantly barraged with stories in popular media that make it seem as if we're really from separate universes.

It goes like this: scientists uncover a small discrepancy in an experiment (often in animals or with older children) and publish the study. Public relations professionals at the scientists' institutes get into the mix, hoping to gain as much press coverage as possible, and then amplify and perhaps exaggerate the contrast to get attention and glory and—wait for it—funding.

But here's the thing: a layperson might perceive a "large" gap as some bridge too far to cross instead of something that scientifically measures as less than 1 percent. In other words, we're constantly asked to believe the sexes are so different that it is, indeed, perfectly natural for women to have fewer opportunities in certain fields and for men not to realize their full emotional selves as caretakers and, *gasp*, loving creatures.

Scientists have another meaning altogether when it comes to reporting "gaps." It's really quite fascinating—and almost tragic—to see small differences amplified into unbridgeable yawning chasms.

IN 2005, JANET Sibley Hyde, a psychologist at the University of Wisconsin, released the groundbreaking study "The Gender Similarities Hypothesis." Unlike most studies, which focus on one particular hypothesis, it was a meta-analysis of studies.

In other words, she took all the studies available about sex differences, analyzed them altogether, and found something at once extraordinary and entirely predictable: in a species whose members share most of the same chromosomes and are homologous from the start, the sexes are really more alike than different.

In only two subject areas were sex differences considered "very large"— or more than 1 percent: throwing velocity and throwing distance.

The rest were all under 1 percent. Across the board.

In math, an area where our so-called sex differences are used to justify underrepresentation of women in high-tech fields, boys did indeed outpace girls at mathematical problem solving . . . with a 0.08 percent gap in performance. This difference falls into a category scientifically regarded as "close to zero." Meanwhile, girls outpaced boys at mathematical computation . . . with a gap of 0.14 percent, or "small."

In leadership, an area where our so-called differences are used to justify underrepresentation of women in politics and CEO suites, girls outpaced boys in perceived abilities in three out of four fields.

Boys and men largely had higher self-esteem and life satisfaction, whereas girls and women generally reported more happiness. Boys and men had higher physical ability ratings, the only area where studies showed performance gaps of more than 1 percent.

The rest of the findings are almost laughably scattershot. Some match up with the societal expectations we still place on kids—boys are considered more aggressive and girls tend toward caring for others more. Remember all of those sexist T-shirts? The ones that call boys aggressive and girls lovely objects? Scientists simply can't separate those cultural influences from the results of the tests, so, sure, gaps may exist—but because of nature or because of the entirely sexist culture we raise our kids in?

Funny thing: even the tests themselves are intrinsically sexist, and no wonder—they were created by white dudes generations ago when it was a socially acceptable case to consider, and argue out loud, that women are inferior. That sexist thinking seeped into the tests.

Want to know how all those sex differences are tallied?

If boys measure higher than girls, the gap is noted with a plus sign.

If girls outpace boys, it's marked with a negative, a minus sign.

It may seem a small thing, but shit like that adds up. These scientists don't exist on some alternate plane. They're part of our culture, too, a culture where it's perfectly "normal" to label tough girls as "tomboys" and softer boys as "girls."

AND THAT'S WHERE the final point comes into play: What's it all matter?

Trying to measure people's natural, innate abilities is a racist, sexist American tradition that dates back for generations, when we were trying to justify slavery and then disenfranchisement, and then Jim Crow, and then mass incarceration, and then underrepresentation in business, sports, government—you name it.

Take a look at the codes embedded in debates like these. Are people using data to explore ways to help people? To, say, find gaps so as to discover new medicines or teaching techniques to help close those gaps? Sure, maybe in scientific fields. But, by and large, when you see everyday people debating

> **Trying to measure people's natural, innate abilities is a racist, sexist American tradition that dates back for generations, when we were trying to justify slavery and then disenfranchisement, and then Jim Crow, and then mass incarceration, and then underrepresentation in business, sports, government.**

sex differences, they are probably using data to justify some type of second-class citizenry, like the idea that women don't belong in certain jobs.

Take the Google guy. Ugh, what a jerk. I almost hate to mention him, but he's really emblematic of the way we still debate, publicly, out loud, whether women are inherently stupid. How easily we slip into these "debates."

In 2017, some asshat programmer dude published an internal memo at Google that, on its face, seemed like a reasonable analysis of the differences between sexes to explain away underrepresentation of women in high-tech fields. Companies like Google, Facebook, and Apple have notoriously poor representation in software development and other tech areas, with only 20 to 30 percent of workers female.

It's because men are better at higher-level thinking, and women are more neurotic, or some such bullshit, the memo argued. Men, in other words, are naturally more suited to the work, and therefore the ratio is fine, and gender outreach is only a politically correct act that makes everyone feel good but that is really ineffective.

Thankfully, Google fired the dude. Can you imagine for a second being this guy's coworker? Knowing he thinks you're inferior because of who you . . . are?

But his philosophy is not singular. Despite scientific evidence of only tiny differences, these cultural myths endure. We have to come to grips with the idea that men, our friends and family, maybe, keep bringing them up largely to excuse away discrimination, not to discover new ways to bridge small disparities.

Programmer and lecturer Cynthia Lee said it best in an essay for the website Vox.com: working in tech is a dream, but to be a woman in the field means always facing skepticism about "belonging."

"There is always a jury, and it's always still out."

How many other fields can you think of, offhand, where the jury is still out on whether women "belong"?

THE REAL-WORLD RAMIFICATIONS of these myths not only leave women out of certain fields for no sound reason but also call into question their basic abilities over and over again.

"I've worked in IT for fifteen years," says my friend Sarah Werle Kimmel. "I have stories."

I met Kimmel through social media circles and frequently hire her to tweak my personal website. I asked her what sort of sexisms or biases she faces as a woman in a high-tech field.

"From the simple 'Isn't there someone else at your company I can talk to about my problem?' before even *telling* me their problem, to assuming I'm the receptionist that can't help them fix their computer," she said, "not to mention the guy who literally said to my face when I walked into their office to fix their server that was down, 'Is there someone else your company can send? It's a really complicated problem.'"

SO, WHAT CAN WE DO?

The point of all this?

See the gross storylines at play. Here's a thing we can do as parents from the beginning. It's really quite simple. We men need to stop accepting the frame of these debates and passing on these sexist notions. Don't put people's worth or equality on the bargaining table, as if whether men and women are equal and worthy of the same jobs and opportunities is a perfectly reasonable thing to debate.

We know differences indeed make us special and unique, and that's awesome and worthy of celebration. But none of these differences should be used to hamstring a person's potential.

Potential is the key word here, and we do a great disservice to all our children by cutting it off based on their sex organs.

Eliot points out that all brains have what's called "plasticity," or the ability to grow. A few scores showing meager differences here and there—differences that may be more cultural than natural—shouldn't be enough to shut down that opportunity to grow.

In other words, Eliot says, boys and girls and men and women can actually grow their brains and increase their abilities to do things, simply given time on a certain task and repetition. It's truly a practice-makes-perfect, or at least -better, situation. Work on something hard enough and long enough, and the brain rewrites itself to become better at that thing—the number of synapses actually increases and test scores go up.

But, look, if we tell girls and boys from day one that they're inherently different and possessed of certain abilities that will determine their life opportunities—and then hand one trucks and Legos and the other dolls, and then dress one in math shirts and the other in tight-fitting flower garb, and then show one an endless series of violent action movies and the other sexed-up cat-fighting drama shows—honestly, the fuck you *think* is going to happen?

Eliot is clear: there are indeed differences between the sexes during development—in utero and through childhood and into adulthood—that definitely account for large or small gaps. But we're also raising our kids next to each other but in different worlds, Eliot argues. And that constant bombardment of cultural expectations can't be separated from studies that reveal gaps—gaps that likely could be closed through simple hard work.

In other words, if we can close gaps through hard work and repetition, we can also widen those gaps through constant reinforcement of bullshit stereotypes that help no one. They only serve to prop up unjust systems and expectations.

We can do better.

You don't have to be a jerk about it, but you can certainly say to friends and relatives something along the lines of, "Well, look, sure, there are differences. But they're small. And they can't altogether be separated from how we raise boys and girls and what we expect of them. Boys better at math? We tell them they are over and over. Girls better at reading and writing in middle school, and being able to 'read' other people's emotions as adults? We expect them to be quiet and polite and studious and caring, so why not?"

Or something like that. I dunno, perhaps just ask them if they're trying to study gaps to help close them or to justify ongoing discrimination, to shrug it all off as perfectly "natural."

You don't have to be perfect at it. But you know the science now. You know it all adds up, that you can't divorce these notions from the sexist and racist society in which we all move around, a society that sets different expectations even from *before* birth for our boys and girls.

At long last, it's time to excuse the jury on this narrative.

—Chapter 3—

THE LOW DAD BAR

In expecting very little from dads, society does two things at once: cut dads out of the everyday lives of our children, and pigeonhole women as the caretakers. It's a lose-lose paradigm we can shift together.

T HIS ALL HAPPENED in the span of a few hours.

I was walking down the sidewalk with my daughter strapped into a chest carrier—a Babybjörn-type thing that left her legs dangling around my belly. I liked that it kept her close to me, her tiny heart thrumming against my chest, and her head facing outward so that we could see and examine the world together.

We had just waved at a cable car rattling up a hill.

"Ding, ding, ding!" We giggled.

And now we were on the way home for a nap, probably for both of us. It had already been a long day.

Then I heard it.

Was that . . . *applause?*

A homeless man sat on the sidewalk, his back slumped against a building. And he was looking at us.

Applauding.

I walked past him and he just kept doing it.

Clap, clap, clap.

"Way to go, dad," he called. "You're doing it right!"

Just hours later, we were at the store, getting things for dinner, when an elderly woman . . . wait for it . . . applauded in the checkout line.

"I just love to see dads and their kids together," she said, leaning in to make faces at Emme. "It really makes my day."

I've been applauded, praised, hugged, congratulated, lauded— merely for being in the same vicinity as my daughter.

THE FIRST TIME it happened, I was shocked. I remember swiveling my head around to see what the commotion was all about. But over the years, I've gotten used to it.

I've been applauded, praised, hugged, congratulated, lauded—merely for being in the same vicinity as my daughter.

It happens all the time.

Just last year, I ran into a girls athletic store to pick up a few bras and a swimsuit my daughter wanted for a family trip.

No bigs.

Literally. Just. Clothes.

And yet, the middle-aged woman who rang up the purchases handed me the bag and said, "You deserve an award. Dad of the Year!"

I kid you not.

An award.

For shopping.

As my wife said, if that cashier had boys, do you think she'd consider giving herself an award for buying *them* clothes? Do you think any cashier anywhere, ever, would put her up for an award for it?

Of course not.

I'm not alone in this experience.

Fellow stay-at-home dad Billy Kilgore wrote a wonderful piece for Upworthy about all the praise he receives simply for being in public with his child.

"Best dad ever!"

"You're taking this dad thing to the next level!"

The bar for dads is incredibly, preposterously, infuriatingly low.

The ramifications are achingly horrible.

Not just for dads.

But for boys, and for moms, and women and girls in general.

IT'S NOT JUST me. It's a thing my dad friends have experienced as well. All over the country.

But there's a weird dichotomy in this, we've determined. A dad at a store or walking down the street with kids—we get applauded. A dad at a park or a "mommy and me" group—we get the side-eye. One dad even had a group of moms confront him and demand just what, exactly, he was up to.

At the park.

With his kid.

I spoke on a panel about racial bias in parenting, and a friend shared his buddy's experience. He's a black man with a white adopted daughter, and the daughter is frequently asked by strangers in stores, malls, theaters, wherever, if "she's okay," if she "needs help." These strangers wait until the dad is out of earshot and then sidle up to his daughter, offering to "save" her.

From her own father.

I get applauded for merely being with my daughter. That guy gets the police called on him.

Sexism, racism, patriarchal structures we all buy in to, knowingly or not, combine to make our life experiences different, but if there's a through-line in them all, it's this: society praises even the least amount of effort from dads while simultaneously punishing moms for not "doing it all."

> **Society praises even the least amount of effort from dads while simultaneously punishing moms for not "doing it all."**

Fellas, we have some issues to explore. But the good news is we can help break this bullshit down—for ourselves, for our kids, and society as a whole— one small talk at a time.

THE THING IS, deep down, if I were being honest, the applause and praise actually feels *good* in the moment.

Rarely do parents get praise for the job they're doing. Occasionally, you might get feedback as the kids get older from, say, coaches or other parents.

"Hey, just wanted to let you know Jimmy was so polite and kind at the party today, always said his pleases and thank yous."

And you'll get a tiny thrill that perhaps amid all the madness and lectures you're doing something right.

Occasionally.

So, I get it. Praise can feel *good,* even from homeless dudes on the street, and even for something as basic as taking the kid to the store—*gasp*—on your own.

But deep down, it also really bugs me. And it should. It should bother the absolute shit out of us.

First, you don't get a cookie for acting like a grown-ass adult. Were you not present during the baby making? Did you not sign up?

Second, these tropes are, in fact, dangerous.

If merely being in the presence of our children is worthy of praise, what's the narrative floating underneath the surface: Who is *really* expected to be in their presence?

That's right.

Moms.

Women.

Even women without kids get hit by the expectation they are supposed to be at home, pumping out children, instead of, say, in the boardroom or the capitol.

"'Have I ever received applause for walking our daughter down the street?' Are you kidding me?"

This is my wife, snorting.

Dopey dads get a cultural permission slip to sit on the couch, drink beer, and not be involved in any household duties or childcare ("*Oh, he's just a dad . . . sigh*") and women are penalized at work and in society in real, harmful ways for daring to step outside of home or show ambition outside child-rearing.

CASUAL SIDEWALK AND shopping applause and praise are not, to be sure, the only messages telling dads the bar is low when it comes to parenting.

The messages are everywhere. In the media. In the news. Maybe even in your own home or friend circles.

Ever see a commercial in which a dad can't seem to make toast?

WTF?

Toast.

I've always been a fan of Sarah Haskins, who created the online show *Target Women,* which tracked how women and men were represented in commercials. (She's moved on to other work, but the clips are available online and are well worth your time, like a 101 class in viewing our culture today.)

This is one of my favorites. Haskins pointed out that, in commercials, single men are often portrayed as super handsome, super sporty, super spy-like, and amazing. Think of any razor blade or sports car commercial, and the guy is just pretty cool, right?

Handsome, mysterious, sexy.

But just a few years later give that same guy a kid in a commercial, and all of a sudden, he can't put breakfast on the table or change a diaper. Seriously, from CIA spy in a suit with the best cologne to not being able to open a cereal box.

This?

Is how dads are generally viewed in pop culture and beyond.

Dads can morph into doughy, unkempt bridge trolls and be praised for having the perfect "dad bod." Imagine the shit moms get from all angles for missing one morning's "calorie count" or for not "putting on her face" or, perhaps, for putting on too *much* face.

For them, there's no winning.

For us . . . well, again, who wrote the rule book?

Now, LOOK, I rarely take offense to shitty dad jokes and media representations of dads. Yes, they're demeaning and make us all look like stooges and imbeciles. I'd roll my eyes and move on if the ramifications weren't so damaging to dads and, worse, moms—and girls and women in general.

Here's where the dangerous part comes into play.

With these tired tropes of doofus dads, men miss out on making pivotal, important emotional connections with their children. We're not supposed to care about the caring and feeding and proper raising of our own kids, let alone the attendant responsibilities, such as the PTA bake sales, the play-dates, the basic emotional labor that comes with having children. Dads are sort of left off the hook on a lot of this stuff, considered too inept or, perhaps, too busy elsewhere—a permission slip of absence never afforded the working mom, who is expected to do it all.

Dads, in other words, are seemingly cut off from the everyday, expected to pop in occasionally for sports or fishing.

We're missing the good stuff, guys.

Here's something else. Every now and then, I hear a divorced dad who has gotten "totally screwed" in childcare and child support proceedings. Men's rights advocates, the lunatic fringe of sad men who think men somehow have it worse, rant about men getting the shaft in divorces.

And you know what? They have a point. Very often, men do.

But it's not because society has it out for men or dads. It's because of the harm the flip side of these tired dad tropes do, the messages they send.

These things are connected.

If dads are so inept they can't make toast or, *gasp*, manage a house for a long weekend, who is expected to do all the work?

That's right.

Moms.

Girls. Women.

People raised with that mind-set will probably rule in favor of women not because they "hate" men or want to "screw over" dads. But because our society is absolutely riddled with the notion that women are first and foremost caretakers.

THAT'S WHAT REALLY pisses me off about the dopey dad trope: the inverse expectations it imposes.

Stay-at-home mom? Here's your kid.

Working mom? Here's your kid.

Single mom, divorced mom, older mom, younger mom? Where the fuck is your kid?

All childcare is ultimately the woman's responsibility in these tired dad tropes—whether they're in commercials or tiny, often innocent-sounding greetings you might encounter at the store.

"Giving mom a break today, daddy?"

"Babysitting duty, daddy?"

Babysitting. My. Own. Fucking. Child.

My friend Chris, a stay-at-home dad and president of the National At-Home Dad Network, got so annoyed by the depiction that his group created a cool T-shirt campaign. The shirt says, "Dads Don't Babysit. It's called parenting."

Is it any wonder that the conversation about "doing it all" only revolves around women? Can they be the perfect worker, earning lower pay for the same work, and bake the cupcakes for the school fair? Meanwhile, men like me can just go punch a clock and come home to watch any sports game we want, peacefully, in a "man cave," while women are expected to do everything else.

LIKE I SAID, the ramifications are dangerous. Yes, women are expected to take on the emotional labor of childcare, no matter their ambitions and careers.

But they're also penalized for it.

A huge component of the gender pay gap comes from the time women take off work to care for kids. The cultural expectation is that women should take time from their job and career to care for kids, whereas men don't face this expectation and are, indeed, punished if they do take time off.

In the end, women lose out on hours, skills, experience, promotions, and everything else needed to keep climbing the salary ladder, because they're expected to drop out and care for kids. A recent study by the Census Bureau shows women earn $12,600 annually less than men before children, and $25,000 less after. Add up $25,000 over a twenty-year career, and that's a lifetime loss of half a million bucks.

There's freedom in that lost money, opportunity, peace of mind.

"This shows that the birth of a child is really when the gender earnings gap grows," Danielle H. Sandler, a senior economist at the Census Bureau, told the *New York Times* in 2018.

THIS LOW BAR for dads always makes me think of our daughter's dentist and how these tropes play out in real life: the everyday emotional baggage women are expected to carry while men can not only shrug it off but also deny it exists.

I've gotten to know the dental staff well over the years. After all, I'm the one responsible for making and getting to the appointments—twice a year like clockwork. I think Dana went to one or two early on to see what the fuss was all about, but it's difficult for a working lawyer to get across town in the middle of the day to pick a kid up from school and schlep her off to the dentist's torture chair.

That is, quite literally, my job.

I'm sure if Dana walked in the door, they'd have no idea who she was; meanwhile, I'm always delighted to see our dentist and her staff—especially the supercool hygienist who gives us free doses of fluoride because our insurance covers only one a year (thanks, dude!).

And yet, despite this dynamic playing out for years, I'll bet you can guess who they call about appointment reminders. No matter how many times I see them, or how many times I tell them that I'm the default parent, I get an email from my wife twice a year: "The dentist called me again."

She's literally expected to do everything—bring home the bacon and root out cavities. (The dentist's office finally corrected this behavior just last year after a few years of telling them.)

Think we're outliers?

Think again.

THE NUMBER OF dual-income families with kids under eighteen has risen from 49 percent of families in the 1970s to 66 percent of families today, according to the Pew Research Center.

The percentage of families in which the dad was the "breadwinner" has decreased from 47 to 28 percent.

Read that one again. Dads make up just a *quarter* of breadwinners in society. Does that match up with the cultural and media depictions you come across? With your friends and family and how they handle everything from childcare to housework?

Meanwhile, with these changes something interesting has happened on the home front. The number of hours dads spent on childcare per week rose from 2.5 to 7 from 1965 to 2011, according to Pew. Housework rose from 4 to 19 hours a week for dads.

In other words, dads are doing more with kids and around the house. Yet, it often feels as if the childcare responsibilities ever fall on moms, and numbers from Pew back that up. With dads doing more, so are moms. Childcare hours have increased for them as well—yet so have working hours outside of the home ("supermom" trope, anyone?).

A "superdad" maybe shows up at school drop-off every now and then, perhaps walks to the park with a child.

A supermom literally does everything else.

First, it's important to see it. Then, it's important to break it.

You'll be freeing and benefiting everyone. (Special note here for my single-parent friends, like my mom, who do it all and get no breaks: We owe you drinks. You're crushing it.)

MY BUDDY DOUG French, who cofounded the Dad 2.0 conference, which harnesses movers and shakers in social media to help change the perception of dads for the better, has seen some gains in recent years. Dads, he noted, are feeling the same work-life balance issues as moms. There's been progress.

"Modern fathers are emphasizing parenting in their daily lives as never before, so they're just learning the challenges of work-life integration that mothers have struggled with for decades," he says.

Though the media depictions of dads often are negative, he notices some positive changes.

"Media portrayals have done a wonderful job of catching up," French says. "When the Dad 2.0 Summit began six years ago, one of the biggest marketing stories involved a diaper company portraying dads as helpless caregivers while moms rolled their eyes in exasperation. Brands have realized that neither characterization is relevant, and now messaging has become much more positive."

That brand was Huggies, and dads went to town on its hapless dad depictions—pressing Huggies to change its portrayals.

This is important because these depictions are what people see and take cues from. It's one of many social scripts that translate into disconnection for dads and do-it-all martyrdom for moms.

HERE'S AN ESPECIALLY annoying and confounding experience that illustrates just how much women are expected to do around the house while men get a complete pass on the life they signed up for.

I can't tell you how many times I've heard working and stay-at-home moms alike say they can't get away for a weekend with their buds because they fear their husbands, who also work, can't handle the home front.

It boggles my mind (1) that this happens, and (2) that it is somehow acceptable, normal, something people casually talk about.

Two adult-ass people decide to have kids together, and one half of that arrangement is considered so inept and clueless that the other can't be away for a night or two without the entire house falling apart?

Two adult-ass people decide to have kids together, and one half of that arrangement is considered so inept and clueless that the other can't be away for a night or two without the entire house falling apart?

Now look, I understand it's challenging. Kids are sometimes tiny life-force takers. Managing and cleaning a house can be annoying.

But, dudes.

Come. The. Fuck. On.

If this is you, let's be honest: get your shit together. Seriously, it's an embarrassment. What are you, four?

Dads, you're missing out on your kids, and you're trapping your partner in a life of servitude. You're perpetuating an age-old societal messaging system that it's all okay, normal to amplify messages women hear at work and on the streets telling them their primary value is being at home, even if they don't have, or even want, kids.

My advice when I hear moms grumble about incompetent dads is always the same: go away. And go away more often. Just go sleep at a friend's house and binge-watch *The Good Place* all night (it's the freaking best).

DESPITE THESE SHIFTING ideas of childcare and housework, something paradoxical is at work in broader society.

A spate of recent studies and surveys shows that millennial men, the youngest generation taking over, hold much more "traditional" views of gender and sex, meaning they view women as inferior—in intelligence and leadership abilities.

So . . . yeah.

What do you do with *that*?

You'd think that once the "dinosaurs" who were weaned on sexism and racism die out, then all would be right and equal and just, yes?

My theory is that these throwbacks to less equitable views come down to the same idea at work with parents and racism. Studies show that well-intentioned parents who want to teach their kids equality actually create tiny racists by pretending to be color-blind.

Well, *pretending* may be a harsh word—in most cases, their behavior is well-intentioned. But nevertheless, this type of color-blindness allows society to fill in views on race instead of parents. And society is still pretty racist.

Probably the same thing happens for sexism. Parents who believe in equality say they are "beyond gender inequality" or "don't see it," and so society fills in the blanks for kids with all the millions of messages of inequality it sends. Society is still pretty sexist.

I had a dad friend my own Gen X age admit to me he was "just traditional" and expected women to stay home.

Tradition is no excuse for oppression.

The same can be said for these tired dad tropes. Just because they exist doesn't mean you have to buy in to them. They're bad for dads. They leave us disconnected from our children and critical home lives.

And they're bad for women, perpetuating caregiver-only roles that lead to everything from endless emotional labor to lower pay to fewer opportunities.

It shouldn't be up to women to change this dynamic.

So, see it.

Help break it.

And don't expect praise for it.

Seriously, check this narrative as you're doing the work. You might be applauded on the street. You might get lauded in the shopping mall.

It's all quite absurd. And there's literally a name for it: the pedestal effect. When men do things traditionally considered "women's work," we get praise for it.

"If you believe in gender equality, it is not hard to understand why it is problematic to place one gender on a pedestal for doing the bare minimum, while another bears the bulk of the child care," stay-at-home dad Kilgore writes.

No more gold stars for doing the parenting you signed up for.

You got this. Let's get to it.

SO, WHAT CAN WE DO?

Sociologist Michael Kimmel may be onto something when it comes to work and household roles specifically.

"There's nothing inherently masculine about work, or inherently feminine about childcare," he says.

He is of the mind that we could radically diminish or even eliminate societal sexism if we simply changed the way we talk about adult roles.

Here's a good, concrete way to talk about it with the kiddos.

It's not *men* who grow up and go to work—it's *grown-ups*.

It's not *women* who grow up and care for children—it's *grown-ups*.

"It's just what you do as a grown-up," he says.

That's the message we're teaching our daughter.

Kids grow up and, well, become adults. That means work, participating equally in family life—working shit out with your partner if you have one and valuing his or her choices and decisions.

"It's very simple," Kimmel says. "Parents need to be a team. They need to be allies."

If you happen to have a two-parent household, and one is checked out or considered incompetent, what are you telling your kids? What lessons are you imparting in the everyday? Is one parent responsible for . . . everything? Work outside the home, and work inside it?

Don't buy in to the trope.

Grown-ups are expected to be involved in their child's school, home life, upbringing, and so forth. Not just moms, not just dads.

Grown-ups.

Adults who have kids.

You can do great good in your circles by taking a pause and considering for a moment who does the work—the everyday kid stuff, house stuff, emotional stuff—and what your role in it has been and whether it lines up with the cultural storylines you see at play.

Don't expect a gold star if you're doing the bare minimum, or even more.

Parenting, childcare, house care, emotional labor—they're just things grown-ups do.

—Chapter 4—

YOU ARE WHAT YOU EAT

We bombard children with horrible messages that appearance is more important than health, but we can make big gains through subtle shifts in how we speak to our kids about simple things like food.

P OP QUIZ: WHAT do you do when you're on a playdate and a mom says, in front of all the girls present, that she and her daughter are "on a diet" and that they're only eating seeds to "get skinny"?

The girls. They're all eight.

That's pretty shitty, right? I think we can agree on that—telling a bunch of kids it's okay to starve yourself to look a certain way.

But how about when your school principal makes several announcements to the entire school about how hungry she is because of the "diet" she's on?

Or how about when you're watching a sporting event with your kid and a commercial comes on imploring women to "try this new diet!" to look healthy, happy, and, of course, sexy?

When a relative says you're looking "a little porky"?

When a seemingly innocent-looking iPad game suddenly stops to hit kids with an ad for another game that portrays hyper-slim-waisted women about to engage in a threesome? (That was unexpected.)

Oh, sure, you can easily call out the playdate mom and say something simple, like, "Oh, that's crazy! Ha ha. We eat the ever-loving fuck out of a whole bunch of healthy food because we need energy and power to get shit done!"

Or something more kid appropriate. Or not. Up to you.

You can pull the principal aside and say, "Hey, come on. Knock that shit off." You can tell the relative to kindly fuck off to fuckville.

Your friends, your workmates, your relatives, they probably "get it" pretty quickly. They're not bad people out to inflict a lifetime of poor eating habits on your kids. Like so many of these quiet, sexist storylines, we simply grew up with them, thought they were acceptable, and haven't really given them much thought.

YOUR KIDS ARE going to be absolutely bombarded with endless messages telling them that, above all, thin is best—the healthiest, the happiest, the sexiest—and that they should probably go on a starvation diet to achieve just that, no matter their individual health needs.

We expose kids to billions of dollars in advertisements that urge them to eat crap-ass, unhealthy foods, while iShackling them at home for fear of "stranger danger" at the playground, so, surprise, surprise, childhood obesity is on the rise. At the same time, we hammer them with endless media depictions and everyday expectations that exalt hyper-thinness as the societal gold standard.

We're doing a number on them, to be sure.

Across the United States, childhood obesity rates have more or less stabilized in the past decade, with 17 percent of kids two to nineteen years old falling into that category, according to the 2017 *State of Obesity Report* put out by the nonprofit Trust for America's Health.

So, that's good news, right? Stable sounds nice.

Unfortunately, that rate is triple what it was in the 1970s, the report shows.

Rates are declining for very young kids (2–5), remaining stable for middle-age kids (6–11), and spiking for older kids (12–19).

What does it all mean in the real lives of our kids? They suffer health consequences: high blood pressure, high cholesterol, depression, bullying, diabetes, and more.

Indeed, many factors are at play here—wealth, education, geography, upbringing, access to healthy food. It all adds up. The report shows a full 90 percent of kids have "poor" diets, only half of them get a full sixty minutes of daily exercise, a quarter of them watch three or more hours of TV and other media a day, all while schools are reducing recess time in favor of class time and better test scores.

These poor health realities don't exist in a vacuum. They coincide with tremendous advertising campaigns that food companies spend billions of dollars on to hook our kids. The Kaiser Family Foundation found that kids are hit with thousands of ads a year; kids ages eight to twelve are smacked with the most.

These incessant food ads and incredible health issues paradoxically exist in a culture in which we depict skinny as the ultimate arbiter of happiness, as the norm.

The Geena Davis Institute on Gender in Media reports that in both prime-time and children's TV shows, the female characters are twice as likely to have "slim" waists than their male counterparts, and that girls and women are far more likely to be depicted as "sexy" or with exposed skin or to be wearing "sexy" outfits.

Common Sense Media shows girls are not alone in receiving these messages that can distort body image. Male toys typically advertised to boys sport oversized muscles not even seen on professional bodybuilders.

What follows? Common Sense Media reports that one in four kids have tried a diet before age seven. A 2012 study in *Miss Representation* (a fabulous documentary about cultural depictions of girls and boys) found that a full 80 percent of ten-year-olds have been on diets.

What a minefield our kids face. We sell them crap food constantly, limit their exercise, throttle their parents' ability to earn or learn or even grab a few fresh apples at the corner store, and then expect them to be super-skinny, hypersexualized objects.

"The media is selling young people the idea that girls' and women's value lies in their youth, beauty, and sexuality and not in their capacity as leaders," *Miss Representation*'s tagline explains. "Boys learn that their success is tied to dominance, power, and aggression. We must value people as whole human beings, not gendered stereotypes."

LET ME TELL you a short story. It illustrates how you might see these dynamics play out before your eyes as you're hanging with the kiddos.

My daughter, then seven, met a girl the same age at a horse show. Turned out we were staying at the same hotel, and the girls decided to go for a swim together.

Yay. Good times.

At the pool, my daughter is in a one-piece suit with a sun shirt over the top of it, not because of some puritanical bent of her parents but simply because she hates to slather on sunscreen. It takes time away from swimming. She's wearing goggles, a comfy outfit, and is happily trying to cannonball into the pool, over and over again.

Her new friend is in a string bikini and is lying on a towel on the pool deck.

"Hey, could you go jump somewhere else?" she tells my daughter. "You're splashing me."

"Well, why don't you just come jumping with me?"

The girl looked over her sunglasses and said, "Because my bathing suit would fall off!"

From the tone, it was meant as an obvious, "WTF, are you kidding me?" comment. But my daughter just cocked her head, confused.

"Well, why don't you just go put on another suit?"

Remember, these kids are seven.

The girl again shifted her sunglasses. "Because I have to work on my tan! Why don't you come up and lay down and work on your tan?"

So . . . she did.

My daughter grabbed her towel, put it next to the girl's, and plopped down on the pool deck.

Now, I know my kid. I started counting in my head the moment she plopped down. I got to seven seconds before my daughter hopped off the towel and jumped in the pool again.

Lying on the deck when she could play in a pool—a *pool!*—instead; it just wasn't in the cards for too long.

Eventually, the other girl joined in and spent half the time swimming and half the time pulling at her bikini, trying to keep it in place.

Here's the thing that broke my heart.

At one point, they were swimming near the side, near where I was busy with a book, eavesdropping like some Jane Goodall of the pool deck, when the girl said something like, "Ooph, I'm starving." It was one of those moans kids make. No big deal.

My daughter asked if we could order some snacks from room service (it wasn't that fancy of a hotel, sorry, kiddo).

The girl stopped her.

"No," she said. "I need to be able to wear this bikini!"

These girls. They had just competed in a horse show. They had just been swimming for a long time on a hot day. And this kid didn't want to eat because she had to fit in a bikini that kept falling off anytime she tried to do the very thing it was supposedly made for: swimming.

Damned if I didn't have a talk with my daughter later to reinforce the notion of healthy eating to fuel our bodies but also, for good measure, clothes to support our activity.

Because here's the thing. If I hadn't been there to overhear this, what lesson would my daughter have received? What would she have taken home?

That she should lay out instead of play to help her body "look" better, and that she should wear uncomfortable-ass clothes, and that she should starve herself just to wear them?

Awesome.

Look, I'm not relaying this to say what a great dad I am (but, come on, let's face it, right?! Here my daughter snorts) but rather to offer an anecdotal example of all the ways I've seen parents pass on some pretty shitty lessons—or at least lessons from society they haven't pushed back on—to their young kids.

I just happened to be there, on duty at the time, to see it. (I hit the vending machine and bought them snacks, endless, delicious snacks—and they fueled them for hours of play. And also more quiet reading time for me....)

I KNOW FULL well I won't be there for the infinite times she'll hear this from friends, movies, magazines, online articles, commenters, random strangers on the sidewalk, men and women who feel it's perfectly acceptable to tell girls and women to "eat a sandwich" or, conversely, to stop eating from the "trough."

"My very thin thirteen-year-old gets 'you should eat more' from a classmate," my friend Ryan says. "She is thin because we eat very unprocessed and I'm genetically predisposed to be thin."

"No matter what you are in our society weight-wise, it still needs to be fixed."

What irks him—and what I think encapsulates the bizarreness and danger of this issue—is the idea that if you're a girl or a woman, there's always something to work on, to be criticized about.

"It bothers me because no matter what you are in our society weight-wise, it still needs to be fixed," he says.

If you're skinny, you need to eat. If you're not, you need to "diet."

In other words, there's no winning. And it comes from all quarters.

COMMON SENSE MEDIA reviewed dozens of studies about diet messages and how kids absorb them.

The results were, well, disturbing.

It's worth a deep dive into what Common Sense Media found:

Children as young as five reported "dissatisfaction" with their bodies; even preschoolers took note about how society judges bodies.

Kids ages five to eight years old who thought their moms were dissatisfied with their bodies had negative reflections of their own.

Body image and the supposed "ideal" image go hand in hand. Common Sense found that 87 percent of ten- to eighteen-year-old females depicted in movies were below average weight.

More than one-half of girls and one-third of boys ages six through eight said their bodies were bigger than their ideal.

By age six, children are aware of the idea of "dieting," and many have tried it. Remember the study I mentioned above? A quarter of seven-year-olds have dieted, and 80 percent of ten-year-olds have done the same.

The kicker?

Between 1999 and 2006, hospitalizations for eating disorders among children younger than age twelve spiked 112 percent.

Well done, society. Well done.

SO, WHAT CAN WE DO?

It's clear that kids emulate and idealize a lot of the things they see—whether with their parents, on the schoolyard, or at the movies and on their cell phones.

So, what's a parent to do?

Like a lot of things, it's pretty simple.

Talk.

Talk with them from very early ages.

Don't let all those messages go unmentioned. *Someone* is teaching your kids about bodies, either casually at the hotel pool or on the playground or on TV and online, where companies spend literally billions of dollars a year to get kids to eat endless crap *and* buy in to skinny-themed beauty norms.

The big takeaway from experts? Don't freak. Be a good role model.

"I think the biggest tips I could offer would be to not make food such a big issue in the house. Keep it light and not serious. Role model good eating habits," says Anthony DeBenedet, a gastroenterologist and author of several parenting books, including *The Art of Rough Housing*.

The big takeaway from experts? Don't freak. Be a good role model.

"Talk about what food is healthy and what food isn't and why. But don't talk about it too much! Eat dessert! Eat McDonald's every now and then. Don't get obsessed on whether something has a preservative in it or is organic or whatever. The more the parent obsesses the more the child will," he says.

Dad Matthew Henry, a former school principal and now a YMCA director, says it's how we talk about the word *diet* that can have a positive influence—that is, *diet* means simply the menu of food that makes up what we eat, not a restriction on eating, as it's more popularly known.

"As a YMCA employee, we have conversations with our children about healthy living. This includes healthy diets that we discuss over dinner (pointing out protein and carbs and the vitamins and minerals in vegetables) and we discuss the importance of eating sweets in moderation," he says.

And what goes hand in hand with all this? Healthy activity.

"We also stress the importance of exercise (which mom and dad model to our kids by going running every weekend and in the evenings)," he says. "We never discuss weight as a method for measuring health."

IN OUR HOME, we eat the ever-living bejesus out of ice cream. And sometimes not even in moderation. We pig out and loaf on a couch and watch movies on weekend nights.

But we also don't watch TV during the week, and we eat usually healthy meals and talk about the value of eating enough good food to provide the energy for what we need to do. We're all sort of exercise obsessed, to be honest. I do running races and triathlons. My wife and daughter ride horses, run, and swim for fun.

Naturally, we're hungry to the point of hangry a lot. So, we try to talk about food as fuel—the good stuff we need to power us through the day.

Here's a thing you can do at home. Whenever I hear kids visiting our house talk about "counting calories," I quickly engage and remind them how important calories actually are—they are literally the fuel that fires our bodies.

Calories often get a bad rap. "OMG, too many calories!"

Have you ever seen a European food label? The calories are listed as "energy," which I think is an amazing way to frame the subject.

You eat some crappy energy, you're not going to have the power you need to do what you want to do. But you eat the fuck out of healthy energy, you're going to feel awesome and have the fuel to go play.

That's the lesson I try to impart when these messages of diets, counting calories, and other bullshit make their way into our home—either through parents or kids who just don't know any better or movies and media content that are fostering some crap ideas about bodies and the "ideal" appearance—which, let's face it, usually means that of super-skinny white girls.

IT SHOULD BE noted that none of this is lost on boys. They, too, idealize and "want" (1) the girls and women in their lives to have the body types they see venerated in the media, and (2) the same big chest–skinny leg body type they see emphasized for men. Common Sense Media says boys are just as susceptible to low self-esteem and body issues girls face, thanks to the onslaught. All those media images of muscle-bound angry men aren't so much for women's sexual preference as for boys' and men's idealized version of what it means to "be a man."

My friend Joanne, mom to two boys, says her kids definitely pick up on it all.

"We are framing it more with the kids about making healthy eating choices and healthy lifestyle and never about losing weight or dieting or being fat," she says. "They are so sensitive and self-conscious at this young age."

Common Sense Media has some good tips on combatting the messages crammed down our throats, not just around eating but also on the supposed ideal body images we are expected to aspire to.

Avoid stereotypical female and male characters in kids' media. That's a pretty big challenge. So, talk about it when you encounter them and share your own values, challenge assumptions about slim and heavy characters, and talk about the way characters are portrayed.

This is my favorite: "Point out characters, athletes, and celebrities who use their bodies to achieve something versus just trying to look good."

That, to me, is the debate winner in a nutshell. When it comes to discussing our bodies and our food diets, it's about fueling and using our bodies to do things—not merely to "look good."

—Chapter 5—

BOYS WILL BE BOYS

*We men need to do a better job raising boys to enjoy a full spectrum
of emotion while no longer shrugging off poor behavior. It all
adds up to serious lifetime consequences for boys—and girls.*

I'LL ALWAYS REMEMBER the first time I heard it. When it wasn't being
applied to me, that is.

"Boys will be boys."

My daughter, less than one at the time, was swimming in a pile of sand
at the playground, alternately smooshing her face into the loam and then
arching her back for air. She'd squeal and smile. She'd sit up, grab some sand,
and watch it slip through her fingers before, for some unholy reason, deciding it looked tasty enough to eat.

Fun times, I know.

Nearby, a boy at *least* a few years older was busy with his own piles of
sand and petrochemicals. Then, suddenly, he turned. It all happened so fast,
and yet I remember it in a slow-motion-movie blur.

He noticed my daughter nearby, her lips coated in a crust of delicious
grime and her fingers encased in drool and grit. He picked up a handful of
sand, took aim . . . and fired, a cloud of sand peppering her face.

Before I could react, a mother sitting opposite me picked him up, moved
him over a few feet, and offered a shy smile.

She shrugged. "Boys will be boys, right?"

I was comforting my daughter at this moment, checking on the sand in her eyes. I just kept thinking, "That's . . . *it*? Boys will be boys? It's over now? And I'm expected to just . . . nod along?"

The French, I found out later, actually have a phrase for that choice comeback you can't quite find at the moment but think of later, say, at the bottom of the stairs while walking away: *l'esprit de l'escalier.*

"Boys will be boys? I think you mean asshole parents will be asshole parents. Honestly, the fuck? You're not even going to talk to him?"

But whatever. I raged in open-mouthed, confused, disbelieving silence.

It wouldn't be the last time.

BOYS HAVE HIT her out of the blue, pulled her hair, stolen her playground toys, pushed her down slides and off swings. In each of these instances, all things kids do from time to time, the nearby parent shrugged and offered, "Boys will be boys."

I've heard friends and loved ones say it.

I have one friend who says, "Boys have more energy and just need to get it out." Read: so, girls in his life just have to take it.

> We consider that paradigm perfectly normal: one can get away with practically anything, and the other has to learn to defend herself.

We're setting our kids up for an incredible world of pain from the very beginning with these seemingly innocuous phrases. "Boys will be boys" is the foundational lynchpin of rape culture, and yet we hear it everywhere, almost from day one.

Follow the thread. Like you, probably, I have friends who are raising boys and who have excused away all manner of bad behavior because "that's just how boys are." I also have friends who are raising girls to defend themselves because of it. We consider that paradigm perfectly normal: one can get away with practically anything, and the other has to learn to defend herself.

One dad from my daughter's soccer team enrolled all his girls in martial arts classes. It was mandatory, he said.

"They need to know," he told me, turning deadly serious. He leaned in, an edge to his voice, and repeated, *"They need to know."*

I'M REMINDED OF Lise Eliot, the neuroscientist who studies sex differences for a living, arguing that we raise boys and girls in the same world but in different cultures.

One is raised to be wild and free and angry and violent, and the other to present herself as a flawless, obedient sexual gift to him, pleasing, for observing or taking, while also learning from childhood to defend herself from him.

Follow the storyline of these seemingly innocuous, everyday phrases we hear all the time.

When they're young, it's "boys will be boys" for him and "sugar and spice and everything nice" for her.

As they age, and begin to explore the opposite sex, the future horrors begin to take shape.

She hears, "He hits you because he likes you."

He hears, "She's just playing hard to get."

Is it no surprise, when these kids become adults, that we ask her what she was wearing/doing/drinking to "deserve" the abuse/harassment/rape from him?

We've collectively groomed them for it, made it a part of everyday speech. We've shrugged it off and built it up at the same time.

Welcome to rape culture.

The Marshall University Women's Center describes it pretty well, connecting the dots from the everyday phrases to the violent ramifications: "Rape culture is an environment in which rape is prevalent and in which sexual violence against women is normalized and excused in the media and popular culture. Rape culture is perpetuated through the use of misogynistic language, the objectification of women's bodies, and the glamorization of sexual violence, thereby creating a society that disregards women's rights and safety."

HAVE YOU EVER seen one of those movies where a detective covers a corkboard with papers and photos and evidence, and then uses red twine to connect the fragments of the crime together? It usually looks like the wild maze of a disturbed person, but then, when you take a step back and start to follow the connections, everything seemingly falls into place. A story emerges that begins to make sense.

That's this story, the story of a million connections that, when added together, form a cultural narrative that cripples our boys from the beginning—
turning them into violent men and not just excusing it all away but also
propping up entire systems and narratives to make it seem somehow
normal.

But make no mistake, guys. We have fucked over our sweet boys.

And in doing so, we're killing our girls.

In media, in government, in popular culture, in the stories and stupid
sayings we pass on at home and on playgrounds, in classrooms, and in the
proverbial "locker room," where talk of raping women is somehow culturally acceptable, we've cut off our boys from accessing their full emotional
selves—we've exalted them and cut them down, and then had the audacity to
lay blame for their destructive waste on their victims.

The results are, quite literally, deadly.

No joke. We're living in the midst of a genocide we are all complicit in
allowing.

These boys are growing up angry, violent, and entitled, and when they're
not later suffering extreme health consequences because of it, they're killing
themselves and each other—or, just as likely, girls and women.

Now, I DON'T want to make secondary the problems we have foisted on boys
for generations, as we try to stuff them into what one masculinity expert has
labeled the "man box"—a one-size-fits-all version of toxicity that doesn't take
into account the full spectrum of feelings all human beings have.

But not more bullshit: if you're a man reading this, you and I both know
we have feelings of sadness, anger, shame, humiliation, happiness, pride,
euphoria, depression—you name it. But do we feel comfortable expressing
this range of emotions around our loved ones? Our buddies? When was the
last time—excepting during a Pixar movie, perhaps—you felt comfortable
enough to cry around your friends?

They're feelings we *all* have, and yet feelings we're expected to suppress
behind swagger, heroism, "manliness," and other ridiculous conventions.

Remember what bell hooks said: "The first act of violence that patriarchy demands of males is not violence toward women. . . . Instead demands
of all males that they engage in acts of psychic self-mutilation, that they kill
off the emotional parts of themselves. If an individual is not successful in

emotionally crippling himself, he can count on patriarchal men to enact rituals of power that will assault his self-esteem."

"Be a man."

"Man up."

"Like a *real* man."

As if there is one template, only one way to do it, and any deviance from it is punishable.

"Don't be a pussy."

"You throw like a girl."

"Come on, ladies."

As if there's not just a difference but a hierarchy, a lesser class.

These messages come early and often for boys.

The ramifications are appalling.

Boys are falling behind in school; men are failing out of colleges, careers, and full lives. They're finding it harder and harder to make friends later in life and suffer the health consequences of loneliness. They kill themselves in tragic numbers because of it all; white men especially—men who thought for so long America, like women, was made solely for their pleasure.

We have inherited a toxic culture and we inculcate our boys with it still. Boys and men who stray from unrealistic, fictionalized masculine mores suffer.

But make no mistake: they do not suffer alone.

These boys grow up to rape girls and women, to abuse them at home and in public, and to kill them in record numbers—at home, and at school, in movie theaters, on city sidewalks, everywhere. And then, outrageously, they benefit from a cultural mythology that asserts it's somehow the fault of the girls and women, that women "embarrassed" them, or "denied" them sex, or "hurt" them somehow.

"Women should not have to be afraid of rejecting a man lest he kills her and others; men should not grow up believing that they're owed sex by women," Jessica Valenti wrote in the *Guardian*. "These should not be tall orders."

The FBI tells us men are the perpetrators in 99.1 percent of rapes, in 73.8 percent of murders, and in 77 percent of assaults. Nearly half of women—43.9 percent—will report some form of sexual violence in their lifetimes, according to the National Center for Victims of Violent Crime. Nearly a quarter of men will report the same, with the violence usually perpetrated by other men.

Men, this is on us. Our boys, our girls—they didn't create these systems and norms. They are inheriting them.

From us.

We owe them, we owe each other, so much more.

From the beginning.

DESPITE OVERWHELMINGLY BEING the killers in our society, boys and men still enjoy a certain macabre privilege about it all, privilege granted from early ages with the language we use to excuse away their behavior with expressions like "boys will be boys" and "he hits you because he likes you."

Here's what I mean. If we know men are largely doing the killing, look at how it's reported; look at how we tell this story.

Psychologist Jackson Katz points out the obvious. Men do most of the violence and remain somehow blameless for it all.

Look at the wording, he says.

It's "women who are killed" or "women who are abused."

Not "men who kill."

It's all sort of scientific and nameless, anonymous.

It just happens somehow.

Blamelessly.

It comes from all angles, this notion that boys and men are "naturally violent" and yet not accountable for it.

I'm reminded of Andrea Dworkin commenting in 1981 on a pornographic image in *Hustler* magazine—a woman tied on a Jeep as a "trophy" by two male "beaver hunters." She writes about this image and porn in general: "He is, he takes; she is not, she is taken."

I saw the very same thing in a Doritos commercial just last year. Two dudes out fishing encounter a beautiful mermaid. There's a pause. Then they're shown at home, with the beautiful mermaid stuffed like a trophy on their mantle.

"He is, he takes."

She is taken.

Margaret Atwood said it best: "Men are afraid women will laugh at them. Women are afraid men will kill them."

Nearly every time I tell a parent of a boy about my work in gender bias and how it impacts girls and women, they politely remind me to "consider the boys" as well, to remember that bias hurts boys too.

And it's true.

No doubt.

We are crippling boys.

We are robbing them of opportunity, in schools, in careers, in interests. We are shutting them off from realizing their full emotional selves with a massive, all-consuming societal messaging system that tells them to "be a man" and sets them on a path toward immense personal struggle and emotional damage.

But we are also creating abusers. We are creating killers—of themselves, yes, but also, in tragic numbers, of girls and women.

What's the endgame? What's going to happen to *your* children?

For girls, it means feeling unsafe as they grow up—feeling like fair game for bra snaps in grade school ("he hits her because he likes her!"), for being sent home from high school because their outfits, their bodies "distract" him, for sexual assault on the way to the car after a night on the town (does he rape her because he likes her?). And it means mental health issues, as they grapple with constantly being perceived as objects for viewing and assessing and taking.

> **But we are also creating abusers. We are creating killers—of themselves, yes, but also, in tragic numbers, of girls and women.**

It means being beaten.

Being killed.

Strike that. Look how easy it is to slip into the comfortable, blameless narrative.

It means, he beats her.

He kills her.

For boys, it means growing up with an overarching sense of entitlement, that every story is theirs, every job, every law, and the idea that girls and women are theirs for the taking. It means a life disconnected from expressing emotion.

Of becoming violent.

Becoming killers.

He kills him.

We need to tackle two things at once: the way we raise boys causes tremendous problems for them but also for the girls and women around them. We've almost normalized the idea that men grow up to be violent, against other men and women, simply because we've been doing it for so damn long. We almost expect it. As if we don't pave the way for it ourselves.

"BOYS FACE ISSUES with gender stereotypes as well and the fact is almost no research is being done on it. There is no rubric for teaching boys emotional literacy or getting support for that," says my friend Charlie Capen, a dad of two boys and the coauthor of the extraordinarily popular humor website How to Be a Dad.

Charlie was raised by a single mom following his father's absence and, later, death, and he saw firsthand the struggles with inequality his mother went through. It informed his life and turned him into a proud feminist intent on equality.

And now, with two boys of his own, he is seeing firsthand the damage the idea that boys are supposed to be so "simple" does. Society is leaving boys bereft of a healthy emotional language to deal with, well, everything. But especially what it means to "be a man."

"Boys go with the flow and continue to hold up the scaffolding of sexism, in part due to education and in equal part due to being treated as distinctly different in nearly every aspect of their lives," Charlie says. "Early learning is particularly important, based on the scant research I've seen. But especially as it relates to nurturing and emotionality. We compound this problem by saying boys are 'simple' and 'easy' emotionally. So, when a boy has complex or complicated feelings or emotions, they literally don't have the tools to deal with it."

Indeed.

The stereotypes simply don't correlate with the everyday feelings *all* men have and yet are expected to suppress.

TONY PORTER, AUTHOR of *Breaking Out of the Man Box* and founder of A Call to Men, which is dedicated to rewriting the idea of what it means to "be a man," said in a famous TED talk that from an early age boys are put in a "man box."

"Be a man. Man up. Don't be a pussy. You [*insert sport action here*] like a girl."

"Boys will be boys."

They all add up to restrict a healthy emotional life for boys—basically, just shove all your emotions away and try to be a 1950s movie cowboy version of a man while you devalue girls and women, think of them as lesser, as objects to be saved and abused, taken.

Get the girl.

Score.

Trophy wife.

"I need you working with me and me working with you on how we raise our sons and teach them to be men—that it's okay to not be dominating, that it's okay to have feelings and emotions, that it's okay to promote equality, that it's okay to have women who are just friends and that's it, that it's okay to be whole, that my liberation as a man is tied to your liberation as a woman," Porter said in his viral talk.

Here's how Porter finished:

He asked a nine-year-old boy, "'What would life be like for you, if you didn't have to adhere to this man box?' He said to me, 'I would be free.'"

Nine years old. And already well aware of the role he's expected to play. It's not a fluke. Sociologists say kids as young as two pick up on expected gender roles.

ANEA BOGUE, A self-esteem expert, author, and host of the podcast *Rad Parenting* (this should be on your list), says society has enforced the patriarchy for millennia, and it's difficult to break out of it in just a couple generations—despite the incredible amounts of evidence of just how bad it is for boys and girls.

"We bring our kids home knowing what colors their rooms should be," Bogue says. "We speak to them differently, play with them differently. Boys are expected to be rough and tumble, and girls are expected to be these wee little flowers."

All the tiny dots add up to define the roles of boys as powerful and in charge and girls as a step below. The messages come from all angles and all traditions. They seep into how we raise our kids, she argues.

How can they not?

"We have yet to have a woman in the White House, and what does it say to girls and boys, women and men, when everything from God to Santa Claus to the most powerful elder in the government are male, when we only have room for that to be a male being?" Bogue wonders. "Those are things we underestimate. We name girls after the father, he 'gives her away,' protects her with guns—these are archaic traditions deeply rooted in the patriarchy."

WHO SUFFERS?

Boys and men, yes.

Greatly.

At the hands of themselves or other boys and men.

The American Foundation for Suicide Prevention reports there are on average 123 suicides a day. White males make up 70 percent of suicides, with middle-aged white men the bulk of that percentage. And let's be clear, boys and men suffer from other violence—sexual violence and psychological violence and intimate partner violence—usually, largely, at the hands of other males.

The FBI reports men are responsible for 90 percent of all homicides. They're victims of 77 percent of them. Let's be clear for the racists in the house: 84 percent of white victims are killed by white perpetrators, and 91 percent of black victims are killed by black perpetrators—a sign that male violence crosses all lines, and that we still very much live in a segregated society.

The Centers for Disease Control and Prevention reports homicide is the number one cause of death for black males ages fifteen to thirty-four. For white males in the same age group, suicide is number two, right behind "unintentional injuries" and right above homicide.

Homicide is number two for Hispanic males, followed by suicide. Same for American Indian and Alaska Natives. Suicide is number two for Asian-Pacific Islander males in the same age group, with cancers and heart disease and homicide high in the ranks as well.

Serial killers, more than 90 percent of them, are mostly men. The same for mass murderers—school shooters, theater shooters, and all the other shooters.

In a civilized society, men should grow old and die of natural causes. Softly, gently, their family around them in loving aid. This should be the thing we strive for.

Instead, the story of our boys and men is a story of violence. In their formative years and young adult lives, men are killing themselves and each other in absurd numbers. This alone should be enough to signal that whatever we have been doing, however we have been raising our boys, has surely gone wrong.

What blame do we all share for raising one-half of our population to be so violent, so angry? What role do we all share in these deaths?

You can draw a through-line from "boys will be boys" to "man up" to "my neighbor didn't seem like a murderer. He was so quiet."

We say these things, we participate in this society, as if there is nothing to be done about it instead of reexamining what we expect out of boys. We are failing them in myriad ways, failing them so badly we take for granted, think it normal, even, that we are raising abusers and killers—of themselves and each other, yes, but also of the girls and women around them.

THE CENTERS FOR Disease Control and Prevention reported that nearly one in five women, or roughly 20 percent, reported experiencing rape, while one in seventy-one men reported the same.

According to the CDC, half of female homicides come at the hands of victims' intimate partners, mostly men.

The United Nations found that the United States has one of the highest rates of physical violence against women in the entire world, with more than half—52 percent—of women reporting physical violence against them in their lifetimes, either by partners or strangers.

Only four countries reported higher rates.

Honestly, men. The fuck are we doing?

We've somehow raised a nation of boys and men who are all at once "heroes" and batterers, all about "family values" and beating the shit out of women. Because, let's face it, these girls and women aren't harassing and beating and raping and killing themselves.

We're raising boys saying it's okay.

We've given them cultural permission slips through everything from songs to movies to playground catchphrases.

We do it at the voting booth and in public office.

Remember that ridiculous fuck hired by the White House to be President Trump's personal secretary? The guy—Rob Porter—who beat multiple former wives and girlfriends? The president called him a "good guy."

This is, mind you, the same president who admitted to sexually abusing women and who had nearly two dozen women come forward to attest to it.

And people still support him, excusing away his admission as "locker room talk."

Then there was his Supreme Court nominee, Brett Kavanaugh, who was accused of attempted rape as a seventeen-year-old. Worst of all, friends and relatives—people you probably know and love—said it shouldn't matter even if the allegations were true, because he was so young.

Honestly, guys, what is this macabre culture we are raising our children in? When we can shoot and kill black boys for having toy guns and Skittles but then excuse away sexual assault by white teens as just an unfortunate growing pain?

Men, check out of that bullshit right now. It doesn't matter *where* or *when* you speak of raping women, it's still raping women. If your circle of friends is comfortable enough appeasing assault in front of you, you're doing something horribly wrong with your life.

It's one thing to say, "I love to fuck!"

It's another thing altogether to say, "I just grab 'em by the pussy."

That's.

Not.

Okay.

No matter *where* you say it.

Look, these voters and enablers might not consider themselves rapey assholes, but in supporting someone who admitted to being a rapey asshole, they're saying it's not a deal breaker.

And why not?

It's ingrained in our culture.

Boys and men can do practically anything to girls and women, and, when caught, it's probably the fault of the girls and women, if they're not "lying" about it, that is.

In the wake of the #MeToo movement, when girls and women disclosed sexual abuse and assault in every corner and avenue of America and around the world, the debate eventually came around to this: What of the abusive men? When can they enjoy life again? When can they make their "comebacks"?

How can I even act around women anymore?

Listen, men. Stop. You sound disgusting. If that's you, you're part of the problem. When I hear men say that, I think (1) they aren't really listening to women, because literally no one is complaining about compliments; you're being entirely disingenuous, and (2) your interactions with women have been problematic if you bemoan the fact that everyday abuses, big or small, are no longer okay and you just don't know how to act anymore.

And if you somehow expect praise for *not* acting abusive or harass-y all this time—*not all men!*—you're also part of the problem, because you're sidelining a long overdue cultural reckoning in search of cookies for being baseline fucking decent. Go talk to your guy buddies about sexually degrading language and behavior if you're such a "good guy." I think women are sick of hearing from us.

ALTHOUGH WOMEN ARE frequently disbelieved or deemed culpable when they report rapes—*What were you wearing? Drinking? Were you asking for it?*—studies show that instances of false reporting of rape consistently hover between 2 and 8 percent.

You may remember the outrage surrounding the Brock Turner trial. He was a rapist from Stanford who was caught in the act by some bystanders, went to trial, and was ultimately convicted. The judge, however, let him off with a lighter sentence than prosecutors sought—six months in jail (he served three months) instead of years in prison.

Or Lyle Burgess, a seventy-nine-year-old businessman from California who raped a five-year-old girl—repeat: a five-year-old girl—and received a sentence of ninety days of house arrest and doesn't have to register as a sex offender.

These might be eye-catching abuses of justice, but they're emblematic of a society that expects men to commit violence and women to be violated by them. Future generations are going to study our continued abrogation of justice—just as, it should be noted, women are largely pointing them out right now.

For every 1,000 instances of rape, only 344 are reported to police, and only 13 cases are referred to prosecutors for trial—and just *six* rapists will be incarcerated, according to the Rape, Abuse & Incest National Network.

Six.

Six out of a thousand rapists will receive jail time for it.

How have we created a culture in which most women report everyday sexual harassment and violence at the hands of boys and men, and yet boys and men are rarely, if ever, punished for it?

The idea of not "ruining" a rapist's life with a long sentence can be traced back to "boys will be boys."

The survivor of the Brock Turner attack read a statement in court that encapsulates the treatment of rape survivors everywhere.

"After a physical assault, I was assaulted with questions designed to attack me, to say see, her facts don't line up, she's out of her mind, she's practically an alcoholic, she probably wanted to hook up, he's like an athlete, right, they were both drunk, whatever, the hospital stuff she remembers is after the fact, why take it into account, Brock has a lot at stake so he's having a really hard time right now."

All of this—the boys will be boys, the women are lying, the rapist's life can't be ruined, when can he make a "comeback"?—this culture trickles down and adds up.

A STUDY PUBLISHED by the American Psychological Association found that men who held what we would consider typically sexist viewpoints—dominance over women and a playboy persona; think "lady killer" used as a compliment—were found to have poorer mental health and a need for professional help.

"The masculine norms of playboy and power over women are the norms most closely associated with sexist attitudes," says Joel Wong, a PhD from Indiana University Bloomington and the lead researcher on a study of nearly twenty thousand men. "The robust association between conformity to these two norms and negative mental health–related outcomes underscores the idea that sexism is not merely a social injustice, but may also have a detrimental effect on the mental health of those who embrace such attitudes."

My friend Whit Honea, author of *The Parents' Phrase Book,* a handbook for what to say to kids in nearly every tricky situation, has two sons and has seen up close the bias at work on them.

"It often seems that society, at least those of us who are conscious of gender bias with a want to correct it, have created an unintentional side effect—namely a backlash against boys, as if they were the problem," he says. "Boys are also affected by gender bias, and that is not their fault. The stereotypes of gender are deeply ingrained, and while the consequences thereof are very clear with regard to girls and women, society is still guilty of encouraging boys to grow into their stoic, 'manly' roles with a 'boys will be boys' mentality that is a disservice to all of us."

Let me be clear: I love these men, my friends. We've hugged and cried in front of each other at dad conferences. I know full well the consequences our patriarchal culture is passing on to our sweet boys. I've lived it firsthand, seen up close the consequences of the broader cultural tropes that seek to keep men in the "man box" of some fictional version of wilderness masculinity, and been a victim and perpetrator of the teasing and taunting of other boys for not choosing a role considered masculine. I ache for those boys. They're entering a culture that will stifle them, tease them, cause them all manner of health issues later in life, and disallow them from experiencing the rich joy of caring (while simultaneously asking, "Where are the fathers?" and laying on their lap all manner of societal ills for not fulfilling roles they were never raised to take seriously).

It can't be overstated. We are slowly killing our boys. We are raising them to kill themselves and each other, to the point we've almost become inured to the absurd frequency and everydayness of it. Some people excuse it away still, saying it's our "nature" or, worse, that men have always done it so . . . **shrug** . . . what can we even do about it?

At some point, the rest of us have to say "enough." Let's do better.

Male dominion, wrote Dorothy Dinnerstein in 1976, is a "chronic strain" on both sexes. She believed that we were in the midst of a transition. A generation later, the transition continues, slowly, painfully—but also, unlike in previous generations, aided by a social media amplification network that gives voice to the everyday experiences of the oppressed and the oppressors.

The codes are readily apparent; you only need open your eyes. It's difficult to lay blame because these narratives are in the air we breathe, atomized into every corner of society. So, I implore you, fellow men, listen and see them unfold around you and judge for yourself—judge who is excused and who takes blame, who has "rightful" claim to bodies and whose "fault" it is—and then go about your duties in everyday fatherhood differently from how previous generations have and hasten the transition to fruition.

Perhaps, as Tony Porter says, we might all yet be free.

SO, WHAT CAN WE DO?

Number one: don't make excuses for bad behavior. It literally starts at home. With you.

Whether it's "boys will be boys" or "she's just being bossy," parents can correct behavior based on the behavior—not on society's expectations of what's okay and what's not depending on gender.

Sociologist Lisa Wade argues that toxic masculinity and rape culture begin in these early stages, when boys are told in ways big and small that they can get away with lots of things.

She maintains that it takes a critical mass of people willing to make a change about what's okay and what's not. Educating peers and parents among us is part of it. "We need to organize around the idea that it's not just boys being boys, that they need to be held accountable for their behavior," Wade says.

That doesn't mean leveling extra harsh punishments but rather not using maleness as an excuse. Are boys inherently uncontrollable and violent? No. Of course not. But society does a pretty good job of telling them they are early on.

By all means, let children be as rambunctious as fuck. Let them run, be wild, be free, be loud, have fun.

But don't allow gender expression or sex to be an excuse for shitty behavior.

It sends a message when you do.

LOOK, I KNOW it's difficult and uncomfortable. I've often failed at finding the words. But I've tried and failed and kept going. You don't have to be an asshole or offer some *Mr. Smith Goes to Washington* speech on the playground, but you can certainly nudge friends and loved ones and strangers at the park in the right direction. Something like:

"I don't like saying 'boys will be boys' because it excuses bad behavior, and I think we all want to raise decent kids, right?"

Bottom line, I'm not saying *one* phrase is the root of all societal ills and if we simply rid ourselves of the phrase all will be well.

Would that were the case.

But it's surely part of the problem. And being aware of it is the first step to writing a new script—one with more hope for boys and girls in the end.

Think about it. You know a boy. You've seen boys in action. They run, sure. They hop, skip, jump, fall down.

Boys read. Boys cry. Boys play video games. Boys cook. Boys, I dunno, like puppies and cupcakes and sprinkles.

So why is "boys will be boys" only brought out when they do something physical, dangerous, stupid, or perhaps violent toward others? Why don't we say "boys will be boys" when we see a boy hugging a friend?

Because it's part of the culture of fear and excuses. It's part of the narrative that is almost imperceptible, slippery, and dangerous: boys, men, can do anything they want.

Kill each other. Rape and abuse and kill women.

And we say it's just who they are instead of taking responsibility for the things we allow to take place around us. Like I said, our sweet boys didn't create this system. We passed it on to them.

Honestly, your biggest battle is going to be confronting friends and relatives and telling them to cut out saying sexist things or doing sexist things. But be that guy. Be the guy your friends are scared to death to say the "wrong thing" to. Make their sexism uncomfortable as fuck if only because we've all played a part in allowing it too long and are finally realizing that each piece is part of a larger whole. Imagine what might happen if more men were willing to be that guy.

Here's something to watch for. I don't think a boy raised in America *hasn't* seen this: boys or men demeaning or even assaulting someone perceived as "weaker"—other boys or girls or women—just for a few yucks from their guy buds. Sociologists even have a name for it: hegemonic homosocial masculinity, or basically maintaining guy order by being pricks to others for a few laughs. Dr. Sharon Bird from the University of Washington wrote about it way back in the early 1990s, with her paper "Welcome to the Men's Club." I wish I had known about that concept much earlier in my life, because it's so easy to see now, all these dudes manscaping the patriarchy for a few good chuckles. It really is disgusting. And so, so easy to stop. Right now. In your own circles.

Just stop laughing.

Say it's not cool.

It might be difficult at first, but our boys and girls depend on you. Make no mistake, they don't need us to *save* them. They don't need white knights.

They need us to show them, and to teach our circles, that we're simply as decent as we pretend to be.

"Before another young man decides to take his misogynist rage out at a school, or a gym, or a city street," Valenti wrote, "let's finally do something."

GROWING UP

—Chapter 6—

HER BEST FRENEMY

We do a lot of damage in raising girls to only be "nice," so let's do a better job in helping our kids express themselves.

I'VE SEEN THIS with my own eyes. It's sneaky.

A few years ago, my daughter returned to school after a long illness and one of her good friends looked at her, seemingly noted the attention she was receiving from well-wishers, rolled her eyes, and turned away without a word. Now, this is a good friend. A nice kid. An awesome kid, really.

But that didn't stop my jaw from hitting the floor. In the grand scheme of things, it didn't seem like that big of a deal. But in young girl world, it was basically a solid right cross—in plain view, with no consequences.

Now, I didn't grow up with the silent microaggressions of girlhood—the things we commonly call "mean girl" behavior today, or what the pros call "relational aggression" or "indirect aggression."

I had to read about them and go to conferences and special talks by experts. There's an entire field of study devoted to relational aggression, and it dates back decades, well before the popularized ideas of queen bees and mean girls. It's fascinating, and I'll get to it soon enough.

But even with no training or education in this field, it would be difficult to miss the behavior. Impossible, even. The in-your-face eye roll. The turned back. The silent, subtle effort to put my daughter in her place.

Standing at the doorway, I would have laid good money on this: if my daughter had spoken up and said, "Hey, what's up?" the girl would have said,

"Oh, nothing." Or perhaps she would have pretended my daughter was making it all up. "What? No, everything's fine, why?"

That behavior, by the way, is called gaslighting.

Here's the thing about "mean girls." We create them. All of us.

GIRLS, MAN. DESPITE the endless bullshit heaped on them, they can often be their own worst enemies. You see it in girlhood, at the workplace, and when a woman runs for the highest office in the land. The internalized misogyny is unforgiving and relentless.

And, yes, the rest of us are all responsible. Because here's the thing about "mean girls."

We create them. All of us.

We tell girls from early ages to be sweet and kind, full of sugar and spice, and all manner of ridiculous, antiquated social programming bullshit, and then we send them on their way without any tools to deal with the anger and frustration we all feel as human beings.

Be kind. Be nice. Sit still. Look pretty.

We give license to boys and expect them to express anger with fists and curse words—*Meet you after school, motherfucker; She was asking for it; Look what you made me do*—and to cram any "feminine" emotions deep into some magic manhole of unfeelingness (creating a Pandora's box of societal horrors in its own right). But we don't give license to or expect girls to express anger. In fact, we call them "bitches" if they show anger and frustration in the same way we allow boys to.

"Parents and teachers expect girls to be able to control themselves more and hold them to higher standards, and so girls exhibit better self-regulation," wrote Soraya Chemaly in the *Huffington Post*. Chemaly is the author of *Rage Becomes Her: The Power of Women's Anger*. "Many parents not only think that boys can't control themselves, but they unconsciously expect boys to be angry and girls to be sociable."

But here's the thing: it's not like girls' anger just disappears into some alternate realm of doilies and dolls. No, it's still going to emerge—but in ways that are both under the radar and socially acceptable.

The eye roll. The back stab. The exclusion. The rumor—especially a sexual rumor. *Especially* a sexual rumor about "stealing" someone's man. Researchers have found, in fact, that this latter example is one of the few instances when hidden aggression can emerge into open, public hostility—because in our society, one of the few times it's acceptable for girls to get pissed off is in a battle over a boy. Think of how many movies you've seen featuring just that trope—women "fighting" over a man.

ALL OF THIS? It's learned behavior. We're teaching it.

Finnish social researcher Kaj Bjorkqvist notes that girls as young as four start out expressing their frustrations the same way boys do: by pushing, shoving, stealing toys, and so forth. But later, girls' aggression is hidden to fly under the radar of parents and teachers because girls are expected to be so sweet and kind while boys, well, "boys will be boys," right?

Check the narrative: we're raising entire generations to express their anger either through silence or violence. It's not hard to imagine what happens as these kids age and people ask, "Why didn't she leave him?" instead of "Why did he beat her?"

We quiet her through childhood and expect her to be "strong," while we condition him to believe we'll overlook his violence to the point of questioning her for what he did. (To be sure, we cannot assume relational abuse goes only one way. Statistics inform us that more men beat women than women beat men, but neither situation is okay. It's not an either-or game.)

The bottom line, guys, is we need to get a handle on what we can get a handle on: each other. We need to have some deep conversations with ourselves about whether we're seeing these tropes play out or even are perpetuating them ourselves. She *can* be sweet, and kind, and nice. That's awesome. We want to raise kind, nice children.

But let's not forget it's okay to encourage our kids—both girls and boys—to express the full spectrum of their emotions.

Difficult truth here. It's hard. I've studied this shit for years, read the books, attended the lectures and workshops, even spoken to experts, but when my daughter was around age ten she said to me, "You *say* you want me to express my anger or when I'm pissed off, but you don't like it when I do it."

Oof. Punch to the gut. Kids know, man. They see through our foibles and hypocrisies. It hurts to admit this, but I'd be remiss not to say I clearly have a lot of work to do in this area.

It's not a new problem, and I'm not alone. But it still stings to realize just how much I've let her down here. That feels like a powerful lesson I hope we men can take away when considering anger and all of the other subjects in this book: to simply understand where we need to do better, and then act accordingly.

ALTHOUGH POPULAR MOVIES like *Heathers* and *Mean Girls*—and a host of books about "bad girl behavior"—have hit the public consciousness in recent years, researchers have been studying hidden aggressions in girl peer groups for decades. Some of the first studies about indirect aggression emerged in the 1950s and 1960s and showed that adolescent girls have a penchant for exclusion and emotionally manipulative aggression.

In short, we've known about this dynamic for generations. But we seemingly do little to address it.

> **"Parents really need to have talks about how you can express your anger, and know that these are really gendered, culturally prescribed, rigid rules about it."**

"Parents really need to have talks about how you can express your anger, and know that these are really gendered, culturally prescribed, rigid rules about it," says Rosalind Wiseman, author of the book *Queen Bees and Wannabees: Helping Your Daughter Survive Cliques, Gossip, Boyfriends, and Other Realities of Adolescence*—which was turned into the pop culture smash hit movie *Mean Girls* and stoked a bazillion articles about mean girlisms. "These rules are unspoken and so often coming from our family, and then a combination of society, our communities we are in, and families," she explains.

It traces back to the idea of the good girl. All the messages of innocence and kindness and hands folded together on your lap in sweetness—that's got to mess with you. How many times have you been pissed off this week? Imagine if the literal mass of society, including your parents, expected you never to show it.

"I FEEL LIKE the damage we do to girls is we disconnect them from their bodies," says Anea Bogue, host of the *Rad Parenting* podcast and creator of the Real Girl empowerment program. "For boys, we say here's what it means to be a successful man—you have to be aggressive, angry, you should be stoic because you're the one who is supposed to protect and provide," Bogue says. "For girls, we put on them just this incredible pressure to please, to be pleasing. It's debilitating."

There's a reason aggression flies under the radar, after all. It allows the good girl ethos to continue in the eyes of adults—even adults who dealt with the same crap when *they* were kids.

As much as we might suppress girls' anger, we by far overindulge it in boys—to the point of excusing away horrible behavior as just a component of their "nature." We tell them to stuff their feelings—except anger—and do a number on them from the beginning, a number that eventually reveals itself in horrible consequences: violence, suicide, depression. (I go in depth about the ramifications of allowing boys only anger and violence as expressions of emotion in other chapters.)

It all adds up.

It is, indeed, debilitating.

"We're really restricting their potential to become whole human beings," Bogue says.

I think of two striking events from 2018 as perfect examples of how our society polices the righteous anger of girls and women—especially girls and women of color—in ways it does not white men like me. You probably recall these events.

One involved tennis great Serena Williams reacting in anger to a perceived injustice—faults and bad calls during the US Open. The other involved a Supreme Court nominee, Brett Kavanaugh, reacting in anger to his own perceived injustice—an allegation of attempted rape. She came under withering scrutiny for showing her anger. He expressed the same level of outrage and vitriol during a Senate hearing—literally, a job interview—and was considered a real "fighter," a leader, still perfectly acceptable for the highest court in the land despite crackpot conspiracy theories and protestations as silly as, "I still like beer!"

Take a breath for a moment.

Recall.

Forget about whether they were "right" or "wrong" when it comes to their perceived injustices. Think only of their reactions and what you saw in our society.

How did you feel seeing these two people—one a black woman from Compton, California, and the other a white man from prestigious East Coast suburbs—expressing their anger at perceived wrongs? Did you notice any differences in how your friends, family, media stories portrayed these events?

Who, I ask, do we allow to be angry? Who gets penalized, and who gets rewarded?

SO, WHAT CAN WE DO?

Fortunately, there's a wealth of helpful research and how-to books on the subject, not to mention parent-daughter clinics to help start conversations. (I attended one with my daughter, and we both noted I was the only man in the room. That's not a cookie-seeking statement but a recognition of the idea that dads might be divorced from the emotional lives of their daughters and that even though I tried I still managed to fuck it up anyway.)

It'd be easy to say a lot of trouble ramps up as puberty hits, but any parent can tell you that "girl trouble" begins much earlier. My own daughter has been on the receiving end—and the giving end. Girls, even girls with parents who are aware of all this stuff, are going to make mistakes, and sometimes they just don't have the right tools to deal with aggression.

I'm reminded of Wiseman saying her two boys, who know of their mother's work on antibullying and her feminist stance, still call themselves "bitches" and "pussies." They know she hates it. It happens, and it's worthy of a talk. I'm also reminded of my own hypocrisies, going so far as to buy a punching bag for my daughter and yet, at the same time, still thwarting her full expression of emotions.

So that's where I'm coming from. There's no one-size-fits-all solution, and I think we can all actively participate in crappy behavior or be bystanders to it. It's in the air, these endless messages of how boys "should be" versus how girls "should be."

IT'S IMPORTANT FIRST to recognize it, and then to offer our girls the tools they need to deal with what is often considered "drama." You'll hear that word a lot—*drama*. It's a catchphrase for all the bullshit that groups can sometimes get caught up in.

Probably the best advice I've heard involves coaching girls to find their own solutions—even solutions you know, as a parent, might not work—and the courage to try them out. The idea is that this process breeds independence and confidence to problem solve—to get herself out of a bad situation rather than waiting for a parent to swoop in and save her. The antithesis of "helicopter" parenting isn't letting them raise themselves like feral animals but rather stepping back and letting them find their own solutions and sometimes fail along the way.

Here's the CliffsNotes version of advice I've learned from reading books like Wiseman's and, one of my personal favorites, *The Blessing of a Skinned Knee* by Wendy Mogel.

The first part involves listening. Don't offer solutions. Just listen and empathize. Then you can move on to wondering what some solutions might be—brainstorming.

Let your daughter discover a solution: dismissing a bully's taunts, confronting a bully, telling adults, and so forth.

For instance, laughing off a mean girl remark. "I know, my pants are crazy today, ha ha!"

Or just owning the source of the dig. "I know my shirt is dirty, but it's all I have today."

The experts usually agree that ignoring things doesn't work out so well.

Then let your daughter implement the solution. If it works, great! If not, more brainstorming. The experts agree that parents should most definitely step in and not worry about helicopter parenting in the face of serious bullying—because at the end of the day, the kids are kids and just don't have the same tools for problem solving and communication as we do.

The bottom line is you want to keep the lines of communication open—no lecturing or finding solutions for them.

PRO TIP FROM a longtime dad, here. My friend Jim Higley, author of the Bobblehead Dad website and parenting speaker, offered me some great advice one day. In raising his daughter, when he sensed there was a problem but she had clammed up, he merely sat with her—just sat there, in silence, hanging out until she was ready, or until she wasn't. No lectures or questions, just time spent sitting there, listening. He said it was a life-changing experience that opened up new ways of communication, especially when he had a deep talk with himself about always needing to "fix things" instead of just listening.

Wiseman echoed this exact method. But there's something else.

Wiseman says the quickest way for parents to shut down communication is to start comparing their own kids to other kids. "If we could stop that, it would be huge. Huge."

But that just tackles mean girls and bullying and friendship drama.

What of anger? Fear?

Bogue recommends a punching bag for girls. It's a great way for them to safely dissipate pent-up anger rather than letting it sit and stew. She also recommends, and helps run, those classes in which a man dresses up in a big padded suit and tries to assault girls, who scream and fight the man off. She says these classes build confidence in what girls' bodies can do, not what they look like.

Parents should also be aware that the very anger and frustration they often feel is often felt by their daughters—even if friends and school and society say they should be nice and not show it.

"Girls need to know—and should be told explicitly—that it's alright to feel anger," Chemaly wrote. "That it's a healthy emotion that, as humans, they have the right to feel and express."

—Chapter 7—

SORRY, NOT SORRY

The word sorry *carries a lot of baggage: as a simple apology,
a social lubricant, and even an expectation—but it's just
one of the many ways we police the language of girls.*

T HIS IS PROBABLY one of the grosser things I've done in a while, a true
asshole move. What really kills me, what makes me feel guilty, is that
I *knew* better—not just that I acted like an asshole. Yes, that. But because I felt the need to do it at all, despite hearing countless women tell me
that it happens.

All the time.

I've heard this called "mansploring"—this idea that a woman can tell a
man something that he'll feel the need to test. Just to be sure. Sort of like
those people who press glowing elevator buttons.

Here's what it looks like. You may have seen it. Or perhaps even done
it. Less than a week after I heard the term, I saw it in action on an airplane.
I was sitting near the bathroom, and a woman walked up, saw the bathroom
was marked "occupied," and began that uncomfortable shuffling wait in the
aisle. A man soon joined her, pointed at the bathroom, and was told by the
woman that yes, it was occupied, and yes, she was waiting in line.

The guy grabbed her shoulders, moved around her, tried the door handle, and then explained, "It's occupied," before moving back to his place in
line. The woman smiled politely and looked down. I stared with my mouth
agape.

What sort of asshole? I thought to myself.

Turns out, I knew exactly the sort.

We're everywhere.

AS THE CHIEF shopper of goods for our house, I see this all the time at the store.

Just about every time I do something wrong—step in someone's way, stand in someone's way, absentmindedly round a corner into someone, leave my cart in a really boneheaded spot—I receive an apology.

"Sorry."

That you walked in front of me.

"Sorry."

That you left your cart right in front of the apples. Dope.

"Sorry."

That you literally ran into me. Jerk.

I'm floored by the number of times I can be out and about in public and do something moronic and receive an apology from a woman.

"Often, women are expected to apologize for things men never have to worry about," writes Claire Warner in *Bustle*, "up to and including our very existence."

I've bumped into women, blocked their way, did that weird little dance in which no one knows which way to go, and much less and much worse, and received an apology of "sorry" before I could spit out my own.

Oh my gosh, white man realizes women say "sorry" all the time! For bullshit *he* did!

I know. I get it.

> **It's not our lived reality, for the most part, and unless we're consciously considering it every moment, we tend to forget it—or perhaps even believe it doesn't exist.**

BUT HERE'S THE deal. I'm not sure we men really *do* get it, no matter how many times we're told. It's not our lived reality, for the most part, and unless we're consciously considering it every moment, we tend to forget it—or perhaps even believe it doesn't exist.

This is problematic.

It's important for guys to point out to guys the many ways we often occupy public space with little regard for others and even more often engage in subtle, everyday cultural systems that oppress girls and women through expectations of obsequious language and action—especially considering all these everyday oppressions exist in a culture in which women are constantly subject to an "intellectual" debate: Are they inherently "different" (read: inferior), are they liars, are they deserving of bodily autonomy?

If we can police women, say, on the sidewalk, why not at the ballot box? In the gilded chambers of legislatures? There's a through-line in there, and we need to be more aware of the ways we connect the one to the other.

"We're expected to be likable but not too flirtatious, confident but not aggressive, and never less than 100 percent put together," Warner writes.

We might not all get together in the boardroom to deny equal pay, or gather together in the capital to deny equal access to reproductive health care. But that doesn't mean all men—yes, even those of us who strive not to be total assholes—don't participate in a society that oppresses all girls and women. It's in our culture, on our sidewalks, in our language and actions, in our music and movies, and it's worthy of exploration so we can first recognize it, and then stop perpetuating it or—this seems key—laughing it off or looking the other way as our male friends do it.

"It is vital to resist those who mock and criticize us for tackling 'minor' manifestations of prejudice, because these are the things that normalize and ingrain the treatment of women as second-class citizens, opening the door for everything else, from workplace discrimination to sexual violence," Laura Bates, founder of the Everyday Sexism Project, wrote in the *Guardian* newspaper.

ALL OF WHICH is to say, I should have known better.

Nevertheless, I wanted to see with my own eyes. I wanted to mansplore the shit out of a single word.

"Sorry."

And then explore the many, many ways we police women in public and how we arrived at a point that it's considered normal, and what lessons we are subtly passing on to our girls and boys.

Who knew that a simple word packed such a punch?

Well, women, probably.

And language experts.

And psychologists.

And writers of all stripes.

There are studies and books and hundreds, if not thousands, of articles devoted to the debate about whether women say sorry too much, too little, not at all, or just the right amount. There's even software you can install to erase any sign of *sorry* or *just* from work missives so as not to show "weakness." But *sorry* is just one example of how our society endlessly polices women's language, bodies, voices, actions, you name it, in ways that make simply being out in public a maze that we men rarely, if ever, have to grapple with.

Lise Eliot, the neuroscientist who studies brain differences, says we raise boys and girls to inhabit the same physical world while yet living in different gender worlds, a pink-and-blue dystopia of toys, clothes, and roles. Knowing how we raise kids, and how we are raised, we can't pretend this construct suddenly disappears in adulthood. Men and women occupy the same spaces and yet live in different worlds, universes I'd argue most men, at best, simply don't realize exist or, at worst, believe it's their birthright to rule over.

SO BACK TO the store.

After years of casual brushes with "sorry" amid the tomatoes and frozen foods, I wanted to be sure I was really hearing what I thought I'd been hearing.

I decided I'd go about my usual shopping, adding in a little extra stupidity just for good measure. I'd take notes about what happened in ten instances in which I was clearly at fault for violating social norms, that is, getting in people's way, or worse.

The first instance took a lot longer than I expected. I grabbed a cart near the front entrance and just sort of parked myself there, pretending to examine a sale on oranges when really I was just doing the very thing I loathe: standing in a doorway. (Seriously, people. It's literally a portal. You move through it.)

I thought this one would be the fastest item on my list of men-taking-up-space idiocy, but it must have been a lull in the shopping day because I stood there for a long, long time—far too long for my own comfort. Just as I was about to give up out of sheer anxiety, I turned around and *wham!* Whacked my cart into a woman entering the store.

"Sorry," she said.

A-ha!

To this day, I feel bad about that one. So pleased to remove myself from standing in the doorway, and so pleased to finally begin my awkward social experiment, I beamed a victorious smile. She hurried along to the potatoes.

So that was number 1. I stood in a doorway, bumped into someone, and earned an apology for it.

Number 2 involved parking my cart in front of a produce section. In a matter of seconds, a woman reached over my cart and offered a "sorry" for me blocking her path.

Nos. 3, 4, 5, 6 all involved walking around and getting in people's way. All earned a sorry.

I was nervous about the more aggressive maneuvers. Should I purposefully bump into someone? Exactly how hard? Any parent lives in abject terror of getting his ankles knocked by a kid-driven cart, so that was off the table completely. I didn't want to physically injure or hurt someone for a stupid social experiment. Instead, I did that awkward dance when you don't know which way to go and just sort of move one way and then the other, effectively blocking the person in front of you.

All earned a sorry.

In ten instances within the span of twenty minutes, I got a solid ten apologies for something I clearly did wrong.

NOW, ON TO the men.

I stood in their way, knocked into their carts, did the awkward shuffling dance thing.

In all, I received a sorry in seven out of ten attempts at being a jerk and two looks that amounted to an unspoken "What the fuck?"

This was all completely nonscientific, and I think, in the end, I received enough apologies from both sexes to call it a wash—which sort of matches up with what researchers have found.

A 2010 study by Canadian researchers published in the journal *Psychological Science* found that (1) women apologize more than men, but (2) they found more instances of offense they felt required an apology. "There was no gender difference in the proportion of offenses that prompted apologies," the study said.

"If that doesn't describe the patriarchy in a nutshell, I don't know what will," writes Warner.

In other words, when both sexes thought an apology was called for—*boom!* Out came the sorry in equal numbers. Men more often simply didn't think they did anything worthy of apology.

This brings me to the hard part.

Listen up.

Here's the thing about my experiment, and something I think we men need to be more honest about. As I was walking around annoying women, I felt no fear.

None.

Zero.

Society basically told me I had every right to do it with no repercussions. In fact, it was very likely I'd be apologized to. And I was.

As I was walking around bumping into men, I'll be honest: there was fear.

Not a fear of death but certainly a tinge in the back of my mind about whether I might soon find myself asked to step outside to "settle this like men."

I'm an average-sized white guy with probably above-average muscle for my age, so I'm not sure I convey "weakling" in public spaces.

Still, the feeling was ever present: I could end up hurt. Physically.

It certainly revealed a lot of fucked-up things about myself. For instance, I could have the audacity to perform an "innocent" social experiment with little regard to whether I was actually hurting people. I made a point not to "physically" hurt someone, but as I was pondering just how fearful I was to mess with the "wrong man," I admit many of the lessons from the Bates's Everyday Sexism Project came back to me, such as the teenage girl who wrote that she was scared to leave her house for fear of being sexually harassed or abused by men.

I could believe that I wasn't doing much harm. But I'd be ignoring a hard truth if I didn't consider just how many women apologized out of fear.

All of them?

I certainly felt it in *all* my encounters in trying to annoy men.

"What if?"

"How should I defuse a situation?"

It was my background noise.

What's really fucked? I could also turn it off the moment the experiment was done. I could move on. Men, girls and women are telling us every day they cannot. It's their constant background noise, and we're the source of it.

I'M NOT ALTOGETHER sure we men realize just how different are the planets we live on and how much of a role we all play in perpetuating the disparities. We have the privilege of devoting zero time to what the entire other half of the population does every day: consider personal safety when, say, simply leaving the house, walking down the sidewalk, grabbing apples at the store, or trying on a new blazer or tie or pants—when girls and women tell us it is the all-encompassing white noise of their lives.

> **It's their constant background noise, and we're the source of it.**

"What if?"

To be perfectly honest, I read and listened to these stories of everyday harassment and felt like I really "got it," but I'm not sure it hit home until I started randomly annoying men in the grocery store, wondering which one might clean my clock in a way my sexism never prompted me to consider with women.

In those moments, I was reminded of Atwood again: "Men are afraid that women will laugh at them. Women are afraid that men will kill them."

I wouldn't recommend men reconstruct my stupid experiment. To this day, I feel sorry about it. But I'd certainly recommend thinking about it for a moment and having a deep talk with yourself: If you randomly bumped into women, would you be scared of violence?

How about men? If you randomly bumped into men, would you be at least preparing yourself for possible violence?

Go on. Give it a thought and see what you come up with.

Now imagine never being able to remove the idea every time you go outside, or even online.

"I assess every man I see on the sidewalk, especially when it's not crowded," a friend told me. "I have to quickly know whether to cross the street, take a different route, whatever."

Even the men who consider themselves "good guys" cast footfalls we don't fully understand the weight of.

MY DAUGHTER AND I attended a girl-power workshop a few years ago in the basement of a sports store. The idea was to give girls the vocabulary and training they needed to deal with bullying, friendship problems, and navigating the world.

A chart offered words that the girls could use to sort out problems. *Sorry* was one of them and was sometimes used in a context of bringing up a problem that hurt a girl. The hurt girl was supposed to say, "Sorry, but when you said *X*, it hurt my feelings."

I piped up and called bullshit, and I remember the look the leader gave me. That look came back to me in the store when I was bumping into men.

"What the fuck do you know?" the look said.

In actual words she explained that for girls the word *sorry* acted as everything from a social lubricant to the fastest way to get past a petty argument and move on. It was a reality that I think boys and men don't necessarily learn, given the bazillion messages aimed at us around something such as "Never give up—never surrender!"

Girls, growing up, do something wrong and an apology is expected.

Boys, growing up, do something wrong and it's . . . you know the answer . . . they're just boys. I've heard the term applied to men. Adult men. "Oh, he's just an inexperienced boy."

Dude's *forty!*

What a horrible storyline we follow: we raise girls to defend themselves, either through martial arts and defense classes or through the proper employment of apologies—good-hearted men literally take them to workshops and studios to learn these things—and yet we devote little, if any, concomitant time to raising boys not to inherit and exacerbate a culture in which this is necessary.

Sure, we tell them to be nice, and to be gentlemen, and to treat girls and women with some Victorian vestige of chivalry in which girls are painted as delicate flowers, but do we take boys to workshops to discuss why we demand girls and women apologize for our faults? Do we sign them up for weekly classes expressly so they'll know how to defend themselves against other boys or men who want to sexually abuse them? Do we take them to workshops to teach them how to navigate the sexism of other boys and men?

We can't train girls to be "powerful and strong," saying how important it is they learn to "defend themselves," all the while believing society isn't so sexist that we consider this an acceptable remedy rather than having more serious discussions with our boys and men about being basic, decent human beings in public spheres.

Like I said in the beginning, I'm really glad you're here. Seriously. We can help shift this culture together. One circle at a time.

PERHAPS I FOCUS too much on the word *sorry*. It is, indeed, just one glaring example of how we men police girls and women while allowing men like us to do whatever the hell we please.

From sorry to *just* to vocal fry (a perceived grating sort of sound in someone's speech) to upspeak (ending sentences with questions?)—where there's a story about a woman in public, there's usually a story about how she speaks and how annoying some guy finds it. It's almost as if, yes, we'll allow women to speak, but they have to say only "sorry."

The radio program *This American Life* did a fantastic episode revealing how both men and women have roughly the same vocal ticks, but listeners only wrote in to complain about the women speakers.

Reporter Chana Joffe-Walt responded to someone who said her voice was too irritating to listen to her reporting, despite her amazing stories. "I'm just trying to speak. Like, literally, the way that the voice comes out of my mouth bothers you? What am I supposed to do about that?" she asked on the show.

Linguist and blogger Debbie Cameron is frequently quoted in stories that examine the way women and girls speak. She's found it's basically no different from the way men speak.

But only women earn scorn for being "annoying."

"We've also learned that some of the most enduring beliefs about the way women talk are not just over-generalizations, they are—to put it bluntly— lies," she writes on her website.

SO ... WHY?

These issues didn't just magically appear overnight. Like many of the problems we've discussed, they're woven into the fabric of our culture, and we pass them down, generation to generation.

It's not, in other words, a surprise that adults today consider it just fine and dandy to police girls and women, that we consider it an acceptable albeit invisible underpinning of society, when that is exactly what we were raised to do.

Let me repeat that: raised to do.

As a child of the 1980s, I find it downright disturbing to look back on movies and songs and pop culture memes we thought important enough for societal deification and then think about how we're still passing them on to another generation.

Movies in which men spy on, or drug, or rape women—not in horrible dramas that explore the issue of assault, but as plotlines in comedies, in romances. Honestly, just do a five-second google on the horribleness of 1980s movies and rape culture. And by all means, yes, consider these were the product of a "different time," but also consider that this time wasn't so long ago, that these were the acceptable themes of our childhood. What impact does it all have on us today? Many of the guys who created these themes are still at work today.

My particular "favorite" movie is about a man who hounds a woman mercilessly for "romance" through stalking and physical dominance before finally "winning her over"—a movie written and directed by a man outed in the #MeToo movement as a serial sexual harasser and abuser. Honestly, I watched that movie as a child and thought, "Oh. That's how you do it." Then I'd go to a playground or high school parking lot and hear boys talking about "scoring."

Or songs. Jesus. The songs.

The Police hit "Every Breath You Take" was basically an anthem for any lovelorn teenager at the time, a smash hit first written by someone—audacious enough to put it into words, to be sure—and then approved by recording companies and then given massive radio bandwidth.

It's about a guy who will stalk a former lover with "every breath" she takes. The chorus says she "belongs" to him. The lyrics read more like a ransom note than a love song, which shouldn't be surprising considering it exists in a culture where it'd be the soundtrack to endless portrayals of men who "just don't take no for an answer." It's not even close to being alone. Does "Jessie's Girl" have a name, or does she just enjoy music history as men's property to be fought over?

They're catchy songs, no doubt. They're still played on the radio today in fact. I wonder how many dads have sung along happily with their sons in the car and not had a talk about just how creepy it is, at least by today's standards.

The pantheon of movies and songs and books is too exhaustive to explore here, but it's not as if the 1980s ended and none of this stuff stayed with the boys and girls raised then. I can think offhand of several music stars today who literally beat and rape women and yet enjoy popular success; a famous DJ doesn't "go down" on his wife—which, okay, TMI—and yet demands it of her because men are "kings"—and somehow, it all seems worthy of debate and acceptance.

Are men kings? Our panel discussion continues after the commercial break, brought to you by Viagra...

THESE MIGHT ALL seem like disparate threads, unconnected, scattershot ramblings of a crazy conspiracy theorist. I think it's truly difficult, if not impossible, for men to fully enjoy the immensity of everyday oppression we perpetuate. Because when we write it down, it *does* indeed sound crazy. Absurd.

But if we listen, we'll realize it's the lived experience of an entire half of the population.

So, put it all together, and what does it look like? To be at least low-level fearful of leaving the house, and then listening to rape culture songs on the radio, and then going to the movies and seeing sexual assault used as a funny plotline, and then going shopping only to have some dumbass stand in your way and have to think about how not to offend him, and then going home again and hoping not to be harassed on the way.

And what is the endgame? What's the sum of a culture that informs us through art and language and appearance that girls and women are lesser and sex objects to be won, and that men can do whatever they please? In all spheres of society?

What if the tables were turned? The reverse is a society men would consider absurd.

Indeed, I wonder how many men hear other men tell them they should be...

...polite and apologetic, and yet assertive and "feisty."

...demure and yet sexy.

...loud and yet not too loud or shrill. Heavens, anything but shrill.

... fit and yet not too fit, skinny and yet not too skinny. (Jesus, we can age into a doughy dad bod and win *praise* for it.)

... dressed up just so: revealing and yet not too revealing.

I wonder how many times we men have been afraid to speak up for fear of being called "bitchy" or "cold." How many of us consider just how much makeup to wear each day to appear pretty but not slutty, and then are penalized in the form of lower pay or less opportunity for not getting it just right. (Yes, it's a thing.)

I wonder how many men hold back tears for fear of being labeled "too emotional" instead of praised for being sensitive, a "good guy." (If he's with a group of other guys, he'll be penalized for ... wait for it ... being a "pussy" or feminine.)

I wonder how many times men fear being harassed, abused, beaten, stalked, drugged, raped, or killed when they leave their house, a bar, their workplace. Or, perhaps, while preparing for a night out, when they consider the color of their tie or their shirt and the reaction it will get them.

Go ahead and ask the girls and women in your life just how often these thoughts cross their mind, and compare that to your own daily experiences.

A teenage girl shared this on Bates's Every Day Sexism page: "It's really bothering me that since I have a bigger bust or a bigger butt that boys think it's okay to harass me. It's honestly sad that I refuse to walk or leave the house by myself because I'm scared walking down the street."

I'm forty-two, and I've lived without this fear all my life. I'm going to go ahead and guess you haven't experienced this either.

And yet it's the world the girls and women in our lives experience every single day.

Should it be on them to speak against it? On us to raise girls to navigate it? Should we expect the oppressed to demand less oppression?

Or perhaps should we see our role in it and have a talk amongst ourselves?

I'M NOT FOR a moment trying to undercut the idea that boys and men are harassed and raped, sometimes by women, but more often by other men. It doesn't matter how big and strong and "manly" we consider ourselves. Actor Terry Crews, a mammoth of a dude, bravely came forward to speak about his sexual abuse at the hands of another man (and was subsequently belittled by other men). But I *am* trying to undercut what I see far too often: the leap of logic is made that because men predominantly do the abusing, it is somehow okay or not worthy of discussion.

If we were being honest, we'd see we don't police boys and men the same way we police girls and women. If anything, I hear men say they are being "feminized" and need better connections with the "wild."

Honestly, the fuck, guys?

No one's asking us to be anything other than polite and decent and to realize we live in a society that has different rules for us.

Remember, the narrative of policing of language and appearance, the things we expect of others and expect to get away with ourselves, form the basis of a society that finds it perfectly acceptable to ask women what they did to anger abusive men and that thinks it's perfectly reasonable to hold public votes on what women can do with their bodies. You can draw a line from one to the other, and let's just drop the charade. In many cases, it's men being assholes.

Because we've been told all along it's okay.

"People who shout at women in the street don't do it because they think there's a chance the woman will drop her shopping, willy-nilly, and leap into their arms! It isn't a compliment—and to call it that disparages the vast majority of lovely men who are perfectly able to pay a real compliment," Bates writes. "It is an exertion of power, dominance and control. And it's utterly horrifying that we've become so used to it that it's considered the norm."

SO, WHAT CAN WE DO?

When it comes to language, it's up to men to stop worrying about *how* girls and women say things and to focus instead on *what* they're saying.

Seriously.

That's on us.

It's also on us to more fully consider the space we take in public spheres and the impact we have on others. The New York City subway system dedicated an entire campaign to "manspreading"—the idea of men sitting and spreading their legs in a way that takes up more space, while women cross their legs or keep their knees together in a way that takes up only a single space.

Look, I get it. When I purposefully squeeze my legs together, my testicles immediately feel the pressure of my thighs, and it doesn't feel all that great. But let's be honest, comfort doesn't come from performing the exact opposite pose, knees fully extended beyond the hips at a stunning angle of obtuseness.

Manspreading may sound like a funny term, but it's emblematic of the so many ways I see men taking up space in public—from loud talking on "very important business calls" to using both armrests to holding doors and demanding praise for it instead of doing it simply out of kindness.

There's a stupid Facebook meme I've seen passed around a billion times about holding doors for women. It's really disturbing and yet not altogether shocking to see so many men agree with the sentiment. In the short video, a man holds a door open for a woman, who walks through and doesn't offer a smile or a "thanks." The man pauses, grabs the woman, and violently throws her back outside—all for having the audacity not to say "thanks."

This short video personifies the myriad ways, I argue, that men move around the world with an expectation of ownership, while women walk around in a state of low-level suspicion, if not fear. The man clearly isn't holding the door open just to be kind—he's expecting something for it, a smile or a thank-you. He has no idea whether the woman can speak at all or is engaged in an emergency phone call, say, and just doesn't realize what's happening. Or, you know, she just doesn't want to. And yet, the man takes umbrage and physically grabs the woman before tossing her aside violently.

I highlight this short video not just because of the disturbing actions it depicts—honestly, do you do things you believe are kind out of kindness or for praise? Because if it's the latter, you're not as kind as you imagine—but also because of the reactions it gets from men.

"Fuck that bitch."

"She's a bitch and deserves that shit. Say 'thank you'!"

I don't remember the exact title, but I'm sure you can find this short video and its comments. A man feels entitled to violently attack a woman on the street because he did something "nice" and she didn't "thank him" for it.

Listen, men. We police girls and women in more ways than we imagine—in tone and words and appearance and endless, tiny ways we can't fathom—and have the audacity to call ourselves "good guys" in the process.

In the end, I'd advise you to take a deep dive into the everyday sexism hashtag and really ask yourself if that's a world you live in: being constantly policed in tone, language, appearance—and then adjust your actions accordingly. And then, here's the deal: you don't get praise for it. You're not extra kind or deserving of cookies for simply listening to people and then deciding to act like a more decent human being. It's baseline, basic human behavior, and it'd be really amazing if we passed those lessons on to our kids.

—Chapter 8—

MOVIES AND MYTHS OF THE "STRONG, POWERFUL FEMALE CHARACTER"

*The stories told onscreen—at movie theaters and online—
often leave out half the population or reinforce the sexism
and underrepresentation we see in the "real world."*

I'M A MOVIE junkie. Let me state that up front. I love them. *Love* them. My pulse quickens at the mere *thought* of raised curtains, dim lights, and Red Vines.

I can't get enough.

But we need to have a talk. Despite some gains here and there, movies are no less sexist today than they were a generation ago.

We're bombarded with constant messages reinforcing the notion that men are angry, violent heroes devoid of emotion and that women are lesser, sidekick sex objects. It's so blatant and in-your-face that you've got to be incredibly wedded to your sexism not to notice.

Seriously, guys. It's pretty bad. And not only does it make for shitty entertainment at this point—honestly, how many CGI robots destroying CGI robots and/or San Francisco do you *need?*—the ramifications can't possibly be overstated: the cultural stories we deem worthy of widespread telling can either inspire new societal scripts or serve to reinforce archaic ones.

We've been tending to the latter for far too long.

So, let's have a walk through some of the worst tropes and stereotypes we continue to see in movies and explore how we can have a chat with the kids about it so we can all demand better.

TAKE *STAR WARS.*

I'm going to do a deep dive on the epic space saga because it has become a cultural touchstone but also because it's emblematic of what happens when we break away, however slowly and subtly, from the boys club idea of movies. What seems like progress can sometimes hide glaring, persistent flaws.

The Force Awakens was a must-see for our family when it debuted in 2015.

But not for the usual reasons.

Sure, I grew up watching the original Star Wars series and have fond memories of standing in a long line with my older brothers to see *Return of the Jedi.* I was excited to share with my daughter a hero's journey that crosses generations and universes. We devoured all the other movies in the series in preparation and were anxious to see how the final three episodes would play out.

But there was something more.

In the incredible buildup to the latest installment, there was a twist. The plot seemed to revolve around . . . wait for it . . . a young woman.

I was thrilled. But I was also more than a little wary.

In watching even the most innocuous family movies with my daughter, I had grown accustomed to getting my hopes up when it comes to so-called strong, powerful female characters only to have those hopes dashed in the theater.

After watching too many stupid shows aimed at kids, I've now gotten used to writer Margot Magowan's aptly named "minority feisty"—the token female character who was billed as awesome and powerful but who ultimately spends her time surrounded by endless seas of boys or men, and more often than not trains the hapless boy hero, who then goes on to save the day and perhaps even "wins" the girl character as a prize.

It's an updated version of Katha Pollitt's "Smurfette Principal."

Or Congress.

In other words, it's nothing new. It's how our culture centers boys and men in film and sidelines girls and women. It's nearly inescapable, like dust, even in the supposed "all-female cast" movies that sexist men are always going on about. (I break down some of those below.)

Like most of these cultural sexisms, *one* movie of girls and women being phenomenally outnumbered by boys and men wouldn't be a big deal, but when the vast majority of them feature boys and men as the main attraction, the onscreen stories we tell can easily turn into real-world realities or serve to reinforce the disparities we see everywhere else in society.

"When your children go to the movies, they learn that boys are more important and get to do more things than girls," Magowan says on her blog, Reel Girl.

Consider who gets to be "in charge" in government, in business, in academia, in sports, and it mirrors what we see onscreen and serves to almost cloak the inequality as "normal."

Even our escapist fantasies, the make-believe worlds we enter for only a few hours to unwind or, perhaps, use to consider deeper truths about the human experience are sexist hellscapes dominated by men, usually violent men destined to also play "savior."

Adults can have intellectual conversations about bias, cinematic roles, story arcs, and so much more, but I wonder: What messages do you think children receive when they see the same sexist storylines over and over and over? As they form an image of the world and . . . who is in charge of it all?

> **What messages do you think children receive when they see the same sexist storylines over and over and over?**

Star Wars, to be sure, was never immune from this charge. The original episodes are practically devoid of women.

The first three episodes were about Luke Skywalker's journey to becoming a Jedi and included the most minority feisty of all, Princess Leia.

But other women?

The original saga offered just sixty-three seconds of female characters speaking who were not Princess Leia.

Seriously.

Sixty-three seconds.

I'm not talking about one movie—I'm talking about *all three* of the originals.

New York Magazine rewatched the series and kept track. Out of a total 386 minutes of screen time, women who were not Princess Leia had just 1 minute of speaking time, according to the magazine's analysis.

You know what those women were speaking about?

Men.

No joke. I rewatched and kept track myself. Nearly every line spoken by a woman besides Leia during those precious sixty-three seconds was about a man. And let's face it, much of Leia's dialogue is about men as well, but no wonder.

Make-believe space is *filled* with them.

What does it tell young boys and girls when enormous male space slugs, tiny male green aliens, male robots, tall and hairy brown male aliens, *short* and hairy brown male aliens all have more speaking roles than actual human women?

Whose fantasy *is* this?

Star Wars, obviously, is not alone. It's not an aberration. Often women exist onscreen only to move a male hero's story along—or, through being murdered, raped, or kidnapped by men, to really give the hero something to "fight" for.

Honestly, once you're aware of this trope, it's hard to enjoy basically any action movie.

You're welcome.

We might see the occasional "fearless, powerful" woman character, but movies are still very much a man's world.

THERE'S BEEN PROGRESS, sure. But when we go out for entertainment, we might see the occasional "fearless, powerful" woman character, but movies are still very much a man's world.

The Geena Davis Institute on Gender in Media tracks leading roles of men and women in movies as well as metrics like screen time and words spoken onscreen, among others, and argues that unconscious bias against women in society has led to often invisible women onscreen.

The institute's studies have found that male characters receive twice as much screen time as female characters and speak twice as much as well. Interestingly, when a movie features a male lead character, the male characters appear onscreen at three times the rate of all female characters. But when a movie has a female lead, the screen time of male and female characters is nearly even.

That's a fascinating statistic. Whenever I write about powerful women lead characters or "all-female casts," I inevitably get responses from sexist men who say something along the lines of how "sick" or "tired" they are of female lead characters and why can't things just be equal?

All this despite the fact that only when there are women leads is screen time *actually* equal.

Funny, these sexist men are woefully silent about "equality" when every other movie features a male lead, so I'm going to go ahead and guess they, like much of society, have serious issues, not with "strong" women, but with women who dare to have a voice or agency.

Seriously, guys. We see this in movies, in business, in sports, in government, and more. This isn't a women's issue.

This is a men's issue. This is our issue.

And why not? Practically every time we turn on a TV or movie for entertainment, we see who is "supposed" to be speaking or doing or violently attacking the computer-generated imagery. What messages do you suppose our kids absorb when we sit down for family movie night and see a screen filled with talking, doing men and absent or trophy-esque women?

Backing up these claims, a 2016 analysis by The Pudding, a website that breaks down data into visual graphics, took a look at more than two thousand screenplays to gauge who spoke more onscreen: men or women. Out of thirty Disney films (Disney now owns the Star Wars franchise), men spoke more in twenty-two of them (including *The Force Awakens*).

"Even films with female leads, such as *Mulan*, the dialogue swings male," said the researchers, Hanah Anderson and Matt Daniels. "Mushu, her protector dragon, has 50 percent more words of dialogue than Mulan herself."

Repeat for emphasis: the male sidekick dragon has more words than the titular "main" female character.

I guess I expected more out of a children's musical about a strong young woman that features the song "I'll Make a Man out of You." (Can't wait to see whether the forthcoming live-action version does better.)

Reminds me of all those women with speaking roles in the original *Star Wars*. . . .

Snark aside, it can't be overemphasized: What messages are our kids breathing in?

THE MOST CURSORY of Google searches about onscreen inequality in movies and TV confirms what even the most casual viewing reveals: girls and women are absent, silent, and, most likely, sexualized.

The New York Film Academy looked at the top five hundred movies from 2007 to 2012 and found women made up 30 percent of speaking characters, nearly 30 percent wore body-revealing costumes (compared to 7 percent of men), 26 percent were partially nude (9 percent for men), and just 10 percent of those movies featured a gender-balanced cast.

The average ratio of characters was 2.25 men to 1 woman.

How, one wonders, does this happen?

Take a look behind the cameras, where nearly every department involved in making a movie is controlled by men—some of whom have used their positions to sexually harass and abuse women in their industry, sparking a reignition of the #MeToo movement, which shined a spotlight on everyday sexual abuse across all industries.

Directors, writers, producers, editors, and cinematographers: dudes, dudes, dudes.

Many studies show men outnumber women nine to one as directors and writers. In the one category where women saw the most advances, producing, men still filled three-quarters of those roles.

I found this bit startling and not at all surprising: out of 250 of the highest-grossing films, 70 percent of them featured ten or more men working behind the scenes in major roles.

Just 1 percent of those films featured ten or more women working behind the scenes.

BIG PICTURE: IT'S not some conspiracy theory how this all happens. It's simply how we're raised, and how we are raising others. It's so smooth and devious, sitting there in a dark theater with your friends, your family, eating popcorn and munching candy, while watching profound inequality play out before you—laughing with it, cheering it—and then exiting the theater together into a world where the same exact scenarios play out on town councils, in legislatures, on sports pages, in boardrooms.

The statistics tell a damning story in representation on and off the screen. But they don't say much about how it happens, how this persistent inequality in jobs and storytelling exists today, how it endures, and how people consider it "normal," how many men can say, with a straight face, that they are "all for equality" but dislike the recent spate of "all-female movies" while mindlessly, blindly, silently, gobbling up movies dominated by men.

Like I said, if they were all for equality, as they claim, they'd be raising their fists and speaking out with the debut of almost every single movie, not just the ones featuring more female characters.

None of it should be surprising. It is, quite literally, how we were raised—how we are still raising kids today.

Men and women making films now were once boys and girls weaned on films in which the disparities were even worse, where the casts were even *more* male-dominated, where women were prizes to be ogled or "won," where people largely didn't think twice about major films like *Star Wars* and *Ghostbusters* and, well, you name it, featuring all males as main characters and in crowd scenes.

The background noise of cultural representation posited that boys and men were in charge and girls and women were sexualized sideshows, punchlines for rape jokes, and subject to endless sexual harassment—with only occasional "feisty" leads surrounded by horrible dudes.

Those kids, the adults of today—us—grew up watching all of this and thinking it was normal, acceptable, right. White men were in charge of government, business, sports, publishing, science, academia—so why would they not be centered in nearly every film? Now in charge, these adults look back fondly on their upbringing, their first experiences at the cinema, their favorite movies and replicate their childhood training onscreen, perpetuating these stereotypes we all grew up watching.

It's a sexist cycle perpetuated by men and women who look back fondly on sexist times and somehow believe they are not today sexist, that they can rail against "all-female casts" as bad, vote for a professed sexual predator, and through it all consider themselves . . . good people.

Come on, man. We can do better. Like the mantra says, "If she can see it, she can be it."

I have to hope that if we also begin to notice the glaring, rampant sexism playing out in nearly every form of onscreen entertainment, we can break it. If *we* can see it, we can call it out.

All this doesn't mean we have to trash our favorite movies of yore. I still like watching the original *Star Wars*, and my daughter does, too. But it's also probably a good idea to point out the issues and to recognize that those movies were made in the past and that we demand better now. Truly, it's as simple as that.

WHAT'S PARTICULARLY MIND-BOGGLING is that, at the end of the day, movie studios are in it to make money, and movies with female leads actually *earn more money* than movies with male leads, according to the Geena Davis Institute. Films led by women earn nearly 16 percent more than films led by men, and movies with co-leads earned 23.5 percent more than movies with male or female leads alone.

Just think how profound the foundation of ingrained, cultural sexism and racism is: despite evidence that female-led movies actually bring in *more* money, movies are still very much a male party—behind the scenes and in front of the cameras.

And when we finally do get the occasional female hero, she's usually dressed in a uniform or outfit no male hero would ever wear on the battlefield—skirts or tight shorts, bras, leggings, and tall boots—outright ridiculous.

In *Miss Representation*—a must-view documentary about the horrible gender imbalances across all media—political science professor Caroline Heldman coined the term "the Fighting Fuck Toy."

"Even though she is doing things on her own terms, she is very much objectified and exists for the male viewer," Heldman says.

Sexist bros making sexist movies for sexist bros weaned on sexist movies. And earning less money at the box office because of it. Awesome.

SO, FINALLY, *THE Force Awakens*.

The idea of a powerful female character headlining one of the biggest franchises in movie history felt like a momentous shift, like a disturbance in the gender force.

On initial viewing, I thought it was truly groundbreaking.

Because the thing is, Rey, the main character, is not the role model for little girls I assumed she'd be.

The Force Awakens has been out for years now, and that's still all I ever hear about it.

"Oh, she's so powerful and strong—a perfect role model for little girls!"

"Finally, a hero girls deserve!"

Enough.

Stop.

Don't keep saying that.

Because the thing is: my daughter, her friends, their circle—and millions like them around the country—they already *know*.

Do you think in their playtime and imaginations that they're *not* the hero?

Please.

Do you think in their playtime that girls *don't* fly the *Falcon*?

That they *don't* beat up jerks with their staffs?

Or tinker, engineer, fly, run, jump, call lightsabers, become the chosen one, and save the universe?

No, Rey is not the perfect role model for little girls.

She's a role model for boys.

INDEED, SHE'S THE *perfect* role model for little boys, and a whole bunch of supposedly grown-ass men as well.

She's the role model they need.

Frankly, she's the role model our expanding universe of epic sexist bullshittery needs, especially when it comes to how girls and women are portrayed in film. The new series is providing, so far, a master class in how to narrow the gender gap onscreen.

Boys can be the unapologetic hero.

Girls can be the unapologetic hero.

It makes no difference to the viewing pleasure of the audience.

Rey is for a new generation of boys and girls who will be playing pretend Star Wars in backyards and schoolyards for years to come.

This is important.

The pretend play following a movie is practically a cornerstone of modern American childhood. I remember being Maverick from *Top Gun*, running around the school playground with hordes of other "fighter pilots" (all males), and I've seen kids today pretending in the schoolyard to be Finn and Rey from the new Star Wars series.

Movies can be a powerful force in reinforcing ancient gender roles, or they can edge playtime—and, later, work time, family time—toward equality. They can open new avenues for kids. After the movies *Brave* and *The Hunger Games,* which both featured powerful women archers, the number of girls participating in the real-world archery scene soared.

What we see can either inspire or throttle desires.

My friend Noelle says it best: "When I was in kindergarten, I played ninja turtles with four boys. It took weeks before I realized that they would never let me be Raphael, like I wanted: I was ALWAYS April. I couldn't be anything else. And I'd have to almost die on a class bench before one of them would kiss me and 'bring me back to life.' At the time, the easiest solution was just to stop playing with them, and no consequences befell me for that. It was years before I realized the sexual significance of all of that 'play.'"

I'M BEING FACETIOUS when it comes to Rey.

She is, obviously, a tremendous role model for girls. In fact, it could be argued she's one of the greatest movie role models for little girls of this age—hence all the attention here.

I've often said I wanted to see a girl hero have the same opportunities as a boy hero. What I mean is, when a story revolves around a boy hero, he usually has adventures and has to save everyone. When there's a girl hero, she also has to figure out where she fits in a boy's world.

I think of Merida from *Brave*. Awesome. Kickass. Brave. But, come on. The entire setup revolves around not *if* she'll ever get married but *when*. How many boy-led movies revolve around marriage plots?

Rey's story is more like Moana's and a perfect model for future female protagonists: they simply get to have adventures. They get to save the day. They get to be the chosen one—not figure out how to snag a man or decide how they'll fit into a man's world.

Rey just gets to do all the cool hero shit. Girls need to see this.

From an entertainment perspective, it rocks. From a cultural perspective, it's a revelation. If there is indeed a connection between the way women are treated onscreen and the way women are treated in real life—and I do believe there is; one reinforces the other—then this is a moment when art clearly is not imitating life, a moment when, in fact, judging by the reactions, art is parsecs beyond life.

So, no, Rey is not a good role model for girls. Yes, she's great for them. There's no denying that.

But Rey isn't just for her.

She's not the role model girls need.

She's the role model everyone else needs.

AND YET ... I HAVE to admit that I didn't really notice this for years, so taken was I with the main character and her hero arc; it has flaws. Big ones.

Take a look at the Internet Movie Database list of cast members, and it shows 186 total cast members, only 41 of which are women—22 percent.

On initial viewing, I thought the film did a pretty good job of filling the screen with more women as key members but also as background members, those characters that just mill around and form the overall population.

I was wrong. It was still an escapist fantasy nearly devoid of women, despite having the window dressing of a lead female character. I think back to the sexist male voices I heard arguing that a woman in the lead was "ruining" their childhood memories, and yet . . . just 22 percent of the make-believe world is women.

Dudes had to have some pretty fragile childhoods for less than a quarter ratio of women to "ruin" it. . . .

Since *The Force Awakens,* several new Star Wars movies have debuted—some of which I haven't seen yet.

The first offshoot, *Rogue One,* was an obvious, disgusting bachelor party from the start. Though it includes tremendous racial diversity and persons with disabilities in casting and should be applauded for that, it was nearly unwatchable for its maleness.

Out of a cast of 145, just 17, or 12 percent, were women. Again, a woman was cast as the lead character—much to the chagrin of sexist men who yet again didn't want their childhoods ruined by yet another powerful woman. But this move was even worse window dressing. Nearly every scene in the movie was dudes, dudes, and more dudes.

The Last Jedi, the latest episode in the saga, had pretty much the same casting issues—18 percent women—but far, far more women in roles that moved the story along. They were central to the plot and had more speaking roles than ever before.

And yet, again . . . 18 percent overall.

WHAT DOES IT say of us men when we see the occasional female hero and then decry the downfall of civilization, when actual female representation doesn't even match up with what we see in representation in government, business, and sports?

Like I said, this is a men's issue, this childlike, angry-boy desire to put up a "no girls allowed" sign on our collective cultural treehouse.

But here's to hoping that if we can see it, we can break it.

SO, WHAT CAN WE DO?

Talk about it.

Talk about it with your friends, on your social media channels, with, most importantly, your kids.

Rosalind Wiseman, author of the Queen Bees books, tells parents to "pick their spots." You don't want to bring it up all the time, or kids start tuning out. But when you're watching something, that's a pretty good opening to point out the crappy female characters who are supposed to be "awesome" but who turn out to be prizes. I think you'll be surprised at how quickly kids pick up on weird gender roles being pushed on them.

They've got eyes and brains, you know.

Here's the bottom line: *someone* is going to tell your child about their expected roles in society. Do you want it to be endless sexist messages from all manner of media . . . or you?

So, talk about it. And don't worry about getting everything "right." Sometimes just pointing out all the sexism and simply asking kids if it seems fair is enough.

We're a pretty big sports family, and commercials during these events are perfect avenues for discussing everything from who gets to speak, who gets to be shown (and which body parts are shown and why), and who takes center stage.

Talk about it with your male friends as well. This is key.

Look, I get it. Chatting in the comfort of your home with your kids is one thing. But chatting about it with your male buddies at the bar is another.

Get over it.

Bring it up. Make your point. You don't have to be preachy about it, but don't be scared of discussing the sexist messages we receive daily simply because you're afraid of getting ribbed by your buds. One circle at a time, fellas. You got this.

I'd also urge you to put your money where your mouth is.

When girls and women are offered as the lead characters, go see the movie. Even if the deck is stacked against these movies—remember the idea that female-led movies outearn male-led movies and still aren't made in equal or greater numbers—it feels important to support them so that moviemakers will keep it up. When *Crazy Rich Asians* debuted in 2018, my friends swamped the theaters and urged all our friends to spread the word because Asian American communities are so underrepresented in movies beyond roles of stereotypically quiet, deadly martial arts assassins. In short, again, put your money where your mouth is and show up. Take the kids. Tell your friends. It's really that easy. Studios might catch on. At the very least, we won't give them a good excuse to continue with the bullshit.

And, seriously, just how many "angry white hero saves the day" movies can one see?

They get *old*.

Not only do they send boys and girls some pretty crap messages of anger and violence, they're also *borrrring*.

Been there, done that.

Let's be vocal for a diversity of voices in the pantheon of cultural mythologies—if not for fairness, then for god's sake, at least for entertainment value.

To BRING IT back to Rey and "talking about it," for my final point, I'll say this: our collective voice is stronger than we imagine.

As awesome as Rey's character is, the original cast photo from the new Star Wars series revealed a glaring lack of female characters. The black-and-white photo showed a bazillion dudes sitting around a room, with only a sprinkling of women.

A social media freakout commenced, and you know what?

It worked.

All that "whining" actually led the producers to do something as simple as swap a male character for a female one, according to screenwriter Lawrence Kasden. He said they switched Captain Phasma from a man to a woman because of the outcry. The movie also populated random bit character parts and scene backgrounds with more women—rebel fighters, random street people, generals, and doctors.

You can literally change the world for the better for all of our kids just by speaking up.

The gender divide in casting is still pretty horrible—22 percent—but I think of how bad it would have been without our chatter.

So, keep talking.

Demand more.

You can literally change the world for the better for all of our kids just by speaking up. One circle at a time.

—Chapter 9—

NOT PLAYING AROUND

Playtimes should be about fun and exploration, but the toys we buy for our kids often undercut the equity and opportunity we want for them.

I WAS AT TARGET with my daughter, and amid the endless parade of toys and games and dolls in pink, fluffy dresses, she saw a skateboard. Her eyes lit up.

"Can I?"

We were there for toilet paper and kitchen towels, and somehow there we were, in the toy aisle. Ah, Target, you sly, mortgage-draining devil.

"Please?" she begged.

It was a long, blue, relatively inexpensive board—something we had been considering for her birthday anyway.

"Let me see there." I grabbed it and double-checked the price and found, sure enough, that it wasn't for her.

"Look, it says 'boys' skateboard.' Sorry."

She cocked her head to the side.

"Seriously?"

I shrugged.

"That's what it says. It's for boys. What can you do?"

At this point, her hands were on her hips and she was struggling to find the words. The look of outraged, silent fury finally broke between gritted teeth.

"But . . . it's . . . a . . . skateboard! It's a . . . *toy!*"

IT ALMOST SEEMS silly, doesn't it? To deny your child a toy because some giant store labeled it for a different sex? "No, you can't have this skateboard—a
skateboard—because it's blue and because a multinational corporation decided it's not for you."

(For the record, I passed on the skateboard because her birthday was
coming up, and we planned on getting her one anyway. Still, it made for a
teachable moment about subtle social messages.)

It might seem silly or absurd to let some company decide which toys are
appropriate for your kids, but how many other facets of society—how many
friends, relatives, schools, strangers at the park—do just that? And
it all seems so damn normal, natural, a perfectly acceptable thing
to do. Some toys are "for" girls and some are "for" boys. You've
probably heard it a billion times by now.

> **Look,
> here's my
> deal: toys
> are gender
> neutral.**

Look, here's my deal: toys are gender neutral. If you're limit-
ing playtime and exploration based on sex or gender expression,
you're an asshole. Not just that, you're perpetuating, from the very
earliest ages, harmful stereotypes that add up to horrible real-
world consequences.

"When you cut off half the opportunities in the world for something you
were born with . . . that's a real shame," says Lise Eliot, author of the book
Pink Brain, Blue Brain.

FOR FAR TOO long, we've bought into a social custom that divides our kids
in the earliest, most important developmental times and sets the tone for
our expectations of them. In some ways, the messages repeat what we may
remember from our own childhood: dolls are for girls, trucks are for boys.
But, in other ways, it's just blatant marketing designed to get families to buy
two of everything—say, a brown leather football for the boys and a pink one
for the girls—because heaven forbid a girl could like a game without a smear
of pink gloss.

Or, in some cases, such as Legos, the toys *used* to be advertised to both
genders, but then the company decided to market largely to boys. And what
happened? Surprise, surprise, girls stopped buying them because they don't
see the toys as "for them." The company later came out with a Friends system designed with girls in mind and received accolades for bringing girls

back into the very early engineering playtime Lego had socially advertised them out of.

Gross.

If they had never created a false split in the first place, girls never would have gone away. But at least now the company can sell two kits to every family, right? One for boys and one for girls. And receive *praise* for it all. It's mind-boggling.

"IT'S ALL MASSIVELY driven by marketers trying to double profits," says Melissa Atkins Wardy, author of *Redefining Girly* and founder of the Brave Girls Alliance. "For girls, the science kits are sparkle science and for boys they're just science. At some point, parents have this 'Ah-ha!' moment and call bullshit," she says. "We don't need to reinforce gender roles here. It's playtime!"

But we've bought into it for oh so long—hook, line, and sinker.

And why not?

In toy stores and schools and on playgrounds around the globe, kids are being told in ways big and small that there are limits to their imaginations and playtime—probably the most critical parts of their development.

Stores blatantly divide their aisles between the sexes—in ways that will nearly make your head spin: for girls, it's pink and fluffy dolls, household appliance toy kits, enormous fake heads for styling with makeup and hair-dos, and hypersexualized miniature plastic bodies with giant eyes and invisible hips; for boys, it's weapons and tech toys and superheroes, sports toys, puzzles, and race cars.

Some stores go out of their way to actually label certain aisles as Boy Toys and Girl Toys. Target used to be the biggest offender—see skateboards for boys only—but changed its policy and turned the toy aisles into something that approaches gender neutrality. Instead of aisles painted pink and blue to denote genders, the toy aisles are now all yellow, with no more labels. (I saw one end cap photo showing a boy with a vacuum. As a lover of Dyson cordless vacuums, podcasts, and general household upkeep, it made me smile.)

RESEARCHERS HAVE FOUND that when toys are gendered, the messages become pretty clear pretty fast.

"We found that girls' toys were associated with physical attractiveness, nurturing, and domestic skill, whereas boys' toys were rated as violent, competitive, exciting, and somewhat dangerous," Judith Blakemore, professor of psychology and associate dean of Arts and Sciences for Faculty Development at Indiana University-Purdue University, told the National Association for the Education of Young Children about a study of a hundred toys. "The toys rated as most likely to be educational and to develop children's physical, cognitive, artistic, and other skills were typically categorized as neutral or moderately masculine."

You've probably noticed something similar.

Boys get the Lego sets, the puzzles, and games, and science-y, space-y stuff, while girls get an endless pink wash of dolls and princesses. My favorite phrase about this comes from Jim Griffioen, a stay-at-home dad turned blogger and photographer: "The Princess Industrial Complex."

Nailed it.

Sadly, everyone loses, not just girls.

Girls lose out on critical spatial development toys—Lego, Minecraft—when we say those are culturally off-limits.

And boys lose out on practicing critical empathy and caring skills that come with doll play and tea parties. If we're raising future dads, it seems silly to shut off nurturing from an early age, doesn't it?

Check out the storyline on that one: Is it any coincidence that from day one we cut off boys from the notion of caring for others, even in playtime, and then see that dads are considered dopes in the majority of cultural depictions and aren't expected to care for kids for even a weekend while "mommy is away," or that male politicians rarely, if ever, get asked "how they do it all," or that women are exalted as the ultimate caregivers and then are punished for it as childcare responsibilities burdened on them alone lead to pay and opportunity disparities—never mind the outrageous violence committed largely by boys and men on other boys and men as well as on girls and women?

Sometimes I wonder if the fix to all this shit is simply more dolls for boys from the beginning.

"Moderately masculine toys have many positive qualities (spatial skills, science, building things, etc.) that parents might want to encourage in both boys and girls," Blakemore says. "Perhaps, to some extent, it is the same for some moderately feminine toys (nurturance, care for infants, developing skills in cooking and housework)."

ACCORDING TO ELIOT, the neuroscientist, nature, indeed, is behind the toy decisions of kids—but in small, subtle amounts. Some research shows that higher prenatal testosterone levels in mothers leads their children to pick more active toys that might be considered conventionally masculine, such as trucks or construction toys. But, similar to the case for brain sex differences, differences in child preferences are incredibly small, certainly not large enough to justify a social stratification that impacts every child.

For most kids, especially before their gender identity forms, there's really no difference at all.

"We see subtle differences in toy preference at twelve months of age, not really anything at six months, but by twelve months we start seeing it," Eliot told me. "But then it takes a big jump at age two or three when boys and girls know they are boys and girls and start to understand what's 'appropriate' for me versus my brother or sister."

In other words, it's absurd to divide toys by gender for very young children—or to throw those silly "gender reveal" parties before they're even born—because the kids themselves don't understand their gender. Sure, they might have visible sex organs ("sex organ reveal party" might be a more apt prebirth celebration), but they won't have an idea of how they consider themselves for at least a few years.

"But then especially after they gender identify, if you hear your child start saying 'that's for girls or that's for boys,' that's when you say, 'That's ridiculous! There is nothing about Legos or baby dolls that are [sic] exclusively for one or the other. Look, dads take care of babies, moms take care of babies. Dads build buildings, and moms build buildings,'" Eliot says.

I'd argue you have to be some form of special asshole to cut your children off from a full spectrum of quality, enriching playtime simply because of societal pressure.

But, really, it's a message most of us have internalized. Boys and girls are "just different," you might hear. Okay, sure. A tiny bit. In some specific areas. And in ways that can't be divorced from the way we treat boys and girls from the moment they arrive. So . . . then what? We should therefore arbitrarily limit their opportunities by slicing out critical development toys for girls or critical nurturing toys for boys?

I don't get it.

IN YEARS OF following how toys are marketed to kids—and trying to raise a daughter to play with whatever the hell she wants to play with—I've noticed a couple things I think a lot of parents have also noticed.

One, girls have an easier time switching between gender expectations. They can play with dolls and power tools, and everyone calls it amazing and awesome.

"She's so powerful!"

> **But give a boy a doll or a purse or some toenail polish, and suddenly he's "girly," as if conventionally feminine qualities themselves are insulting.**

But give a boy a doll or a purse or some toenail polish, and suddenly he's "girly," as if conventionally feminine qualities themselves are insulting.

Think of how many things we divide by gender—clothes, sports, chores, jobs, pay—and which things we herald as "amazing and awesome" in society. Then consider where it all begins. The clothes we put them in, the toys we give them—these set the tone for all the rest of it.

My friend Chris posted a photo of his boys and their dolls on his social networks and received an absolute blizzard of disturbing notes about the "feminization" of his boys. The same thing happened to my friend Aaron when his boy chose a purse as a prize. You would have thought they were actually beating their children, from the social media reaction of it all.

Look, I get it. We are deluged by these messages everywhere—in toy commercials, trips to the store, visits to the playground. Sometimes the messages are blaring and ridiculous. But often, they're subtle to the point of seeming innocuous—to the point that if you call it out, people ignore it or say you're making too big a deal out of it, or that it's "natural."

I posit that it's the opposite, that we've considered it "natural" instead of "manmade" for far too long.

BACK TO TARGET. In the weeks following the premiere of the new Star Wars movie, toy lovers discovered something sad—but all too predictable.

There was no sign of the lead character, Rey. Indeed, the toy aisle had Star Wars storm troopers, villains, aliens, Jedis, fighter craft of all kind...and no Rey.

Even a boxed set of characters featured all of Rey's friends and enemies and a bunch of random, helmeted villains instead of her. The Monopoly game included pretty much everyone except her. There was even a Millennium Falcon set—which she famously flew and became the freaking *pilot* of—and still no Rey.

She was the main character in this movie and apparently all the new Star Wars movies to come, and yet was not available for kids in action figure form. Believe me, I had to search high and low. I checked out every big store that had a selection of Star Wars toys and couldn't find more than an occasional mention of Rey.

We weren't the only ones to discover this.

An entire Twitter campaign emerged about her absence in the toy aisles, featuring the hashtag #wheresrey.

Can you imagine a line of *Raiders of the Lost Ark* toys not featuring Indiana Jones?

It just wouldn't happen.

It would be downright silly.

Toymakers claimed it was a well-intended omission designed to keep Rey's big role in the films a secret.

I call BS.

John Marcotte, author of the website Heroic Girls, which does an amazing job of tracking gender bias in marketing and toys, found that time and time again popular female action figures are girl-washed out of the toy aisles. Rey wasn't the first. There is a clear pattern, and it's not a "well-intended effort." It's not "natural."

Gamora, the green alien from the Guardians of the Galaxy series, was also excluded from toy sets.

Black Widow, the popular buttkicker from the Avengers series, was replaced in a toy set that featured her most pivotal moment—jumping out of a plane on a motorcycle—by a male character. In the toy aisles, her coolest moment was taken over by a guy.

Seriously.

It's like replacing Rocky in the final bouts with, well, anyone else.

Hard to imagine, I know, but it happens all the time with female leads—either they are grossly underrepresented or they are replaced altogether.

Why?

Marketing. Gender roles. Societal reinforcement. We've made it nearly impossible for boys to play with so-called feminine toys without attracting derision and disdain.

"The worst thing you can be as a boy is feminine," Melissa Atkins Wardy says. "All the men I've ever met in my life eat food. So why would you also not sell kitchens to boys? It's crazy."

SO, WHAT CAN WE DO?

The Center for Early Childhood Education at Eastern Connecticut State University studies the influence of culture on play.

"We have found some surprising gender differences in our study," Jeffrey Trawick-Smith, a professor at the university, said in an interview with the National Association for the Education of Young Children. "Many of the toys nominated by parents and teachers were used most often and in the most complex ways by boys. This included items that seemed gender neutral from an adult perspective. What set the highest-scoring toys apart was that they prompted problem solving, social interaction, and creative expression in both boys and girls."

The center found results that upend the refrains you constantly hear when discussing marketing and toys: that companies are just giving us what we want.

"Interestingly, toys that have traditionally been viewed as male oriented—construction toys and toy vehicles, for example—elicited the highest quality play among girls," Trawick-Smith says. "So, try to set aside previous conceptions about what inspires male and female play and objectively observe toy effects to be sure boys and girls equally benefit from play materials."

When I'm buying toys for, say, birthday presents, I largely stick to science toys or books for boys and girls. It's just what my daughter likes, so I assume other kids might like them as well. If I happen to know the kid well, I buy what fits her interests—whether it's a doll or a ball glove.

What I don't do is take guidance from some random corporate giant—or assholes who shake their fists and rage about "tradition." The research just doesn't back it up. I know I sound like some anticorporatist nutcase (I'd marry Target if I could; ugh, I know), but it's really about making choices, not having them made for you—or worse, for your kids. There must be a Venn diagram somewhere showing the number of white guys I've heard shouting, "Personal freedom!" with one breath and then with another, "Conform to traditional gender roles!"

So, if your girl wants a skateboard, buy it. If your boy wants a doll, do the same—but be prepared to have talks with people, your friends and family even, who won't like it.

Consider that for a moment and tell me if you're okay with this: you don't give a second thought to buying a girl a skateboard, but would you have to have a heart-to-heart with a boy about a doll purchase? Would you have to prepare him for scorn and ridicule?

Sadly, that's our culture.

We can give girls endless dolls and "nurturing toys," but we have a hard time doing the same for future dads—and then, here's the kicker of it all, everyone complains later about how dads can't even care for kids for a weekend, or that judges screw over dads in custody cases. It's literally in our cultural atmosphere, everywhere, to downgrade men as uncaring and to pigeonhole women as the ones who "do it all"—with lower pay and constant threats of violence and harassment from these same grown-ass men who have been told since childhood that nurturing and caring just ain't their bag, that violence and destruction are more in line with their "natural" state.

No joke. They're connected, linked by the expectations of what we consider "natural" for boys and girls and then, later, men and women.

Look, you're not a "bad" parent for buying pink shit for girls and blue shit for boys. I bought my daughter a pink batting helmet. Later, she wanted a blue one. Cool. They both fit her best. All I'd say is just be aware of whether you're cutting kids off from critical play opportunities because it's what they want—or because it's what they're learning to want from your expectations or societal pressure about what they "should" want. What I mean is, don't block avenues of fun and development for bullshit sexist reasons.

TRAWICK-SMITH FOUND SOMETHING else interesting in the center's studies on toys and what appeals the most to the greatest number of kids. It will hopefully give you some guidance on how to go from here.

Basic, he says, is better. "These toys are relatively open-ended, so children can use them in multiple ways."

—Chapter 10—

THROW LIKE A GIRL

*Although boys and girls play sports in roughly equal numbers,
culturally, sports are still very much a "man's game."*

"MOUNTAINS," SHE SAID, shaking her head. "There are literally more pictures of *mountains* than women."

She paused. Tilted her head. Chuckled morosely.

"Well, it *is* a nice mountain."

We were flipping through the sports pages, hoping to find some news about that day's upcoming US women's soccer match.

Nothing.

In fact, there was barely a mention of any female athletes at all.

For any sport.

As an impromptu test of equality in coverage, we quickly added up all the photos. Out of seventeen total, there were more images of mountains (one) than female athletes (zero).

Sure, sports have long been promoted as the "domain" of men, the proverbial man cave of supposedly strong men who nevertheless have childlike fits of exasperation at the idea of "sharing" fields or coverage with women.

But come on, man.

Zero?

Not one fucking photo of a female athlete?

Unfortunately, it wasn't an aberration.

My daughter knows full well my disdain for our local paper's abhorrently sexist sports page. Its lack of coverage of women athletes is all at once glaringly obvious and disgusting—but also par for the course when it comes to national coverage of athletes who happen to be women.

HERE'S WHAT I mean.

Even the most casual observer of the sports pages would notice a distinct lack of equal coverage. But so obvious was the *San Francisco Chronicle*'s misogyny that I decided to do a weeklong review of its coverage and send it in to the editors, in the hopes of improving things.

Here's what I found:

Over the course of a random week in 2017, the *Chronicle* ran 204 sports stories. Thirty-two stories related to athletes who were women, or roughly 15 percent of coverage. About half of those stories were brief, one-paragraph update-style stories.

It published a total of 115 photos, with 20 showing women in some way. Five of those photos, for instance, were of the paper's very own columnist, not actual female athletes, and a few others were the spouses or girlfriends of male athletes. The paper published zero photos of husbands of female athletes.

During this same period, just to make sure the *Chronicle* wasn't some crazy outlier, I looked at the coverage in the *New York Times* Sunday sports page and saw similar figures: just four of eighteen stories centered on athletes who were women.

To follow up on this quasi-experiment, my daughter and I performed another check in 2018—on Mother's Day, no less.

The *Chronicle* published thirty-one photos. There were more photos of horses (one) and mountains again (two) than female athletes (zero).

The *New York Times* published twenty-four photos in its sports pages. There were more photos of horses (four) and even horse tack (one) than female athletes (zero).

SO, WHAT GIVES?

Neither of these papers is an outlier.

This is our culture, our shared experience about whose stories we find important enough to tell.

Sports is, indeed, a bastion of boys and men—to the point that women were not so long ago physically barred from participation and to this day continue to be the object of ridicule among both obnoxiously sexist assholes and well-meaning people who are simply repeating dreadful cultural tropes.

Insert "You run/throw/cry like a girl" here.

It's not difficult to trace a through-line from childhood taunts that paint girls as weak and lesser to national news coverage and cultural participation that reinforce the notion.

The Tucker Center for Research on Girls and Women in Sport at the University of Minnesota, in the best-known recent study of media coverage, found female athletes receive just 4 percent of sports coverage. This matches the twenty-year study of national sports media by University of Southern California and Purdue sociologists, which also shows female athletes receive roughly 4 percent of coverage.

> **It's not difficult to trace a through-line from childhood taunts that paint girls as weak and lesser to national news coverage and cultural participation that reinforce the notion.**

A 2015 Gallup poll asked who is most likely to be sports fans and viewers. Of respondents, 66 percent of men, as you might imagine from the endless coverage of them, claimed they were sports fans.

But here's the thing. Women weren't *zero*.

Or 10 percent. Or the *Chronicle*'s own 15 percent, or the *New York Times*'s 20 percent.

A full 51 percent of women claimed they were sports fans. Other studies have shown female viewers of sports make 31 (NHL) to 35 percent of the audience (NASCAR).

Add this in: Billie Jean King's Women in Sports Foundation, which tracks progress after Title IX, shows there are roughly 4.4 million boys and 3.2 million girls involved in high school sports and that the number of female athletes continues to climb from an initial three hundred thousand girls in 1972, when the Education Amendments Act explicitly barred discrimination on the basis of sex in educational programs.

The point of it all?

Girls and women play sports in numbers far greater than media's unequal coverage gap would pretend. Half of women say they are sports fans. And roughly one-third actually tune in regularly to sports.

How does that possibly justify coverage that ranges from 4 to roughly 20 percent? Or everyday coverage that features more representations of nature and horses than female athletes?

Obviously, it doesn't.

SOMETHING ELSE IS going on here. News decisions about who receives coverage don't just materialize out of the ether. These are decisions made largely by men, men raised under the constant messaging that girls and women are lesser, that sports is a man's domain, that people only want to watch men play with their balls.

The absurdity of all these statistics and viewership among women and the distinct lack of coverage of women's sports leave out one key aspect: men love watching women's sports, too.

Think of the 2015 Women's World Cup final, which drew more viewers than the NBA and NHL finals that year. Then there's the Olympics, the full-grown WNBA, and the ever-growing NWSL.

The lack of coverage of female athletes is purposeful, buttressed by the idea that—and I've heard this plenty of times, as a former newspaper reporter—no one really cares about women's sports, that it's an economic disaster in the making to cover them more.

It's really a horrible chicken-or-the-egg scenario carted out to excuse a sexist system.

People won't "care" about women's sports to equal degrees until men's and women's sports are covered in equal degrees—but they're never covered in equal degrees because editors keep thinking no one cares.

And who suffers from it all? Our kids.

They learn from early ages that sports are for boys, and that it's perfectly fine to leave girls out of the picture despite their enormous and growing participation in sports. We tell our kids to be powerful and strong and that they can do anything; yet we show them something else entirely every time we open the paper or turn on the TV—and in the way we talk about sports with our buddies.

It's worthy of some critical self-examination: Do we tell our girls they can do anything, and then undercut women in certain fields? Don't kid yourself. Our kids notice.

TAKE A LOOK at another example. I'm a huge Portland Thorns soccer fan. Tobin Heath is a fleet-footed god walking among us. But if you go on the ESPN soccer page in search of scores and game times for the biggest women's professional league in the United States—the league that features our biggest stars—you have to scroll down past B and C league teams from practically every continent before you get there.

ESPN can't possibly argue that its website analytics show no one is interested when the website basically makes the league impossible to find.

These are decisions made by people who think it's somehow normal to give half the population short shrift, not because it's right, or just, or even a money-making proposition. But because the idea that it's okay to do so starts in our shared childhood milieu, when even today well-meaning parents tilt the playing fields in favor of boys.

It's a messaging system playing out in every backyard, ball field, and playground.

> **It's a messaging system playing out in every backyard, ball field, and playground.**

FROM THE MOMENT my friend's daughter started playing baseball, there was only one question: When would she switch to softball?

"When your daughter plays on 'boys' teams,' you definitely get an earful. Some good, some not so good," says Michele, who lives in Georgia.

Her eleven-year-old daughter, Gabi, is a hard-throwing, all-star baseball pitcher who has played on "boys' teams" for years.

"From when she first started playing baseball at the age of five, in general, people would always be surprised to see a girl at first and then would recognize and comment on her skill immediately," Michele says. "That's a good thing. But so much of the time it would be followed up by questions like: 'Will she play softball?' or 'When will you switch her to softball?' or 'How long will she play for?'"

Michele says she doesn't have anything against softball. It's just that her daughter *likes* baseball. Why should society's expectations keep a child from a sport she likes?

But even for five-year-olds, baseball fields are the domain of boys, and it seems fellow parents—parents like you and me—aren't afraid to reinforce this notion from the bleachers.

"I still get the questions about softball. And most often people will say, 'What is she going to do when she gets to be around fifteen–sixteen and the boys are so much bigger?' They say things that imply that unless she's a big, strong boy she won't be able to play," Michele explains.

It's a series of conversations she's had many times over the years, and she's honed her replies.

"There are many responses to this. First of all, not all boys/men who play are huge. Teams need a diverse group of players that offer skill sets to do different things. For example, there will be home-run hitters on teams that are not fast around the bases. Typically, a position like shortstop is not going to be your biggest player. The other thing I tell them is that it doesn't matter. She will play as long as she's competitive."

Notice the story that is passed on to kids: any boy can be a perfectly average benchwarmer who may or may not get playing time, but a girl playing alongside that boy basically has to be the reincarnation of Joltin' Jo Weaver (she hit for 4.29 in 1954; sorry, Ted) to be considered "good enough."

As Michele ticked off the micro-obstacles her daughter faces, seemingly innocent-sounding questions that challenge the girl's presence on a ball field, I began to wonder whether as a society we aren't still embodying some Victorian-era protectionism of girls, who, in that notion, are more apt to have fainting spells than, say, turn two from the hot corner.

For years, women were kept from long-distance running events such as the marathon for fear that the mileage would hurt them. Or, worse . . . their baby-making abilities.

"It was feared that anything longer was going to injure women, that they wouldn't be able to have children or they somehow turned into men," Kathrin Switzer told NPR on the fiftieth anniversary of her famous Boston Marathon run in 1967. That was the first time a woman officially wore a bib and entered the race. (Switzer gave credit to the woman who, the previous year, had jumped out of the bushes to run the course unofficially.) In her contest, Switzer was grabbed by race officials, who tried to force her off course while running.

"You're going to get big legs. You're going to grow hair on your chest. It was hilarious, the myths," she recalled. "And, of course, when people hear myths, they believe them because to try otherwise might mean damaging yourself. So people were afraid and they just went about their lives that way and restricted themselves."

It's the same protectionism of our precious girls that my own daughter has faced. I've heard parents tell their sons not to throw "too hard" to her, or to go easy, never mind she can bring the heat, catch nearly any worm burner or fly ball, and round the bases at speeds probably beating, or at least rivaling, those of these prepubescent boys. But never mind the notion that she can actually play, or "keep up," with the boys—think of how many messages we send to boys that they have to "go easy," while girls are told they are both "weak" and yet "must prove themselves" against the cultural norm of boyhood.

These are just a few examples rooted in childhood. It gets worse later on as girls grow into older athletes.

Much worse.

LIKE I MENTIONED earlier, Billie Jean King's Women's Sports Foundation compiled studies showing female athletes receive 4 percent of media coverage—a statistic apparent to anyone who opens any major sports page or turns on any sports TV show, which almost undoubtedly features a round of men angrily yelling at each other.

"Sportsball!"

A 2012 study shows the popular *ESPN Magazine* showcased female athletes on just over 3 percent of covers. (Color me shocked, then, at where it places our country's best female soccer players, buried behind endless pages of C league amateur men.)

Here's a question that embodies the issue of poor coverage of female athletes: When you think of *Sports Illustrated* magazine and women, do you think of athletes or . . . swimsuits?

Coverage like this trickles down.

It tells boys—and their parents—that male athletes are more important, that their stories are more important to tell.

It also tells girls they're not just second class but barely human at all—objects, not athletes. It starts at young ages on crappy fields and follows the girls into college, where fewer sports scholarships are available to them, and into the pros, where they often get lower pay and crappier fields and little to no support.

It's not a sports problem. It's a cultural problem.

There's no evil control center with some villain pushing buttons, making it all happen and cackling maniacally. It's us, allowing it to happen in front of our very eyes. In the bleachers.

I ALWAYS REMEMBER a great editorial written by soccer player Carli Lloyd and published in the *New York Times*. As you may recall, Lloyd scored a hat trick in the final of the Women's World Cup in 2015, securing yet another trophy for us all—a feat accomplished three times by the women's team and never by the men's.

And yet, the men's team was paid more not just in salary but also in everyday perks. When traveling, for instance, the men's team received $15 more per diem, and hundreds more for appearances, and thousands more for making World Cup rosters.

"Our beef is not with the men's national team; we love those guys, and we support those guys," Lloyd wrote. "It's with the federation, and its history of treating us as if we should be happy that we are professional players and not working in the kitchen or scrubbing the locker room."

The women are expected to win the cup every four years, whereas it's practically a national miracle if the men's team makes it out of the first group stages. In fact, the men's team didn't even qualify for the 2018 World Cup.

The final game of the Women's World Cup was the most watched soccer game in the United States—ever.

It beat out audience figures from the NHL final and the NBA final.

Yet the women's team is paid considerably less than the men's side— in salary and in everyday expenses like per diems. The sad thing is, with all that winning and audience pull, the women's side actually earned *more* money than the men's side in its World Cup year—yet the players are paid less and have crappier fields and less support, according to Lloyd.

"Simply put, we're sick of being treated like second-class citizens," she wrote. "It wears on you after a while. And we are done with it."

(As of this writing, the women's side negotiated a new contract that met its needs and is now preparing for the World Cup in France. The men's side is still "rebuilding" for 2022.)

Step back and examine the broader cultural story we tell our kids: girls are expected to shuffle off to "girls' sports" at an early age. Boys who can't sport are labeled weak or "girly." Adults feel comfortable telling children they "run like a girl." Clothes for children are made roomy for boys and skinny for girls. Colleges offer more scholarships for men. National media outlets treat women's sports as a third-tier joke in which coverage is more likely to focus on appearance rather than ability, if, that is, it features them at all.

And parents—parents like you and me—have soaked it all up from the time we were children ourselves to today, when nearly every media message we inhale says girls and women are lesser.

We're caught in a web—a web of sexism that reinforces these notions every day on the ball fields ("You throw like a girl!"), in media coverage (4 percent), and in pay disparities for pros (higher audience figures, three World Cups, and lower pay).

It's a tough web to break.

HERE'S THE KICKER.

The benefits of sports for girls are just overwhelmingly positive.

Mind-blowingly positive.

King's foundation shows study after study after study finds girls in sports have healthier body images, do drugs less, have fewer unwanted pregnancies, do better in school, and actually reduce their risk for breast cancer and osteoporosis.

As a society, we *know* this. Parents want their girls to play team sports. Remember those participation figures in the years after Title IX was enacted? From three hundred thousand to three million? Everywhere you look, girls are playing more and more sports—yet these micro-obstacles and macro-obstacles remain in their way.

It's only been a few generations since Title IX went into effect, but pay for professional female athletes (despite better ratings and outcomes) and college scholarships for girls are still lagging behind those for male professional and student athletes. College men earn 55 percent of the scholarships, despite the fact there are actually *more* female athletes in college, according to King's foundation.

Given the benefits of just a few hours of sports a week, why shouldn't our culture do everything it can to ensure girls have the same access to play and lifelong sporting opportunities as boys?

CROSSFIT PROVIDES A pretty good example of how to do just that.

Hear me out. It's worth a look.

I know CrossFit gets bagged on because, well, it's basically the sport of exercise, combining weight lifting, running, and swimming into timed events—and the joke is that people who do CrossFit can't shut up about it.

And yet it provides a pretty good model for competing and equal support from its parent organization.

I don't even *do* CrossFit, but I've loved how the sport has developed in a way that puts the stars of both sexes on equal footing. It's been fun and really sort of amazing to watch.

Competitions account for the physiological differences between most men and most women—and mix up the weights they have to lift, with men lifting heavier things for their events.

After that, the events are basically the same. Run a mile. Lift some weights. Do some pushups. Run another mile. Men and women compete on the same stages, perform the same activities, and receive what seems to be the same adulation from fans.

And the coverage from its parent media organization is full-on equal. As is the pay, and the support.

The result is that both men and women have the same opportunities, and the fans have bought in equally, it seems.

Basically, any run-of-the-mill CrossFit fan can tell you who is the previous year's men's champion and women's champion. Can your run-of-the-mill fans of basketball, soccer, baseball, or hockey say the same for men's and women's professional teams?

Perhaps CrossFit being so new has something to do with it. The federation is not an entrenched organization that was created at a time when women were excluded from many facets of society, let alone sports. But its model of equality in competition, pay, and coverage feels like the endgame here, something for other organizations to study.

THE SOCIETAL IMPACT of empowering cultural stories can't be overstated. There are amazing links between ample sports coverage—and media representations—of sporty girls and actual sporty, healthy girls.

The Geena Davis Institute on Gender in Media found that in the years following movies with heroines who were archers (Merida in *Brave* and Katniss in *The Hunger Games*), girls' participation in archery rose by 105 percent.

"It's not surprising to me that Hollywood's depiction of inspiring female archers has contributed to the sport's phenomenal growth—it's another demonstration of the powerful impact fictional characters can have on girls' aspirations," Davis said when the study came out last year. "As I always say, if she can see it, she can be it."

But first, we have to stop being shocked that girls like sports and that they can perform just as well—or just as average even—as all the boys. Then, we have to give them better role models and more coverage and more support—from athletic fields to clothes to simply the idea that playing around and playing sports isn't about gender.

"The greatest hurdle for my daughter and girls like her will be to simply prove they are good enough," my friend Michele says. "She has to be better or most people will not consider her to be a serious enough player. There will always be naysayers and those who don't support girls playing with boys; however, in my experience, there are many who do. We have been fortunate enough to find coaches and organizations who have no problem with her playing because they know she is an asset."

THE BOTTOM LINE is we have to recognize all the obstacles girls face even today and be aware that girls and women from different cultural backgrounds, ethnicities, and ability levels face similar and yet slightly different obstacles—and deserve no less than equal support.

Girls are playing more sports, and it's doing great good for them, and yet even well-meaning parents and coaches still toss out the same microsexisms they learned growing up. And it's all reinforced by shamefully poor media coverage and sad disparities between the sexes, such as availability of appropriate play clothes, college scholarships, or coaching opportunities after playing careers are over.

Fortunately for our girls and boys, there's you.

Parents on the sidelines have tremendous power to change the dynamics of unequal sports access and coverage simply by changing how we talk about who is allowed to play.

You can be a total asshole about it and say girls deserve less access and coverage because "that's just the way it's always been."

Or you can demand better.

> Parents on the sidelines have tremendous power to change the dynamics of unequal sports access and coverage simply by changing how we talk about who is allowed to play.

SO, WHAT CAN WE DO?

When it comes to women's sports, I use this analogy to discuss sexist coverage, lack of support, or whatever. Usually, when the topic comes up, a sexist man says something along the lines of, "Well, women will deserve equal pay/support/audience when they compete at the same level and pull in the same viewership." Or some such bullshit.

But it's not that black and white. Would that it were.

Here's the analogy, something to think about and perhaps keep in your pocket for when this topic comes up with your buds.

Imagine a company hires you and me to run lemonade stands.

The company gives you some shitty, rotten lemons, a few planks of wood, a handful of nails, maybe a hammer—who knows?—some ice, and maybe a mention or two in an ad campaign. Then off you go.

Now me. I get amazing, beautiful, organic lemons, raw sugar, spring water, a construction team to build my stand. The company promotes my stand online and on TV. I get sent off to management seminars and have endless gobs of money to pay workers and keep the stand neat and tidy. Outside of the company support, TV shows are dedicated to discussing my lemonade stand for hours on end. People listen to radio shows about my badass lemonade on their way to work. Parents buy their children T-shirts with my logo on them, and stores don't even offer the other stand's goods. Coaches around the world yell at their charges that they throw "like that other stand!" My stand is held up as the better, stronger option not just by my company but also in all facets of society, while those same facets consider the "other stand" not just different but weak and deserving of less attention.

Now, who do you think is going to sell more lemonade?

And here's the key: What sort of asshole would I be if I just shrugged and pointed at my sales stats to say I was doing better and therefore *deserved* better pay? What sort of monumental slowcoach of sexism would I have to be to think winning a rigged game was fair?

That's basically the scenario faced by women in soccer, basketball, business, and government—you name it. Just endless generations of support for boys and men, and then a cultural expectation that, somehow, things should be equal by now, but if they're not? Women deserve even less. It's only "natural," some argue, instead of created and maintained systems designed to bolster one and limit the other.

THAT MIGHT HELP open a few eyes to the obstacles girls and women still face.

The Women's Sports Foundation offers easy tips to help parents tip the scales toward equality.

Attend women's sporting events. Watch them on TV.

Support companies that advocate for women's athletics. Encourage the media to cover them.

Coach a girls' team.

These are my suggestions, and some from friends:

Don't use jerky language. Don't degrade a boy by calling him a girl: "You throw like a girl." We've all heard it. We can all stop using it and call it out when we hear it. It's just one more tiny hurdle in the way of progress.

Buy sports equipment for birthday and holiday presents.

Work out with your kids. It's great for everyone.

Take your sons or nephews to watch their female siblings or cousins play sports.

Encourage your town's cheerleading squads and bands to visit both boys' and girls' events.

Show your daughter articles or books about female athletes you consider role models.

Explain that it's okay to be feminine *and* athletic. Tell your sons it's cool to not like sports at all.

My friend Michele, whose daughter is the all-star baseball player, has some words of wisdom:

"My advice is simple—let your daughters know that you will not only support them if they choose to play a sport, but that you will be their advocate as well."

—Chapter 11—

ONLINE HARASSMENT

Girls and women are harassed, abused, and belittled online in ways boys and men can't fathom, and the repercussions are chilling.

A FRIEND OF MINE posted a story online about a controversial topic. It doesn't matter which one. This happens all the time, no matter the topic.

Within hours, his story took off. Went viral.

The threats began almost immediately.

People, usually men, threatened him and his family. They posted his photo. His address. Photos of his home.

Soon enough, he had to dismantle his entire social media presence and even take his family—in the physical world, not the online one—into hiding.

All because of some things he said online. Ironically, these are the same crowds that have bemoaned the idea that people take things "too seriously nowadays" and that everyone's "too PC."

To this day, he considers deeply whether something he says online might endanger his family again. People have called this cyberbullying, but that term doesn't go far enough. If terrorism is defined as the desire to in-fluence outcomes based on fears of violence and intimidation, let's call this what it is: online terrorism.

Now, the interesting thing—and by *interesting* I mean horrifying—is the way the online harassment and abuse took a predictable turn from these aggressive, violent, abusive men. They didn't just threaten him to the point of his seeking police intervention but also belittled his "manhood."

You've probably seen it online or perhaps even participated in it. He was targeted for violence for some words he said, but he lost his "manhood" in the process.

No one threatened to rape him. They threatened to rape his wife, repeatedly.

He was, in other words, soft, unmanly, worthy of ridicule and violence and some sordid fantasy in which his wife would suffer for it all.

He was, in their words, "a pussy"—feminine.

Catch the narrative: lesser.

HE IS BY no means alone. And it shouldn't be surprising that the online community resembles the physical one, with girls and women taking the brunt of oppression in the form of sexualized violence.

> "Harassment and vitriol are the price you must pay online, to be a woman, a person of color, a disabled person, anything other than a straight white male."

It's not a scientific study, to be sure, but I'd be surprised if you found something different in your friend circles. I have a lot of male friends who are writers, and I can count only one who has ever—ever—received a rape threat for something he wrote online, and even then you had to know the terminology to get it.

Nearly all of my female writer friends have.

Surprise, surprise, this matches perfectly with their physical-world experiences. Nearly zero of my male friends have been victims of everyday sidewalk sexual harassment from men, and yet nearly all of our female friends have been victims of it.

"Harassment and vitriol are the price you must pay online, to be a woman, a person of color, a disabled person, anything other than a straight white male," says Ebony Adams on the *Feminist Frequency* podcast, which tracks cultural tropes and sexism, especially in the gamer and online communities. "There is a price you have to pay simply for existing and letting it be known that you exist."

Her colleague Anita Sarkeesian came under brutal online assault for merely outlining in a series of wonderful videos all the horrible sexist tropes perpetuated by the video game industry—which creates the games our children are playing and internalizing as "normal." (You should google her videos; they're simply amazing cultural journalism about the tropes we quietly inhale.)

Rape threats, death threats, career threats. Sarkeesian had to literally go into hiding because of the violence. For merely pointing out egregious sexism, she was immediately subject to onslaughts of it—a form of online terrorism with a sexual bent rarely directed at men.

This online sexual terrorism is meant to do a couple things: extinguish everyday voices that challenge the white supremacist patriarchy and that have heretofore rarely had worldwide platforms, and solidify narratives in this moment of tremendous social transition that have existed since the beginning—men are the "norm," women are the variant.

"Even 'innocuous' harassment, when it's coming at you en masse from hundreds or even thousands of users a day, stops feeling innocuous very quickly. It's a silencing tactic," wrote Lindy West in the *Guardian*, referring to her experiences writing online and receiving harassment known as trolling. "The message is: we'll stop when you're gone."

West endures endless threats of sexual violence and death for having the gall to say women of all stripes deserve equality, and she famously confronted a "troll" who did something almost unthinkably egregious: impersonated her dead father online to attack her. Imagine that, would you? A man going to great lengths to investigate her life, discover her father had died, and then spend the time and energy to create social media accounts in his name all to send emotional abuse her way.

It is egregious beyond words.

But it's the virtual world our children inhabit the moment they open their phones.

THESE MAY SEEM like extreme examples. But you've probably never walked around as a girl or woman. They tell us again and again this is their everyday experience.

A 2017 Pew Research Center study found 41 percent of Americans have been subject to online harassment, and 66 percent have witnessed it. Nearly 20 percent reported abuse like the above, sustained or sexual threats or stalking.

In other words, line up five of your kids and their friends. Imagine their faces. Nearly half of them will be harassed online in ways you might think are "innocuous."

One of them will suffer sustained, sexualized, threatening abuse.

Which one will it be, do you think?

Interestingly, the study shows men are more likely to report being subject to online harassment, such as being called names or being threatened. But women, and especially young women, are far more likely to be subjected to sexualized harassment or abuse, with 21 percent of women ages eighteen to twenty-nine reporting it compared with 9 percent of men. More than half—53 percent—of women say they have been sent unsolicited, explicit images (read: dick pics).

In all, 35 percent of women report harassment as either extremely or very upsetting, compared to 16 percent of men. Divides like this continue. According to Pew, more than half of women say online abuse is too often excused away as "not a big deal," whereas 64 percent of men—and 73 percent of men ages eighteen to twenty-nine—say people take too much "offense" at it all. And 70 percent of women—a full 83 percent of those eighteen to twenty-nine—view online harassment as a major problem, while only half of men, across age groups, share this view, according to the study.

Well. Duh.

We enjoy a privilege of not having to deal with it as much. Who, then, bears the responsibility to see that it ends?

If men are not subjected to everyday sexual harassment, abuse, and threats from other men in their everyday physical lives or when they seek work or escapist fun online, of course we will not consider it a big deal, and many will go so far as to insist it doesn't even exist, that women are making too big a deal of it all, that people are "too PC."

But that doesn't mean that it's not happening just because we enjoy a privilege of not having to deal with it as much. Who, then, bears the responsibility to see that it ends?

Make no mistake, the ramifications are horrible.

A 2014 study from researchers at the University of Mary Washington's Psychology Department found ongoing sexual harassment leads to the same outcomes as sexual assault—depression, post-traumatic stress, and "insidious trauma."

The researchers studied physical sexual harassment, not online, but if we've been listening to the women and girls in our lives, it's not all that difficult to make the connections. Wherever they are, sexual abuse follows. From men.

It adds up.

"Women become caught in a catch-22; if they speak out about how they are treated, they are likely to be labeled as 'overly sensitive,' and if they say nothing, they have to live with these experiences without the chance of social support or vindication," the researchers wrote.

I don't think we men can truly fathom the emotional drain of everyday sexual harassment online or in the real world. I don't think most of us have to give it much thought, other than, perhaps, not doing it—as opposed to being subjects of it. Yes, to be sure, men are sexually harassed and abused. But men are also largely the abusers. I'm not sure we're fully cognizant of the life-sucking drain of it all—in dealing with not just the big traumas but also the littler ones, the everyday ones: parsing emails from work colleagues who seem, on the face of it, professional but who are also condescending in perhaps a gendered way, or thinking about whether we've just been threatened with rape for having an opinion. We can, more or less, go on with our lives, stumbling cluelessly from one meeting to the bar to the parking lot to the online forum, without having to navigate an endless gauntlet of sexualized aggression and violence. We like to think we treat people equally, or that we rise based on our merit and our deeds, but I'm not sure we fully recognize just how little baggage, comparatively, we have to carry or operate under the weight of at every moment.

We'd recognize if we'd listen, I suppose. And perhaps inwardly reflect on how our behavior impacts others.

IT MIGHT BE reasonable to explore the "reasons" men feel free to be sexual abusers and harassers online. The obscurity of identity, dissociation from physical reality, loss of face-to-face contextual cues that let you know you're being hurtful. I've heard people say these online behaviors are almost like "road rage."

Something just . . . happens.

And it's true. It does sort of happen. Even people we think are otherwise reasonable have done both of these things. I have. I've let myself slip into "road rage" to the point of cursing at other drivers or flipping them off. And I've "told off" people online, going so far as to call relatives sexist and racist for their support of a racist and sexist man.

But here's the thing. Here's where the narrative comes into play to excuse it all away.

John Suler, professor of psychotherapy at Rider University, explored these ideas in his groundbreaking analysis of the "online disinhibition effect." In other words, he explored why we can be assholes online.

Several factors come together to form an environment where people feel freer to be jerks online than they would on the street. To name a few, there is anonymity, sure, but also the idea that the internet feels more like a "game"—there is a "real" world versus the "online" one, despite the idea both are made up of real people—and there's often a time break between when we read things and when we write things, unlike in interpersonal conversation when we can immediately see the impact of our words.

Whether it's "road rage" or "online anonymity," there is a hidden narrative that says these actions are somehow "not us"—that we are different people, somehow, depending on the circumstances.

It might be good if we realized we can be both the guys who smile and say polite "hellos" to people and the guys who "blow a gasket" online and write horrible things to other people—there is not "some other guy" out there pulling this bullshit, no one but . . . us.

Our bad behaviors are no less a part of us than our good behaviors, in other words. It's a good idea to remember this while we're online: although we are capable of performing a full spectrum of behaviors, we might choose to publicly demonstrate the "good ones" and ensure our friend circles do the same.

I SAY ALL this because it's good to understand the underlying motivations and factors behind why people can be jerks online, to recognize the psychological effects that can shape our actions online and in the real world.

Yet we cannot forget that it all comes together in a sexist society that treats men and women fundamentally differently. The sexism in the physical world will of course follow us into the online world.

But here's the key: our social structure is changing in ways we can't quite fathom, and we are raising our children to inhabit both the physical and the online spheres. We are, right now, crafting the traditions and social mores for a new form of civilization.

So, we have a choice.

We can choose to pass on the vestiges of our male-dominated culture, which originated thousands of years ago based on written law, religion, and mores, as "normal" and "natural," letting them form and shape online communities for generations to come, or we can recognize the inequities of the past and strive to make online social spheres less like the current physical ones. We can recognize our previous wrongs and not repeat them as we build together this new, electronic civilization. Quite literally, today, in the midst of this technological earthquake, we have the power other generations in transformation had but neglected to realize or perhaps care much about.

Oh, it might seem lofty and innocent. But we're mistaken when we think we have nothing to do with the culture we allow to exist around us, with what we see as "normal."

LET ME BE crystal clear, men.

I think we can do better in these as-of-yet infant stages of the internet experiment to help craft a more equitable society online, a place where our sons and daughters won't be subjected to the same sexual violence they commit or are exposed to on the sidewalks.

Just because you personally don't engage in these sexually abusive behaviors—online or on the sidewalk—doesn't make you a "good guy."

We don't get to wash our hands of the problem and walk away, as if we hold no responsibility to eradicate it. And what's more, doing our part to help eliminate this problem—with our sons and daughters and friends and family—doesn't make us "good guys" either.

Working to end sexual harassment makes us, at best, baseline decent.

SO, WHAT CAN WE DO?

First of all, don't be a jerk online. (Tall order, I know. I can be a jerk online sometimes as well.) But if you're going to be, don't bring violence into it—especially sexualized violence and threats. You can make your point without it. Just don't. Stop it. And stop your friends when they do it. It's far simpler than you imagine, and if it's not, you'll at least know which of your friends are problematic.

Make your guy friends just as uncomfortable discussing horribly sexist things around you as you imagine they'd be in the company of the "gentler sex."

So, that's your friends. Your buds. Hopefully, among ourselves we can broaden the circles of our reach to help eradicate online sexism and sexualized threats. But what of our kids?

Michael Oberschneider, a child psychologist and author of screen-free children's books, shared some excellent advice with the excellent On Parenting section of the *Washington Post,* and I share it here because it makes a lot of sense.

"Have tons of conversations," he said. "And have guidelines in place as a family." Think about "screen-free" zones, where kids can unwind without online interference, and consider content blockers, depending on their age. Be aware of their online activities and check in, both in conversation and in browser history.

I tell my daughter this: don't for a second think anything you say or do online is "private" in any way. From apps to social media to random emails, consider that they could be hacked or shared without your consent, and then, before you know it, your parents or your friends or your grandma are seeing exactly what you said or did.

And here's the thing. I don't say this to help you avoid someday being "found out"—that is, you secretly harbor and let loose some bullshit opinion and suddenly your racist and sexist ideologies are there for the entire world to pick apart. I think we've all seen this happen—and perhaps delighted in it.

That seems like the morally and ethically wrong way to go about it. Rather, don't *not* say or do hurtful things online because you think it might one day be "discovered" and you'll be damaged by it. Don't do or say hurtful things online because you'd be hurting others. In other words, try to be decent.

ALONG THOSE LINES, be aware of just how much your behaviors influence your children's behaviors online. If you're calling women "sluts" and "bitches" online, your kids are going to follow suit. Your boys will think it's okay; your girls will think they are lesser and defined only by their sexuality.

Robert Faris, a sociology professor at the University of California, Davis, also shared some important lessons in the parenting section of the *Washington Post*. He says kids won't model exactly what we do, but they will see what we consider "priorities," such as status or social climbing or "being cool." If we do that ourselves, our kids might see that as important, and then engage in bullying behaviors online to gain popularity. He suggests parents know their children's friends, invest in relationships long before problems arise, and stay involved in kids' online activities.

Bottom line, you, me, our kids—we're going to mess up online. So, save some grace for that. But as we develop this new social structure, let's do our best to recognize the wrongs we've inherited in the physical world—the hierarchies and traditions—and then try to do better online.

Perhaps it's too late already. But we're still in the infancy of this new civilization. And we can chart a different course. Today.

—Chapter 12—

LIKE, MATH IS SO HARD!

From Barbie dolls to depictions of scientists in popular movies, we tell boys and girls early and often just who the "smarter" sex is. Let's stop doing that.

BEFORE OUR DAUGHTER started kindergarten, we toured probably a dozen schools, both public and private, around the Bay Area. At one of them, a fancy-schmancy private school just outside of San Francisco, we were positively floored by the math and science centers.

From geometric building blocks for younger ages to fully built science and maker labs for the older grades, the school looked as if it came out of central casting for a movie about high-tech science schools. To this day, I have yet to see anything as nerd glorious as this campus.

Yet, it was the walls that attracted my attention.

As our tour group listened to the science teacher explain all the techy gizmos and doodads (English major here, clearly), I noticed the walls were positively *covered* with posters of famous scientists. On its face, it all seemed so normal, motivating even.

Look at all these role models, children. You, too, can do this.

Yay, science!

It took all of a few seconds to note that out of the twenty posters, only one woman was represented. It was like the sports pages, or the halls of government, or the boardrooms of big business.

A good ol' boys club.

But at school. As a motivational, encouraging, feel-good fount of inspiration, no less.

We might lecture kids on equality. But we sure as hell show them we don't mean it.

Math and science hold a special place in our shared storylines and become an early driving force in unequal opportunity later for our kids.

We might lecture kids on equality. But we sure as hell show them we don't mean it.

BEFORE DIVING INTO data showing just how much girls and women are underrepresented and underpaid in math and science fields, and the underlying forces that perpetuate these problems from childhood onward, it's critical to check the histories of these fields.

Bottom line? Men have been debating the worth, dignity, intellect, and equality of women for centuries, millennia. We know this. But these particular fields somehow remain cultural "safe spaces" for sexist men to continue those debates today—but subtly, earnestly, all of it ostensibly couched in science and pseudoscience about "differences." Make no mistake, these aren't "debates" so much as excuses—excuses trotted out to explain away historical oppression while also shrugging off its modern lineage as if it's all perfectly "natural" instead of created and maintained discrimination.

Here's what I mean, and you may have seen this, too. When "debates" erupt about why girls and women are underrepresented in math and science fields, you'll hear everything from the "biological differences" between the sexes to some bullshit about boys reaching for trucks as infants and girls reaching for dolls, or that girls and women just "choose" different fields.

And in all of this, you might notice that these sexist men—let's face it, it's usually white men who consider themselves "intellectuals"—never say anything along the lines of, "Gee, girls and women *are* underrepresented at tech jobs or academia; perhaps we should really get at why and do something about it so all ideas are brought to the table and we're better off as a society."

Please.

You've heard this shit before, I'm sure of it. You've heard a man say instead something like, "Well, girls and women are underrepresented in these fields because of 'differences' that just make boys and men better at math and science, so that's why men have always been better at it."

Left unsaid is the same underlying theme that has been following this debate for generations: women are lesser, deserving not just of past injustices but current ones as well.

Math and science and technology hold a special place in the sexist structures because they provide socially acceptable avenues for the continuation of age-old sexist notions. In these fields, women's inherent intellect is called into question openly, publicly, as if females are obviously an inferior class and therefore rightful subjects of discrimination.

Come on, man. You don't have to buy in to the sexism just because it's everywhere.

IT'S IMPOSSIBLE TO discuss the modern-day inequalities without first digging into the deep, rich history of oppression. Since the Renaissance brought us into modernity, men have not just advanced to the highest levels of math and science to become legends but through law and custom kept women from doing the same.

Rosalind Barnett, senior scientist at the Brandeis University Women's Studies Research Center and author of several books on this subject, wrote a short history of the barriers women have faced in science. Whereas men could advance to study at universities during Renaissance times, women had just four life options: marriage, maid work, prostitution, or convent life. It's why you can name every single Ninja Turtle and no famous women scientists from the same era as these Renaissance-inspired teenage mutants.

It's not like these barriers suddenly fell. They were carried through the Enlightenment and into the early American experience, where, sure, things improved and some women were able to attend women's colleges. But it wasn't until the 1960s that women could obtain doctorates at what we consider our top universities, such as Harvard and Princeton. I'm not saying women didn't indeed contribute enormously to the scientific cause during these times, but they did so despite enormous, sexist barriers.

Barriers that never magically vanished.

Barriers we have bought in to and should probably stop passing on to our children, because we're crippling their opportunities almost from day one: cutting off girls from critical, high-paying, world-changing fields, and also cutting off boys from enriching arts and literature fields, or cutting them off from college altogether through some absurd overcorrection to right historical wrongs.

Or, then again, maybe the field has finally leveled and we're only now finding out that boys are "inherently" worse at academics, that they're just "naturally" dumber, or that they're just so . . . different . . . that they are deserving of discrimination?

I kid.

But it does sound silly, doesn't it? Downright outrageous when you apply the same line of thinking to boys? No one goes around positing that they are intellectually inferior and deserve to be underrepresented in high maths, but how many times have you heard some dude say the same thing about girls or women?

Like I said, check the narrative. Just because one way is socially acceptable doesn't make it right.

SCIENTISTS HAVE DONE some interesting studies over the years to figure out where all of our biases about the mathematical abilities of boys and girls come from. Here's the thing. These biases can't possibly be divorced from the endless messages sent about "differences" between the sexes, and then how we raise them, what we expect of them. Hell, before kids are even born, people are throwing "gender reveal" parties to celebrate their visible sex organs (remember, gender identity doesn't solidify until between the ages of two and three) and planning everything from outfit colors to room decor based on sex alone.

As much as we'd like to imagine we treat boys and girls the same, we don't.

As much as we'd like to imagine we treat boys and girls the same, we don't. By and large, we expect girls to sit still and look pretty, and we expect boys to be wild, dirty, exploring hellions.

When you shop for these new humans, salespeople will helpfully guide you to certain colors or sayings depending on your child's sex. They'll direct you to boys' toys that are all about tech and building and science-related things, while girls' toys are all about nurturing or housecleaning or appearance.

Studies have found that parents have higher physical risk tolerances for boys than for girls. Studies even show just how differently we speak to children of different sexes and give them different toys. Boys dressed as girls for this research received what are considered socially "feminine" toys, whereas girls dressed as boys were given "masculine" toys.

It all adds up, this air we all breathe.

And it obviously doesn't stop at home. It follows these kids to school.

One recent study, published by the National Bureau of Economic Research, explored how teachers treat boys and girls differently beginning in elementary school.

Sixth graders were given a test, and then teachers, who could see the children's names on the tests, rated their performance. In those tests, boys outpaced girls and earned higher marks. The same tests were given to outside observers to grade but the test takers' names were not revealed. In that batch, girls were rated higher. The study followed the students through high school and discovered that boys, even those who received lower marks by the outside, blinded test scorers, went on to receive higher marks than girls in national tests. In other words, merely being told they were better led them to believe they were, and they ultimately *did* better.

The researchers also found that not only did the girls go on to perform worse than the boys but also they avoided advanced placement courses. In fact, just 18.5 percent of American students who take advanced placement tests in computer sciences are girls. In college, women earn just 12 percent of computer science degrees.

In short, the researchers found that boys performed worse than girls in early tests but were rated better and then went on to hold the bulk of college degrees and, later, work positions in related fields.

"Our results suggest that teachers' over-assessment of boys in primary school in a specific subject has a positive and significant effect on boys' achievements in that subject in the national tests administered during middle school and at the end of high school, and it has an asymmetric significant negative effect on girls," note the study authors, Victor Lavy and Edith Sand.

ON IT GOES into the workforce. Researchers found incredible parallels to school experiences.

A technology recruitment company, Speak With A Geek, did a fascinating experiment in 1999. It's an oldie by now, but a goodie.

It sent out five thousand applications to eligible tech companies in which all identifying characteristics of applicants—gender, race, background—were hidden. Candidates who were women received 54 percent of the callbacks. But when identifying characteristics of candidates were provided to the hiring companies, women received just 5 percent of callbacks.

These results are echoed by a famous study from Skidmore College by social psychologist Corrine Moss-Racusin. Her team created two fictitious résumés for a research assistant and sent them out to colleges and universities across the country.

The only thing different about the two résumés?

The name at the top.

One was "John" and one was "Jennifer."

Across the board, John was rated as more competent, more hirable, and deserving of a higher salary and more mentoring. Again, his résumé was exactly the same as Jennifer's—with the only exception being their gender—and he was found to be deserving of $4,000 more a year than Jennifer.

These types of tests have been repeated over and over, in field after field. It's not that recruiters and bosses—that you and I—are trying to be outright sexist and discriminatory. Some are, sure. But for the most part, it's simply in the stories we've all been fed since birth: math and science are for boys. You have to actively connect the dots, step back, and intentionally try to do better.

And even then, you probably won't.

THIS IS WHAT our daughters are up against—a quiet, multilayered, multigenerational, atomized system of biases that say in ways big and small that they are lesser, that they are *deserving* of less. It's how pay gaps develop; it's how their résumés get pushed aside; it's how they're quietly mocked or made fun of in labs or made to fetch coffee instead of making discoveries.

What's it look like in practice? In the real world? It can be a blatant denial of advancement, pay, or participation. It can be sexual harassment or assault. Or it can be subtle, perhaps even well-meaning behavior.

My friend Sarah says the sexism in computer sciences has followed her wherever she goes.

"It's a really complicated problem," a man told her at work, after she was called in to fix a technical problem. The man requested someone else to do the work—a man.

Or the time when she'd been working as the de facto department manager for a year, only to be told she'd have to report to the man she had been managing—who also happened to have a lighter résumé. She resigned.

"I still get pissed about that one," she told me.

IT WOULD SEEM as if, knowing all this, people might have tried to do something about it. Well, good news, they have!

After years of only grudgingly admitting girls to science classes, and against a backdrop of cultural debates that argue girls suck at science, people have found it difficult to attract girls to science. Shocker, I know.

One of my favorite albeit rage-inducing examples of this comes from the Carnegie Science Center, a major science museum in Pittsburgh. It offers Boy Scouts seven courses, from robotics to weather to chemistry, and offers Girls Scouts just one class: "Science with a Sparkle," a class on how to become a cosmetics chemist.

The center responded to the ensuing internet outrage at the time this became known, saying it had indeed offered more and different classes for girls, and welcomes girls into any class, but the only ones that girls actually attended in great numbers were the "sparkle" classes. Oh, and a sleepover.

This example encapsulates the argument, I think. Are girls really only interested in cosmetics science? Or are they told over and over again that math and science are not for them? Combine that with so many societal messages about their looks being their most important characteristic, and is it any wonder that a science class about appearance is the most well attended?

The posters, the science classes designed around appearance, the computer science classes with a "boys-only" feel—they add up. Each, on their own, might be a small point, but kids get the message.

And the real-world consequences for our kids? Entire avenues of exploration shut off from them because of their gender. If you don't think early education reinforces this idea, think about the science fields you grew up with and consider how they might have shaped your thinking about who is a "real scientist."

You're not alone.

Take a moment to google "cartoon scientist." Our cultural notions of who "looks" like a scientist are deeply embedded in our collective psyche.

> **Our cultural notions of who "looks" like a scientist are deeply embedded in our collective psyche.**

HERE'S AN APPALLING statistic. You've heard of the Nobel Prize, right? The preeminent honor for basically any field of expertise—from science to literature to peace?

From 1901 to 2016, women have earned 4 chemistry prizes, in contrast with 171 men. In economics, it's 1 to 77. Physics is 2 to 202.

In all, including literature and peace prizes, women have earned just 49 Nobel Prizes, compared with 836 for men. The bulk of women recipients are in the peace and literature categories.

It doesn't take a rocket scientist to link social constructs like these—men are scientists worthy of awards—to popular notions of scientists we see onscreen and how we tell stories about them. Remember the Star Wars spin-off *Rogue One*—the one where a whole bunch of fragile dudes had a fit because one of the lead characters was a woman? Well, remember when the movie trotted out a field of scientists and engineers in a pivotal scene? There were, I lost count, ten white guys and no one else. Like, this is a universe with Yoda and Chewbacca and, I don't know, whatever the fuck a Kowakian monkey-lizard is.

And they couldn't find *one* scientist that was a woman? An alien, even?

These depictions are no different from "cartoon scientist." When we, as a society, consider *scientists,* we have a type in mind.

And that trickles down.

THE ROOT OF it all is that our girls and boys are told from elementary school that science and math is a boys club—and this notion is reinforced in college, with fewer scholarships and degrees for women, and in the professional world, with lower pay and fewer opportunities for women. It's reinforced with seemingly well-intentioned workshops for girls that focus on appearance, and it's reinforced on TV and in other media images in which female scientists are either stunningly attractive or goofy/ditzy or simply invisible. These images fly in the face of the female scientists and doctors I—and probably you—know in real life.

A friend of mine, a pediatrician, said when she was growing up, her parents always wanted her to marry a doctor. That was, seemingly, the best she could do. Marry one.

When she got to medical school and relayed this story to her peers, many agreed they had been told the same thing. What did they do? They bought special lab coats with a message on them: "Be the doctor your parents always wanted you to marry."

SO, WHAT CAN WE DO?

First, stop buying in to the notion that you can have a public, open debate about whether women are "smart enough" for math. Be aware of the narrative: these debates aren't happening to find gaps and close them to help everyone in society advance. Rather, the issue is raised usually because sexist people are trying to excuse sexist systems.

"Are women smart enough for the high maths?"

Ugh. Gross.

Stop.

Parenting 101: try not to be an asshole.

Think about what our kids see when we do this: we're setting a horrible example that it's reasonable and socially acceptable to question the intellect of whole groups of people.

LIKE MOST OF the subjects in this book, there are a million tiny issues to be addressed and the record set straight. One of them is the idea that it's only crusty, snooty male math nerds who are looking down their noses at girls and women rather than an entire culture devoted to believing boys are "just better" at some things, such as math.

In other words, it's all of us. So, we can do our part, starting from early ages.

I asked my friend Sarah, the tech-savvy consultant, about ways to "fix" the problems early on, and she suggested we become more blatant about combatting bias with our language—how we discuss math and children, both boys and girls.

"I would just make sure that kids know that anyone can be anything," Sarah says. "Like, pointing out things like, 'Wow! That girl really knows her computers! Awesome!'"

How WE TALK about who is "good" at math and science is one thing.

How we recruit people into college or top tech jobs is another. Studies have found that blind résumé reviews work in achieving some level of parity, so why not keep that up?

Then there is the idea of the "growth" mind-set versus the fixed mind-set. Can you work hard and get better at something, or are you doomed to suck at math, say, from the beginning—is ability fixed? Researchers say kids who are encouraged to struggle and work hard—those praised for their effort—perform better in later tests than kids who are told they are "smart."

Here's how it works in practice: kids who are hard workers are presented a tough problem and try to figure it out, whereas kids who were labeled "smart" tend to stop trying when presented with a hard problem. They don't want to be found out, so to not blow their cover, they just stop trying.

Basically, praise effort—in boys and girls.

And find role models. I think back to the posters in the classrooms we visited and have been on the lookout for similar disparities displayed in the school she now attends. If I found them—thankfully I have not—I wouldn't hesitate to call them out and even buy some equalizing posters myself. Kids need the role models. If they can see it, they can be it, as the saying goes.

It's why I took my daughter to see the *Ghostbusters* reboot—an example of battling many biases at the same time. One, the movie remake featured an all-female cast as heroes. Two, most of them were unapologetic in-your-face scientists. Three, they dressed like normal people, not male-gaze, sexy, fantasy superheroes. Four, the female leads got to play the type of characters boys have looked up to for generations. When we see groundbreaking role models like this, we need to support them. (The movie also scared the shit out of her and she refused to sleep for two days, so . . . pick your teachable moments.)

Pop quiz: How many men did you hear lamenting the fact that the original Ghostbusters series featured "an all-male cast" of ghostbusters? How many did you hear complain about "an all-female cast" with the new movie?

Why do you think that is?

HERE's AN IMPORTANT point to consider. Girls might be underrepresented in tech fields, but they're earning a lot more college degrees than boys and are catching up, or leading, in many of these fields now. It's important not to believe we're raising one up while hurting the other—that's an ancient di-chotomy that buys in to the idea that this is a zero-sum game, that taking the math pie and giving it to girls means there's less for boys. That's not how life works. There's pie for everyone. So, let's be aware that we don't want to hurt him while praising her.

As parents, we can be the role models kids need. And we should be saying that kids can do math. Kids can do science. Kids can grow up to be scientists and math freaks.

Which brings me to this last point: stop being a jerk—especially in the rampantly sexualized world of gaming, a techie boys club in which female characters are almost always objectified and in which female players are treated to endless online abuse and real-life threats when they speak out. If you see your kids engaging big time in the gaming scene, keep watch and keep the conversations going, experts say. Gaming is a great way to get kids interested in tech—and to open avenues of conversation about how the tech world can impose stereotypes on kids.

—Chapter 13—

BLACK GIRL MAGIC

Lofty goals of raising "color-blind" children do more harm than good. Instead, experts agree it's important to talk with our kids about race and obstacles people face because of differences.

REAL TALK, FELLAS. As my fellow dad and technology writer Tshaka Armstrong says when discussing race, "It's time to get uncomfortable."

To that end, I'm going to talk specifically to white dads like myself, white dads who, whether actively engaged with antiracist or racist movements, can continue living their lives as the societal "norm" against which all others are judged. People who look like us spent generations erecting obstacles to racial and gender equality, and we need to take a hard look at what role we play in reinforcing them instead of condescendingly speaking to "all people," as if "all people" are somehow responsible for their own oppression, or throwing up our hands and pretending it was all in the past. We either, at worst, are yet complicit or, at best, are unknowing beneficiaries.

Because, make no mistake, our American culture was stitched together for generations with our collective benefit in mind, and we need to fully examine which of those threads remain and just how much power we have over others. If you're suddenly up in your feelings, thinking you—and white people in general—don't yet hold enormous power, consider this: white people, led by white men, can pool our votes into such a dynamic force as to elect the most openly racist and sexist president the country has seen in a generation and yet also enjoy a cultural myth that "no one listens to us" or that we're the "forgotten men" or—this is my personal favorite—it's somehow the fault of "white women"—who, yes, supported him, but not nearly to the extent white men did. We have the power to rule and the audacity to throw a pity party about it, as if we deserve sympathy for electing someone who is openly hostile to people who don't look like us.

Honestly, the fuck?

Oh, yes, I'm fully aware of so-called internet intellectuals who would have us believe that everyone has had it rough in the past, that other cultures have done worse things, and that the almighty individual just needs to "work hard" to make it. I'll be the first to join you in arguing that we need to teach our children to work hard—amen on that one—but the rest is reflex guilt born out of a desire not to fully examine our own complicity in racist and sexist traditions and the systems they created and support today. We simply can't ignore that the playing field in this country has been tipped for hundreds of years in our favor, and I don't know how any father can just throw up his hands and say, "Work harder then," instead of, "Hey, let's make it level first, and only then can we go on about hard work."

Let me put it this way: don't gloat for winning a rigged game. And rigged it is.

Don't gloat for winning a rigged game.

Like the good man said, uncomfortable.

Here's something horrible to begin with: black girls are suspended from school six times more than their white peers, research shows.

Black girls are often considered "loud," "sassy," and laden with "behavioral issues." Basically, the same traits we desire for today's white girls—outspoken and opinionated with leadership potential, the token "strong, powerful female" characters—are considered "too much" when it comes to black girls; Asian American girls are mostly given a veneer of invisibility with an expectation of being "shy and quiet." Man, we sure do pull a number on each other, but experts agree it's better to talk about our biases and stereotypes than to let them fester and grow.

To that end, it's worth a deep dive into what's going on in schools, because they are the gateway to how our children experience broader society. They're often the first brush our kids have with a fucked-up predominately white cultural narrative that says "black Americans" in the same sentence as "inner cities" or "crime" or "issues" or "thugs," as if those are perfectly reasonable streams of public consciousness to follow and discuss.

Put a pin in that. We'll soon enough explore these early racist structures, down to the code words your supposedly "color-blind" white friends and family haul out to distance themselves from the racist policies and people they support, and then examine how all of this adds up to actual deaths caused by racial stress.

NEW RESEARCH FROM the Yale Child Study Center shows something interesting and quite conflicting when it comes to young kids, race, and education.

Black boys, like black girls, are suspended at rates much higher than their white peers. To get at why, the researchers asked teachers to evaluate groups of kids on video to find troubling behavioral issues. The researchers used eye-tracking technology to see where the teachers turned their attention—and sure enough, the study found that teachers focused most of their attention on the young black boys, even when the kids weren't doing anything wrong.

Are black boys suspended at higher rates because they're doing something wrong, or because teachers are constantly monitoring them, perhaps looking for something wrong? It's not an intellectual feat to jump to the fact that white women called the cops on black people merely for sitting in Starbucks or Waffle House, or napping, or barbecuing in the park—all real events of 2018. Or that police arrest black people nearly four times more often than white people for marijuana crimes, despite little difference in actual use, according to the American Civil Liberties Union.

Hard truth—just so you don't think I'm pointing at white structures and mores without realizing my own responsibility in them—here's something pretty racist about myself. I told my daughter about these suspension and attention studies, saying, "Isn't this *fascinating?*"

She took a beat and responded, "I think you mean appalling."

As the Avenue Q song goes, "Everyone's a little bit racist." It's impossible to grow up in a racist and sexist society and not have some of it slough off onto you. Look, I'm not saying every white person is offering racial epithets or hoisting the Confederate flag (yes, obscenely racist. And traitorous to boot). But there's a lower-key racism I think white people like me need to unearth and consider. I can call these studies "fascinating" because I have the privilege to consider them academically, to turn them over in my mind, and then walk away. They don't affect me personally.

But no doubt, they form the bedrock of the black experience in America, and it begins when all our kids get together in school.

But no doubt, they form the bedrock of the black experience in America, and it begins when all our kids get together in school.

"The emotional and mental somersaults that people of color have to do daily at work, in school, and socially to be respected first, then hopefully listened to and heard is exhausting," says Carol Cain, esteemed travel writer and blogger.

So, here's the deal, dads who look like me: we can say "not me" and perhaps feel smug about it. But being "nice" or "not racist" is baseline work. We don't deserve a medal or an award. We don't deserve good feelings for not being horrible.

We've simply tried to clear the lowest bar of decency.

Perhaps, instead, we might consider what role we play in it all.

To be sure, it's complicated. A host of factors collide.

Those same teachers in the Yale study who focused most on black boys, as if looking for trouble, next focused most of their attention on white boys.

And then on white girls.

And then, finally, on black girls.

So, what gives?

First, the age-old trope of "boys will be boys" leaves teachers to expect more disturbances from boys, and so teachers are on the lookout for them, while they expect girls to be sweet and kind and nice, and therefore deserving of fewer circumspect gazes.

But that's just gender at play. Add in race, and you've got intersected layers of crazytown.

If the focus appears to be on black girls the least, why, then, are they suspended at rates higher than that of their white peers or even black boys?

Weird, right?

Bias. Fear. Mythologies born out of a nation formed in bondage and narratives passed down generation to generation. America has a lot to unpack.

SUSPENSION AND HARSHER punishment are just two of the sexisms girls of color face. Fewer scholarships, lower pay, fewer job opportunities, absurd maternal and infant mortality rates—those are just a few of the things awaiting them as they age.

Why?

Have you ever heard the term *intersectionality*? Civil rights advocate, lawyer, and scholar Kimberlé Crenshaw coined the term to explain the collision of racial and gender bias. Black girls, for instance, don't just face the sexisms their white girl peers face. They also face racism that white girls don't—an amplified burden where the two components of race and gender intersect.

When it comes to why black girls are suspended at higher rates and receive stiffer sentences than their white peers, the National Black Women's Justice Center in Berkeley, California, which was founded to help explain why, has a couple theories. Like a lot of the sexisms discussed in this book, there are seemingly endless tiny dots, and they all add up.

One component involves the amount of attention each student receives. According to the justice center, white kids get more attention from teachers than black girls do. But not for any obviously racist reasons. Younger black girls are regarded as more self-reliant and on track, and therefore in need of less attention. The message black girls internalize, however, is that they're not as deserving of help and education as other kids, according to the justice center's research.

Other factors are zero-tolerance policies that seem to single out outspoken black girls, higher instances of sexual assault and bullying among black girls, and more responsibilities at home that take away time and attention from school duties, according to the justice center.

Add these up, mix in some weird mythologies America has built up around black girls (they're aggressive, highly sexualized, loud and obnoxious, while also self-reliant and "on track"), and you've got a recipe for some serious trouble.

BLACK GIRLS MATTER, a report by the African American Policy Forum with the Columbia Law School, documents some pretty harsh statistics about major city school discipline rates. Black girls in Boston are 28 percent of the school population but were 61 percent of the students disciplined, compared to 5 percent of their white peers.

Monique Morris, cofounder of the justice center in Berkeley, has written extensively on the intersectionality of race and gender and a dominant white culture to help explain why black girls are all at once ignored by teachers because they're regarded as self-reliant and on track but then disciplined at high rates and perceive themselves as unworthy.

Hostility toward each other, distrust of systems and teachers, the feeling of being outspoken yet expected to fit into society's general view of girls as quiet and nonobtrusive—these add up to thwart education for black girls, especially those in zero-tolerance systems.

Let me amplify Morris's thoughts here.

"These, and other examples, signal that our work to improve the educational experiences of other girls must address the messages they have internalized about the value of Black femininity and the opportunities they have to bring their whole selves to the learning experience," Morris wrote in an essay for Your Black World. "Too many have learned to be hostile toward one another, and to dwell in a state of self-loathing. Their behaviors are often the result of years of being told they are not worthy. For many of these girls, this is the foundation for why they act out, and to challenge the adults who present themselves as authority figures."

Research seems to corroborate this finding about worthiness. The Yale researchers found something else of interest in how teachers treat kids of different races: black teachers were harsher on black students in doling out punishments, and white teachers had much lower expectations of good work from black children. The white-person bar for black kids, in other words, was pretty low.

Again, it all adds up.

Race, background, socioeconomic status, family life—we all come from different places—but we all enter institutions and cultures set up by rich white folk, and the institutional messages and cultural expectations remain. Not just that, for generations white people either through law or through force have kept people of color from the same opportunities they enjoyed—enslaved them, imprisoned them because of their heritage (thinking of you, Japanese American friends), denied equal housing, equal education, equal representation. In other words, the playing field may seem level today, but only to the people who set it up in the first place and didn't allow others even to play the same game until a generation ago. I don't say this to impugn every white person alive today. But I'd be remiss in leaving out historical facts that paved the way for our current "norms."

Our past may be just that, but it'd be silly to pretend it doesn't have a profound impact on how we raise our own children today.

WHAT HAPPENS, THEN, when these black children who have been policed and suspended and punished since their introduction to society enter the workforce?

Well, congrats! Lower pay, fewer opportunities, and less generational wealth to pass on.

The Institute for Women's Policy Research, which has been tracking the gender pay gap over generations, found that in 2017, compared to what white men earned, white women earned roughly 82 percent, black women earned 67 percent, Asian women earned 93 percent, and Hispanic women earned 62 percent.

In 2016, the accounting firm Deloitte teamed with the Alliance for Board Diversity to examine representation on *Fortune 500* business boards. The good news is that minority representation has been ticking upward. The bad news is that business is still very much a white man's club.

The study found that at the top five hundred businesses, white men held 70 percent of the board seats. White women held 16 percent, and minority women (black, Asian, Hispanic) held 3.8 percent. Is that because minorities aren't "working hard enough" or because our systems were fucked from the beginning and are only very slowly coming around? We simply cannot argue this is the natural order of things instead of purposeful, created institutions that benefit people unequally today.

In terms of wealth, the *New York Times* featured on its Upshot online data section an astounding interactive graphic about the wealth gap between white families and black families. The feature relied on Yale studies that showed black families held $5 in wealth for every $100 in white family wealth.

Even the study authors were taken aback by the figures.

"It seems that we've convinced ourselves—and by 'we' I mean Americans writ large—that racial discrimination is a thing of the past," study author and Yale researcher Jennifer Richeson told the *Times*.

"BLACK WOMEN AND white confront different challenges in today's corporate offices because they entered the white-collar workforce from different gates," says Tai Wingfield, senior vice president of the Center for Talent Innovation.

The center's study, *Ambition in Black and White: The Feminist Narrative Revised,* shows black women were more ambitious for powerful work positions than white women, yet received less mentoring and had fewer advocates among senior employees.

The study posits that black women were more ambitious because their mothers and grandmothers before them had always had to hold down jobs and seek more money for their families. Clutching pearls and baking cakes for a workaday, commuting office hubby wasn't always an option in the black American experience. This is one reason early feminism frequently left out women of color, because while white women were debating whether to work or stay home with the kids, a lot of the black women were already "having it all" with lower-paying jobs. The study shows much more ambivalence among white women for positions of power, mentioning that the idea of the caretaker role for white women has been hard to shrug off, while people of every other ethnicity have had to hold down multiple jobs just to get by.

And all along, it should be noted, white dudes like me have been ignoring them all, but especially black women. Remember the image of the black schoolgirl receiving less attention from teachers because they think she is doing okay and is self-reliant? And, paradoxically, too loud and brash and deserving of stiffer punishment when she speaks up?

That continues for black women in the workforce.

"What's keeping capable, ambitious women out of the C suite today," says the coauthor of the study, Melinda Marshall, "is what's held them back since the dawn of the women's movement: black women cannot shed their cloak of invisibility, and white women cannot put aside expectations that they be perfect mothers and wives."

EVERY TIME I think of these studies, I am brought back to TV host Bill O'Reilly, a horrible shitbird who was forced off the Fox News channel for his repeated sexual abuse and harassment of women.

Why, I keep thinking, do I agree with this guy, at least in one regard?

Well, he was considered the "voice" of so many people and held a prime-time TV slot on a major network to air his views. In one of his TV show clips, he went into one of his angry white guy apoplectic rages about how black people have to work harder than white people to get ahead. He literally said that. And the thing is, I found myself . . . agreeing with him.

Black people, and all people of color, do indeed have to work harder to get ahead. America has erected obstacles for people of color that I simply don't have to face, and I think O'Reilly was onto something when he said this.

But then—and this is key—he sort of threw up his hands, as if to say, "Well, that's life. What are you going to do?"

And that was the end of the matter.

Here's my central thesis and lessons I think are important to pass on: if you recognize we live in a society that makes existing, let alone succeeding, more difficult for people simply because of race or gender, do you have a responsibility to do something?

I agree with O'Reilly's initial premise—indeed, it is borne out by data—but I don't agree that it's just the natural order that can't be fixed or worked on, that we just shrug it off and say, "Well, work harder, then," as if we have no responsibility or don't, at the very least, enjoy the privilege of the opposite: *not* having to work as hard to succeed. I don't want to raise children in a rigged system and then have the audacity to tell them their hard work alone—rather than systems and traditions created and bent in their favor and then also maintained generation by generation—had everything to do with their success, their opportunities, their very health.

People who benefit unequally from racist, sexist systems have a moral imperative to work toward more equitable treatment of all. First, they must fully understand the history of how these narratives developed, exploring the racism and sexism behind them, and then work to untilt the playing field, to tip it in a more equitable direction.

People's lives depend on it in a way I'm not fully sure white dads like myself can fully comprehend.

HERE'S WHAT I mean.

Black women are two to three times more likely to die in childbirth than white women, according to an astounding analysis by the *New York Times* last year. Black babies are 2.2 times more likely to die than white babies.

People who benefit unequally from racist, sexist systems have a moral imperative to work toward more equitable treatment of all.

These figures are worsening year by year; the gap between white maternal mortality rates and black maternal mortality rates is larger than it was in 1850.

"It was narrower then when black women were slaves," reporter Linda Villarosa explained on the *New York Times* podcast *The Daily*.

These deaths are the driving force behind the United States ranking thirty-second out of the thirty-five most developed countries in maternal mortality.

Villarosa explained that latent cultural bias creeps into medical schools and hospitals as horrible stereotypes: black women experience less pain, need less medication, and have "thicker skin." They are also not listened to as much as white women are and often don't meet their doctors until already in labor.

Wealth, education, region—it didn't matter. Black women with advanced degrees or their babies die at rates higher than those of white women with an eighth-grade education.

The reason? America is racist AF.

"Something happens to black women because of the lived experience of being black in America," Villarosa says.

The ceaseless, all-consuming, toxic racial stress of simply being black in America wears down the body and makes it more susceptible to illness. It's called "weathering," and it has been found to be the key ingredient in these deaths.

"Racism and race are baked into every single thing in our society and medicine is not immune," she says.

PARADOXICALLY, DESPITE INCUBATING and exacerbating a racist and sexist atmosphere with all manner of horrible outcomes—including outrageous numbers of baby deaths in a culture of "pro-life" axioms—researchers have found that white people generally just don't want to talk about it. What's more, we get pissy and defensive when called on it.

Racial bias expert Robin DiAngelo dubbed this "white fragility" and saw it firsthand in years of leading discussions about race, racism, and white privilege. "It became clear over time that white people have extremely low thresholds for enduring any discomfort associated with challenges to our racial worldview," she writes.

Look, I get it—if you're a white guy like me, you might be feeling a bit itchy at all this racial discussion, and especially at the idea that you are probably party to perpetuating unequal systems that put you at the top as the cultural norm, and others under you as the cultural "other." To be honest, it made me tremendously itchy as well. I don't think white people are raised to talk about race and gender bias, or, when we do discuss it, we're expected to pretend to be "color-blind." It's often well-meaning, but it's also an obstacle to equality. We pretend everyone rises because of merit and hard work, and yet we're blind to the unfair systems we inherited.

If you think all this is bullshit, okay, I hear you. But really nothing I've said has been historically outrageous.

White men founded this country. Built its systems. And restricted the rights of others, if not outright killed them. None of this is a shocker.

All I'm asking you to do is consider whether any of the past atrocities have been incubated long enough to maintain purchase today and then consider if you have a moral duty to help change course by speaking simply to kids about it: telling them early on about our shared history and then teaching them it's perfectly okay to see differences and to talk about them.

I'M GOING TO leave you with two thoughts before imploring you to take a deep, sustained dive into American experiences different from your own.

First, think about this essay for a moment. I think it fits neatly into the racist constructs white men like me fit into when considering "others" in America.

If I am honest, I'd admit this very essay perpetuates racist ideas while urgently trying to bring them to your attention.

How so?

I'm talking about the black experience for girls in America here, and it's largely focused on problems and punishment, on data and studies about poor outcomes. And yes, indeed, it's all true.

But that's not the sum of the black experience in America, is it?

Watch how it plays out: the white narrative, when considering the black narrative, far too often follows a stream of thought from "black" to "bad," or at the very least from "black" to "issues."

It's how otherwise nonracist white men can bemoan the "absence of black fathers" without realizing that this bias against black men probably leads them not to hire black men, which leads, perhaps, to higher unemployment rates in black men or higher incarceration rates than for white men. Plus, copious research shows that black fathers, all things equal, actually spend *more* time with their children when at home than white fathers do.

It's how we can consider it socially acceptable for politicians to talk about black people and then immediately segue into "inner cities" and "crime," as if that is the sum of the black impact on America. Or how media messages from the 1980s and 1990s warned of the waves of "crack babies" and black "superpredators," while white babies in today's opioid epidemic are given, just as black babies should have been, sympathy.

It's how even well-meaning white people can write to other well-meaning white people and urge them to discuss others' humanity, as if someone's inherent worth, dignity, and equality are worthy of debate. I honestly don't know how to square that, because I don't want to not discuss race and therefore, in silence, pretend that our systems and narratives don't need attention.

But I also don't want to pretend it's okay to debate someone's basic humanity. Medical doctors and scientists, yes, should by all means explore what characteristics might divide us and then find ways to help us. But I fear far too often us laypeople engage in everyday discussions that put someone else's life, liberty, and pursuit of happiness up for debate.

So, I leave you with this second thought. Ask yourself, white dads, just how many times in your life your inherent intelligence or worth has been subject to public debate. How many times have you heard people discuss your equality? How many times have you heard someone say, "Let me just play devil's advocate for a moment," and then go on to question your humanity or your intelligence? Do you want your kids to put someone's life in the balance?

JAMILA MICHENER, A poverty scholar at Cornell University, retold on her Twitter account an experience she had while lecturing recently. With genuine curiosity, she says, a student asked for her thoughts—again, in a public lecture—on the "cognitive inferiority" of black people.

I amplify her response here, because I don't think it's a notion white dads like me have to consider on a daily basis.

"The feeling is this: my present, my equality, my ability—can be reasonably questioned and must be consistently justified, explained, and even defended. Ironically, if that defense is too ardent, then I can be doubted and depicted as angry, emotional, or lacking objectivity. At the same time, if my defense of the intellectual capacity of black people is not ardent enough, then students of color will feel abandoned and other students may believe that ideas about the inferiority of black folk are a run-of-the-mill part of academic discourse."

What traces of this acceptable discourse do you see in your everyday circles? Can these bits be traced back to the gross narrative lineage of our ancestors—who first debated the worth of "savages" and then debated the "worth" of slaves and then debated the "worth" of women and then debated the "worth" of civil rights and still today debate the worth of a population that is policed, shot, and incarcerated at rates higher than others, that is afforded lower pay and fewer opportunities, and that lives with a toxic racial stress so profound that it is killing babies at rates unseen since our ancestors enslaved them?

SO, WHAT CAN WE DO?

Morris, of the National Black Women's Justice Center, has some good advice for tackling the inequality of discipline in schools.

Engendering a feeling of safety and of being listened to at school is paramount.

Be on the lookout for zero-tolerance policies that just happen to target kids of color. It's well and good to say you have zero tolerance for bad behavior among all students, but why are black kids punished more often and with harsher punishments?

Overpunishment is not the only factor at play here. The *Black Girls Matter* study shows black girls' accomplishments are often underpraised, and then the cloak of invisibility begins to set in. Is it a shock that it took some fifty years after she played her part in the early space program for black NASA programmer Katherine Johnson to get her due public praise? She wasn't hiding, for god's sake. Her story has been well known in black media for decades.

Set a high bar. Then celebrate kids—all kids—meeting it and beating it.

Also be on the lookout for fairness, and who is being "protected" or "punished" for unfairness.

Here's what I mean.

Educator and activist Kelly Hurst started a nonprofit called Being Black at School to educate educators on unequal enforcement of school rules. This anecdote that she shared with Illinois's NPR station sums it up perfectly:

"You know, the black students that I had to discipline, that came to my office, almost 100 percent of the time would say, 'I absolutely did that behavior. I did that thing they said I did. But so did some white kids, and they are sitting in those classrooms getting an education, and I'm in here, and I'm going to get another consequence, and then I'm going to fall further and further behind.' That's a systemic issue."

Educators and parents should be on the lookout for signs of abuse. The *Black Girls Matter* study shows higher instances of sexual abuse—and even abuse by peers—among black girls. Imagine trying to fit in to a zero-tolerance policy while struggling with the aftereffects of rape or posttraumatic stress disorder. The study showed higher instances of "acting out" if personal counseling needs weren't met.

It's not just "big things" that can lead to trauma. *Psychology Today* showed a link between the microaggressions of racism and posttraumatic stress disorder. In other words, simply being black in America can cause you mental trauma. The article talked about little things—a scowl, a comment, perhaps a shifting away from a black kid at the lunch table or moving a purse out of reach. You try living in a world in which everyone treats you as a threat or an oddity, and see what that does for you. Remember the study on mortality rates and racial stress? That's the outcome here.

BEYOND SCHOOL, WHAT we can do as parents and consumers is pretty easy: talk about it. Research. Dive deep into cultures you may not fully understand.

But, please, don't for a second believe it's up to oppressed populations to educate you on their oppression. Do your own damn work. As activist and educator DeRay Mckesson often says, "Google is free."

I have a racist, sexist shitbird relative who, although he grew up in the midst of segregation in a state with a huge KKK following, claims we are living "in the most racist times ever" thanks to having had a black president.

Come on, man. Don't do that. Let's get something straight. The internet has been a great leveler in bringing more stories to the broader cultural fore, and that makes some white people incredibly itchy—because they grew up thinking America was about their stories, their jobs, their rights, as if they literally owned everything. Sharing others' stories is uncomfortable for many. But that's something racist white people are going to have to get used to.

And you can help! Once you find something you like, amplify it for your white friends. Because here's the deal. Oppressed groups don't need to hear about what a "good guy" you are for being baseline decent—that is, "not racist." They need you and me to discuss with each other and our peers just how fucked the systems, and the narratives that support them, are.

So let's get to work. Let's raise our kids to see color, to understand the system has been rigged from the start, and to know we can help unrig it—and only then, once the playing field is level, can we feel good about "making it."

THE LIFETIME CONSEQUENCES
OF OUR EARLY LESSONS

—Chapter 14—

PAY DAY

You know there's a "gender pay gap," but you may not realize how big a role we play in perpetuating it at home by telling our boys to be "leaders" and our girls to be "caretakers." It all adds up to lower pay for women and fewer opportunities for girls—and boys.

THE GENDER WAGE gap. You've probably heard of it. Unless you, personally, do something to help change the storyline on whose job it is to care for children and elderly parents and perform household duties, your kids are going to suffer from it as well.

Here's the deal. Women earn on average roughly 80 percent of what men earn, and less depending on their race. In real time and dollars, that means if men and women started working in January of this year, all women would have to work until April of *next* year to earn as much as men did in one year alone, with black women having to work until August, and Latinas until November.

That loss of yearly income adds up and becomes an absolute hammer.

US soccer star Abby Wambach put it better than I ever could in a graduation ceremony speech at Columbia University last year: "What we need to talk about more is the aggregate and compounding effects of the pay gap on women's lives. Over time, the pay gap means women are able to invest less and save less so they have to work longer. When we talk about what the pay gap costs us, let's be clear. It costs us our very lives."

Current forecasts from the Institute for Women's Policy Research show white women will close the gap in 2059, while, like they had to with voting rights, women of color will have to wait a while longer: 2124 for black women, and 2223 for Hispanic women.

> "When we talk about what the pay gap costs us, let's be clear. It costs us our very lives."

No, it's not because horrible men put up signs in want ads saying, "No women need apply" or "No jobs for Negroes." (At least, not anymore.)

No, it's not because some human resources drone decided to simply divide up the men and women, separate them further by race or ability or sexual orientation, and then distribute unequal paychecks based on all those factors. (At least, not anymore.) But would it were that easy today! The sheer number of discrimination lawsuits would close the pay gap immediately. Like, yesterday. Those workers would *own* the companies by now.

No, it's not as if bosses are frankly telling women that men are paid more because they have "families to support." (At least, not anymore.)

No, rather, like so many of the subjects in this book, it's the little things. And how they add up.

IT'S THE WAY we raise girls to nurture and boys to be violent, girls to be nurses and boys to be doctors.

It's the school subjects we push away from one sex and push the other sex into.

It's the way we expect women to do school duties and we praise men for "babysitting" their own damn children.

It's the way we expect women to take care of the family through household care and men to take care of the family through working outside the home.

It's the way men feel okay excluding women from meetings or business events because . . . men will try to rape them after too many drinks and they know it? Women will "lie" about it? I never did get this one. But surely the fragility of men to not consider themselves rapey assholes after a few drinks or to not consider women as anything but sexual objects factors into it.

It's the way white people call the police on black women for golfing, or asking for utensils at restaurants, or napping.

It's, in other words, a lot of seemingly disconnected things that nevertheless form a sexist culture in which, surprise, sexism happens. Including, shocker, in the workforce.

In this particular area, and this is absolutely key here, fellas: we dads can do tremendous good—not just in closing inequities in pay and opportunity for women but also in changing the face of family life in favor of more loving involvement of men at home and valuing our familial duties at home, which are equally as important as work outside of the home.

It's damn time we had a collective come-to-Jesus moment about this.

TWO THINGS ARE worthy of quick consideration before we take a deeper dive into the gap.

One, when you hear *pay gap,* dudes want the details. They want the data. Holy shit, do dudes want the data. And I'm obviously not saying that's a bad thing. So, we'll explore the data to suss out exactly what the pay gap means. From what I've been able to discern, I don't think anyone is really arguing that a gap exists but rather *why* it exists: some people contend that women simply "choose" lower-paying jobs or to exit the workforce for childcare; others, like me, say these "choices" have problematic generational societal pressures behind them.

Which brings us to point two. Like every other inequity we've explored so far, we simply cannot remove the data from societal norms and our expectations for boys and girls, for men and women. In other words, we can't have fever-pitched debates about the data and then pretend the cold, hard numbers exist in a vacuum. There's an entire societal messaging system driving the data, and it comes into play long before we see the gap at all.

But, okay. That said, let's take a look at the data.

Here's a snapshot of the overall workforce to lay some groundwork.

Women make up roughly 46 percent of the overall workforce. We're no longer in the June Cleaver epoch—as if that was an actual thing for minority populations at the time instead of a white culture advertising campaign of feminine domesticity. Put a pin in that. It'll be important to remember that generations of mainstream culture perpetuated damaging stereotypes.

Yet, despite making up roughly half of the workforce, women are drastically underrepresented in the highest echelons of business. In 2017, women held thirty-two chief executive officer positions in *Fortune 500* companies. Yes, thirty-two out of five hundred. But by 2018, the number fell to twenty-four.

When Susan Faludi wrote *Backlash: The Undeclared War Against Women in America* in 1991, she noted the number was two.

Two out of five hundred.

So . . . progress? Or a sign that business dudes just think women can't be company leaders and have thought so for generations?

In tech, as an example of an exalted field of work, women make up 30 percent of the rank-and-file workforce at giant tech companies like Apple, Google, Facebook, and Twitter, and the gap in executive positions is even larger.

So, the pay gap. You find it when you take all the workers who are women and look at their median income—the one in the middle between the highs and lows. Then you do the same for the men. The Institute for Women's Policy Research says the ratio of these median incomes is 80.5 percent, leaving a gap of 19.5 percent.

Put another way, all women earn 80 percent of what men earn, with women of color earning even less. The gap is closing, slowly, to be sure. It used to be women earned 59 percent of what men earned in the 1970s, and then up to 77 percent in the 2010s, and now it's at around 80 percent.

This takes into account all jobs. But the gap exists *within* the same jobs as well. Some fields, such as law, see the highest gaps; others, such as pharmacy work, see very low gaps.

What's particularly relevant, according to the Institute for Women's Policy Research, is that the gap exists within fields once considered traditionally "masculine," such as construction, labor, maintenance, and so forth.

But it also exists in traditionally "feminine" lines of work, such as nursing, teaching, secretarial work, and others.

In other words, men are by and large paid more overall and in nearly every field.

WHAT GIVES?

Again, it's not as if head honchos are hiring women and simply saying they'll be paid less than men (anymore, but remember this was legal not too long ago). This is where, I'd guess, many arguments go off track because far too many people are looking for blatant signs of discrimination. When they don't find them, they brush the whole thing off as a myth or explain it away as simply "choices" made by individual workers.

It's sort of like when you see men assess the statement of a female sexual harassment survivor, poring over the words like so many Columbos only to declare, "Nope! Not legally rape. Everything's fine then. Carry on." As if the rest isn't, at the least, problematic.

It's certainly easier to brush it all away than to consider just how complicit we all are in the ongoing inequity of valuing, and paying, more for male labor than for female labor.

"It's hard to find the smoking guns," says Barbara Goldin, a Harvard economist, in a *Freakonomics* podcast on the subject. Goldin has been studying the pay gap for years and is often cited as a leading expert. What's interesting is that her appearance on this particular *Freakonomics* episode is often shared as both proof that a gap exists and also a defense of the myth that it doesn't.

It's worth a quick detour into what she's found.

For starters, she says the gap doesn't have much to do with discrimination, nor does it have to do with "unequal" bargaining and negotiating tactics between the sexes. In other words, the cultural trope that men just "bargain" harder and that women don't "lean in" enough might play a small role but certainly not enough to explain the entire gap. It's one dot. A small one.

> **It's certainly easier to brush it all away than to consider just how complicit we all are in the ongoing inequity of valuing, and paying, more for male labor than for female labor.**

She cited a famous study that tracked the careers of roughly twenty-five hundred MBAs from the University of Chicago's Booth School of Business. Right out of school, women who joined the workforce were paid on average $115,000 and men were paid $130,000—a 12 percent gap (not the 20 percent gap seen across all levels).

Here's where the critical part comes into play.

As the study followed those same workers, it found men after nine years had an average salary of $400,000, whereas women earned an average of $250,000—a 46 percent gender wage gap.

What, pray tell, usually happens as young people out of school begin to age?

What major life event often follows?

"So much of the gap happens at the moment kids are born," says Sarah Kliff, a Vox reporter who is probably the best tracker of pay gap data. (It's worth a dive into her podcasts and short videos on the subject for more details.)

For men, when children arrive, the upward trajectory of pay continues. It's a different story for women.

"For women, there is a nose dive in earnings they never recover from," Kliff said on a Vox podcast exploring the wage gap.

Interestingly, the wage gap begins to narrow again as women continue to work and age into their forties, fifties, and sixties—when childcare is not so paramount.

SO, THAT'S THE data. There's not much of a debate, from what I can tell, around the idea that men and women are, indeed, paid differently. There is a debate, however, about whether the pay gap develops because of individual choices rather than societal pressures and expectations about who is responsible for childcare.

This is when we have to consider our shared storylines and structures.

It begins early, often in tiny, seemingly innocent ways, and you can do something about it in the way you speak to—and, more importantly, care for—your children. Because it all trickles down. Kids soak up our language and examples, they see endless media messages and real-life examples of what it means to be a "professional," and it forms the bedrock for how they view society and begin to consider their roles in it.

My friend Karen, who dressed her daughter up for Halloween in doctor's scrubs, remembered the reaction from other adults: "Everyone said she was such a cute nurse. I admire doctors and nurses equally, but it was interesting to hear."

My friend Melissa shared a similar story about her daughter and professional expectations for girls. "Emma told her teacher she wanted to be a doctor when she grew up and the teacher suggested that she should be a nurse instead."

Who usually gets paid more, do you think? Doctors or nurses?

Health care is not, clearly, the only professional field with cultural barriers that put men and women on unequal footing. Politics, business, major sports, tech—there are plenty. Like, when I say "policewoman" or "firewoman," you know I mean *all* people can be officers or firefighters, right? I'm being facetious, yes, but it's a small example of ways we have long normalized which roles "belong" to which sexes, and it's impossible to leave out how these all add up, how they either open avenues for boys and girls or cut them off.

This idea of culturally assigning roles has different formulations, not just around sex but around race as well. A certain vein of men and women argue that affirmative action means "unqualified" minority applicants are "taking" jobs from more-deserving people rather than simply a program that tries to mindfully widen the pool of qualified applicants.

Sociologist Michael Kimmel says there's a mythology in America about "whose" job it is—"it" being all jobs outside of the home—and how white men have lived in fear of someone "taking" their jobs: immigrants, women, refugees, the affirmative action slouch, etc., etc., etc.

"For many men, the idea is if you don't make it, whose fault is it?"

All to say, let's not forget that we often culturally assign expected roles, even in childhood, and maintain a narrative that certain people "deserve" those jobs.

PLENTY OF OTHER inequities are at play as well, including some very important ones you may be perpetuating at work or at home.

I have a friend who is a lawyer, a field where the pay gap is large and where women, and especially women of color, are underrepresented at high levels.

Let me repeat what she told me about her role at work and the pay inequity she has seen. It highlights the quieter and yet seemingly "reasonable" ways these pay gaps develop—especially if people are relying on data alone as the ultimate arbiter.

She began working in law at the same time as several partners at a smaller, boutique firm and noticed that the pay for the male partners quickly outpaced hers. She talked to the partners in charge of pay and was told to simply look at the hours each partner billed that year.

That seemed simple enough. Everything could be boiled down to raw data—hours billed. Bob billed more hours, brought in more money, and therefore deserved more pay.

It all *seemed* equal and fair.

But the thing is, all the junior male partners who billed more than her were pulled into meetings by senior partners, when she wasn't. They were invited to dinners, when she wasn't. They were invited out to drinks, when she wasn't. They soon became familiar faces to senior partners and their clients and were given more work, despite the fact she actually *lobbied* for more work than them and was denied.

At the end of the year, how "fair" would it be to simply add up all the hours billed and compensate everyone on that basis as if no other factors were involved?

Now, you might say, my friend just needed to "lean in" and demand more. Ahh, but she'd be screwed over for that, too.

Lean In, the group dedicated to workplace equality and a big proponent of urging women to ask for more, found something interesting in a study—something that led it to question the idea that women simply need to demand more. Turns out, women *have been* asking, like my friend at the law firm. But they've been shut down.

"Women who negotiate for a promotion or compensation increase are 30 percent more likely than men who negotiate to receive feedback that they are 'bossy,' 'too aggressive,' or 'intimidating,'" according to the study.

The study found everything my friend found: women have less access to senior mentors, fewer shots at promotion, and lower pay, to boot. It reminded me that not every woman's experience is the same. Whereas the Lean In study found only 40 percent of women wanted to become top leaders, compared to 56 percent of men, I recall the Center for Talent and Innovation's research that black women have the highest aspirations for leadership roles but the least opportunity and lowest pay.

I'D BE REMISS not to examine the sexual dynamics at play here. Vice President Mike Pence is not alone in declaring he won't dine or socialize alone with women or drink at functions when his wife is not present. This has become known as the Pence Rule, and I have seen countless otherwise reasonable men who claim not to be sexist champion this idea. Honestly, the fuck? What an absurd notion to normalize as somehow socially acceptable.

It should be considered as blatantly discriminatory for men to say this as for companies to post "no women hired" signs, because how does this play out in the real world, when intimate mentorships are needed and business

drinks and dinners grease the wheels of industry? Could a senior male partner spend a long time alone with a junior female partner? Invite her out to
drinks just to chat? It's the sort of bonding that goes on behind the scenes for
male colleagues but that my friend noticed rarely happened for her.

What an incredible injustice, all this. Women get penalized for not at-
tending important functions, because men fear it might lead to sexual encounters. I think that's putting it kindly. I've seen men argue that they just
won't be able to "help themselves."

Well, hard truth, dudes. You might be wondering whether
a simple after-work drink might lead to a sexual encounter, but
if the #MeToo movement has taught us anything, the woman
you're meeting might be wondering whether the encounter will
lead to you sexually harassing or assaulting them.

All this is more of a men problem than a women problem, and I think we need to get our shit together.

All this is more of a men problem than a women problem,
and I think we need to get our shit together in this regard. The
consequences, no matter how "good a guy" you think you are,
add up to pay gaps simply because of the sexist relational dynamics we think are acceptable to maintain. We can't openly
admit to not having important business dinners with women
because we're afraid we won't be able to "help ourselves" and
then also pretend we can simply add up billable hours at the
end of the year and that treats all workers as equal. Please. We need to call on
ourselves to do better.

SO, FINALLY, WE come to the crux of the matter: men. Dads. People like you
and me.

If the pay gap widens once children enter the picture, why does it predominately affect women?

Here's an enlightening take. Sociologist Kimmel was a backer of the
"bring your daughter to work" day movement to demystify the office for girls
and show them what it was like and how to get there someday. In the 1990s,
he helped start a "bring your son into the home" movement—to have fathers
show sons important household chores like vacuuming and cleaning and
cooking.

Guess which one is still a popular thing?

"We didn't get any public support," he says.

Beginning at home, we're still raising boys to do work in the office or factory and girls to take care of the house or also "have it all" with a job to boot. It follows kids into the workforce, with the expectation that, eventually, all women will stay home or that their roles will be fundamentally different from men's.

In 2015, the Pew Research Center released a study of eighteen hundred people that showed how the sexes divide housework and childcare.

It asked who does the bulk of child scheduling and school stuff. Even though both men and women worked, 54 percent of moms said they did more, 39 percent of couples split it evenly, and just 6 percent of dads said they did more.

It asked who did more household duties, and 59 percent of couples reported splitting chores equally, while 31 percent of moms said they did more, with 9 percent of dads reporting they did more.

It asked who took care of sick kids, and 47 percent of couples reported an even split, while 46 percent of moms said they did more, and 6 percent of dads said they did more.

The thing is, these numbers are growing. Dads *are* doing more around the house and at school and with their kids, and that's a good thing, and that should be celebrated. Dads of color actually spend more time with their children than white dads do when given the chance, despite the near constant lamentations from racist white people going on about "absent black fathers."

But the numbers are still pretty low, and they exist in a world that still portrays dads as dopey and moms as do-it-all martyrs.

HERE'S AN EXAMPLE you might recognize. Every time the Olympics rolls around, P&G unleashes its seemingly heartfelt campaigns about all the shit moms do to get their charges from carpool to the Olympic podium. It's a small example, sure, but it really exemplifies destructive cultural norms and how we're constantly hit with media messages that reinforce familial work disparities and make us believe it's all somehow okay, sappy and touching even. Worthy of earned tears.

For one, it leaves dads out of the picture altogether, despite the fact that when it comes to sports, dads do more—from coaching to yelling at children from the sidelines to populating every angry sports program in the world, let alone the actual playing and coaching fields of professional sports.

But, okay. That's fine. That's not what really gets me. I'm not about to "not all dads" this debate. No, what gets me is how it pigeonholes women as the only possible caregivers and the consequences of this notion. Look, I get that staying home and dealing with kids is a tiring, thankless job—just give me two minutes in the bathroom, *please!*—and it's awesome when people, let alone society at large, recognize this and applaud it.

But check out the stories we tell each other. Is it really so different from what you hear from moms who say they can't even get away for a weekend because dopey dad can't be counted on to pack a lunch? Think about what these shitty commercials say: no matter what else women have going on, they have to get the kids up, get them dressed, get them fed, schlepp them across town and back, pick them up when they fall, and then shovel them off to Olympic glory. But, wait, don't forget to buy one of our household products because when you're done with the kids and your second shift at the factory, you're going to have to clean the toilets.

See? P&G just *loves* moms.

Awwww.

I do understand it feels good to be praised. But I can't wait for men and women alike to say we've had enough of these dated, damaging tropes. Like I said, it's a small example, but it's both emblematic and a reinforcement of what our cultural norms are: moms have to, truly, do it all. And dads get praise when we do, like, a quarter of it. Aren't there even books that showcase men doing everyday housework labeled as "porn" for women, as if the very idea is both hilarious and titillating. "Dads! Vacuuming! I *so* get off on that."

It's impossible to separate these ingrained cultural notions from the real consequences they lead to.

Partly, it feels as if moms might say they've had enough of it all and call bullshit. "Like, you take the kid to practice, dude. I have a board meeting." But that also feels like blaming the oppressed for their continued oppression. I hear dads say they "try" to do more, but moms don't "let" them, and to be sure there is probably a truth in that. I feel itchy if I see my wife cleaning, because, frankly, that's *my* job. I chose to stay home to do it. It's rare when she has to pack a school lunch. That's my job. So I *do* understand the idea that roles might be closely guarded out of a feeling of responsibility or sense of worth. But if we were both working full time outside of the home, I'm sure we'd find a different arrangement.

If all work things are equal, inequities in house and childcare feel like more of a dad problem to me—a problem we can help fix by stepping up, by, wait for it, leaning in. At home.

SO, WHAT CAN WE DO?

In her reporting, Vox's Kliff found that men, when they take time off after babies are born, get penalized more than moms. In other words, it's expected when moms do it, but not when dads do it.

We have shitty expectations for childcare, but also shitty child leave policies. Iceland gives new parents who are couples nine months of leave, with three months for new moms, three months for new dads, and three months to be split up between them. Rates of men taking leave skyrocketed, because it was use it or lose it. Interestingly, Iceland's pay gap isn't nearly as large as ours (6 percent compared to 20, but Iceland also has laws that require pay audits to find inequities). But other countries that have more childcare leave still have large pay gaps, Kliff reports.

What's needed, instead, feels less like a government intervention and more like a new societal norm—a messaging system from male friend to male friend, dad to dad, that men are in charge of childcare and house duties as well.

Kimmel says childcare should be something all "grown-ups" do—not moms, not dads.

Look, yes, if you happen to be in a relationship and one of you happens to work outside of the home and the other in it, you can be adults and figure out how to split up duties. I take on the house chores, school duties, and after-school duties, while my wife deals with a lot of the stuff we might have to sign off on as well as vacation planning. If I were being honest, I'd say she cooks too much, but she enjoys cooking, like a hobby. I do all of the dishes—all of the endless, endless dishes. If we were both working full time outside of the home, I'd be sure I was doing my fair share, because that's just what adults do.

(I know I've been leaving out single moms and dads who, truly, do have to do it all. Praise be to you. Seriously, thanks, Mom. I don't know how you did it.)

As for couples and household duties, my friend Kristin puts it best:

"There's a treasure trove of articles online about the 'mental load' or 'emotional load' of motherhood," Kristin says. "Men should be self-auditing with questions like, 'Are my wife and I equally healthy? equally exercising? equally rested? equally able to sustain relationships beyond this family? Or am I taking advantage of my wife's willingness to do all the menial labor, carry all the mental load of parenthood, and wear herself into the ground?' Just as importantly, women have to be willing to share these responsibilities with their spouses."

Kliff wondered whether we don't, indeed, need a different sort of ad campaign, and hilariously created one in one of her Vox podcasts, to help socialize the notion that men should equally care for the children they helped create.

Take time off work to care for babies if you can. Bring your kids to your friend groups, just as you might imagine young moms do.

"Show your friends it's a normal thing for men to take care of babies," Kliff says.

I see my stay-at-home dad friends' and my loving Dad 2.0 convention dad friends' heads exploding right now. So, I'll say, if you're already doing this, great! Keep it up. You're rocking it.

If you're not, recognize it. And get on it.

It quite literally can reshape the cultural face of our country toward equality for all—in pay, healthy emotional lives, and opportunity.

BUT THAT'S AT home. Yes, it has links to what happens at work. What can we actually do at work?

A lot!

First off, don't pretend the field is level. Don't be that guy—the guy who refuses to mentor, give work to, or even dine alone with rising employees who are women and then tallies up billable hours and punishes them for it.

Don't pretend as if everyone is getting a fair shake in America, because they're not. Race, gender, mythologies about our roles in America—they all add up, from the time a teacher tells a girl she'd make a great nurse when really the girl wants to be a doctor to job interviews when women face panels of white dudes who don't give them access to the same opportunities and then dock their pay because of it.

Start from there. Start from simply believing that perhaps your experience isn't everyone else's.

In 2015, 90 percent of candidates who filled CEO roles came from within a company's managerial pipeline. Guess how many of those CEOs were women?

Zero.

None.

Are you telling me those companies had *only* men qualified to do the job? Seriously?

It's more likely they had only male managers "next in line"—but only because those guys were given the opportunities to advance all along the way, while women were called "bossy" or "pushy" for trying to get the same damn things. In business, men are aggressive and leaders. Women are bitchy and shrill.

Again, stop pretending the field is level. We are reminded from day one that it is not.

The good news is, you can simply be aware of this.

The Lean In study, in collaboration with McKinsey & Co., outlined a few ways to help rectify gender inequality in the workplace.

First, talk about it. Lay out your company's goals and be continually open about it. The ideas of fairness and equality shouldn't be relegated to an occasional meeting but should be part of a company's culture.

(Interestingly, this works at home with the kids as well. Talk to your girls and boys continually, constantly, about the ways gender and race and nationality and religion play roles in our everyday lives. It ain't all negative. It's sometimes pretty damn fun.)

Another great, but underutilized way to achieve parity comes at the beginning—during the hiring process. Blind résumé reviews (cover the name) minimize gender bias, but only 4 percent of companies studied use this practice. The study also recommends setting hiring and managerial pipeline targets and then holding managers accountable for meeting them.

WORKPLACE AND FAMILY flexibility. Push it for everyone, not just women. Think about that: if it's just a "women's issue," it props up the stereotype that only women can care for kids—leaving managers to see them as unworthy of promotion, and leaving men bereft of some quality time with their kids.

When men talk about kids, reproductive health care, parental leave, and anything related to caring as if it's all a "women's issue," they're doing it wrong. These are family issues, grown-up issues. You can do tremendous good in framing them this way when chatting with your kids about it all.

When was the last time you heard about a male partner or male office badass expected to "do it all"? Be a boss *and* raise a family?

Interestingly, the Lean In study found that 42 percent of men don't eye leadership spots because they fear it will disrupt work-life balance. You know how many women say this?

The *exact same number.*

While both men and women want the same thing—work-life balance—a million media messages and everyday conversations team up to make it appear as if only men want top boss slots.

You may recall a mountain of articles about how women need to be more confident, need to lean in, or just need to say yes to new gigs and then work it out. Guess what other metric shows men and women on equal footing? Confidence. Thirteen percent of both men and women said they wouldn't want a top job because they were not confident they'd be successful.

And who gets promoted anyway?

The bottom line is companies, like families, need to talk more about gender equality—get it out in the open and make it a part of everyday culture—and then hold themselves accountable for working toward it.

—Chapter 15—

WAITING FOR MADAM PRESIDENT

It's no surprise women are vastly underrepresented in government positions when many weren't allowed to vote until a couple generations ago and are still denied today, but what example are we setting for our kids when we discuss our leaders?

SOMETIMES I LOOK at President Trump and wonder, how does he do it all?

How does he juggle being president *and* father to a young child?

What, I wonder, is his go-to cookie recipe?

And how much time does he devote to considering that fine line between projecting power and decisiveness and not coming off as "cold" or "bitchy"?

Must be tough.

Look, I'm not sexist, but something about his voice just . . . bugs me.

He sounds shrill.

Talking about running again in 2020 seems too ambitious. Selfish, if you ask me. Doesn't he think of his family? Shouldn't he be home with his children instead?

Don't get me wrong. I'd vote for a man. Of course. Just . . . not this one. He's too bitchy.

And I don't mean to judge, but those colorful power ties make him look sort of bulky. I wonder if he'd consider more slimming earth tones?

> **Don't get me wrong. I'd vote for a man. Just . . . not this one. He's too bitchy.**

Sometimes he sounds really angry. I bet he hates men. It sounds like it. You can just . . . tell.

Or maybe it's just his time of the month, you know? Probably can't trust him with our nuclear arsenal, being so emotional and all.

Sometimes I wonder how he finds time for PTA duties. The playground won't fix itself. I bet his cupcakes are a hit.

Giving a State of the Union address in rule-mandated heels must be exhausting. Ugh. Poor guy. And yet, so inspiring and powerful!

He should wear more pearls. They project respectability. And mix up his blazers. Who wears the same color all the time anyway?

Sometimes he looks like he just needs a man to fuck him real good. He's so uptight.

I wonder what his nighttime face routine is?

Does he hold meetings with men . . . alone? Does he ever dine alone with a married man? Seems sort of risky, if you ask me. I'd never hold a meeting with a man all by myself.

Honestly, he should smile more.

OBVIOUSLY, I'M BEING facetious here.

Very few, if *any*, male politicians are confronted with these "how does he do it all" questions or any of the bullshit above.

But they're de rigueur for any female politician.

And our children are watching. They're gobbling up the subtle cues we give about who is a "leader" and who is not.

I've witnessed my own family members label Hillary Clinton a "cunt" for daring to serve her country while getting absolutely pissed off at me for calling them sexist. What a mindfuck, that. They could vote for the most openly sexist president in a generation, call women "cunts," and then have the audacity to claim that not only are they *not* sexist but they actually support women.

I'm sure you've also seen women politicians be targets of sexualized invective in ways male politicians never are. It's impossible to avoid in America.

The preceding tropes serve to reinforce the notion that, above all else, a woman's duty is at home, tending to children—certainly not running for office—and that her body, her emotional state, her reproductive health, and her household duties are all fair game in ways they never are for men. Imagine, if you will, the sheer number of "think pieces" you would have seen had Clinton had an eleven-year-old child while running for president—endless, mind-numbing "just asking" pieces about whether a woman could, truly, have it all.

Power *and* parenting?

Heavens. How does she *do it?*

It's a debate I don't remember having for the previous three male presidents who had school-aged children while in office. They could have a quick game of catch and be praised endlessly for it.

And how many have you seen about the current president?

"Our candidates get that question all the time—I get that question all the time: 'Where are your children?' Uh, they're with their father," said Andrea Dew-Steele, a buddy of mine who started Emerge America, which trains Democrat women to run for office. "It's changing a little bit, but men just don't get that question."

> **Women in American politics have always had to walk a fine line between political ambition and their relationships to home life, children, and men.**

WOMEN IN AMERICAN politics have always had to walk a fine line between political ambition and their relationships to home life, children, and men—roles that go back to the nation's founding when Abigail Adams implored her husband to "remember the ladies" and John Quincy Adams responded that he didn't think men wanted to be ruled by the "despotism of the petticoat."

Honestly, can you tell me this notion has disappeared?

I'm going to go out on a limb and say you, like me, have heard at least one of your male friends, who probably considers himself "just old-fashioned," say something along these lines: women belong at home, tending to "womanly" things, like the house, or petticoats, or their periods. How many politicians or news stories or talking heads have you seen intimate something similar?

"Blood coming out of her wherever."

It ain't new, is what I'm saying.

America has created this Wild West, John Wayne-esque mythology of men as freedom-loving wilderness brutes.

But dudes have always been afraid of women in charge and have sought to undercut their authority by labeling them as "emotional" (as if the current president's Twitter feed doesn't put that trope to rest forever) or out of their proper homebound realm, or, as Adams would argue, secretly out to rule men.

It's everywhere. And we need to break this shit down from the beginning, because it's all conspiring to keep us from having our best country possible.

Before we get to the place we find ourselves today—with women making up 51 percent of the population and roughly 20 percent of representation across nearly all levels of government—it's worth a brief historical tour of how white men, in both language and law, sought to keep women and people of color from voting or running for office and of how many of the rotted offspring of these dangerous roots remain today in phrases and ideologies you may be passing on to your children.

LET'S START WITH voting.

I think it's a myth that the Founding Fathers just sort of "overlooked" mentioning women specifically when it came to voting so that women therefore had to fight to be included and that slowly, year by year, things will edge toward equality in representation. It's what I vaguely remember learning as a child: women weren't included, then they were, and now everything's going swell.

But that overlooks the purposeful, systematic efforts white men have made to keep women and people of color from voting.

Case in point: many people think women (well, white women) won the right to vote in 1920.

But women had the vote early on, until states started stripping it away.

One of my favorite historical anecdotes comes from Elizabeth, New Jersey. Around the turn of the 1800s, women got together, went to the polls, and created a voting bloc so powerful that their preferred candidate won. Soon after, in the election of 1806, the town of some thousand residents saw six thousand votes cast. It was madness. White people, black people, women, men, even children—they all came out to vote, often multiple times. Men would cast their votes, go home to put on costumes, and then go back to the polls to cast their votes again dressed as women.

Turns out the state constitution of New Jersey said "all inhabitants" could vote, so in some cities, all inhabitants did just that.

States got wise. Fast. Throughout the 1800s, state by state, men got together to restrict voting to white dudes, if they hadn't already. Then, not long after, depending on the state, the same men got together and started handing the rights back.

Wyoming Territory did it as a way to attract women west, given how few of them there were in the outerlands. Jeannette Rankin, the first woman elected to Congress, won her seat just a few years before the Nineteenth Amendment was passed.

Think about all that for a second: in granting and denying and granting all over again certain rights, white men had to get together in gilded rooms to consider and actually cast votes on the basic humanity of other people, to debate just who was worthy of rights.

What I'm saying is, it wasn't accidental. It wasn't some slip-up or forgotten mention in the Constitution that, golly, overlooked some people. I think that's sort of a soft mythology built up over the years to excuse away the determined actions of white men to restrict rights, part and parcel with the way racist people today say the Civil War was fought over "states' rights" instead of white people seeking to keep black people enslaved.

In short, it *sounds* better. But it ain't the truth.

No, white men kept women from voting for generations.

Purposefully. Systematically.

Do you think these efforts have suddenly disappeared, that everything is okay now? That was all in the past and an America built and maintained by oppression is fine now?

To be sure, women sought to correct these wrongs and had to fight white men in the streets to do so. (Again, voting rights didn't just magically materialize.)

With the Nineteenth Amendment, white women won the right to vote in 1920. But consider just how long it took for other women, and you tell me if this is all ancient history.

Native Americans were supposed to have the right to vote in 1924, but New Mexico, in 1962, was the last state to enfranchise them. Sort of.

Thanks to Jim Crow, poll taxes, lynchings, and all manner of violence, white people kept black people from voting en masse until the Civil Rights Act of 1965.

But let's not pretend for a second that everyone got together and sang "Kumbaya" after that.

The law had to be reinforced in the 1970s, 1980s, 1990s, and 2000s—and then, in 2013, the Supreme Court decided that because we had elected a black president, America was suddenly postracial, and it cut back on some parts of the law.

And what happened? Some states immediately sought to make it harder for people of color to vote. And by states, I mean white people in power representing those states.

Like I said, it's not ancient history. It's just the continuation of it.

HERE'S THE BOTTOM line: men wrote laws to keep women from voting or holding office and often physically abused or threatened the oppressed to keep these systems in place; they have created laws to this day to prevent equal participation in government.

Where does this sordid past and present leave us?

With the idea that gross underrepresentation of women and people of color in government is somehow normal rather than an outcome created and maintained by our laws and our everyday customs that keep women "in their place."

Emerge America keeps track of women in governmental positions.

As of the summer of 2018, only thirty-seven women have ever served as governors, in just twenty-seven states, basically half.

Half of the United States has never had a woman in the governor's mansion. A black woman has never served as governor. (As of this writing, Stacey Abrams had just lost the Georgia governor's election, following a race plagued by disenfranchisement. Full disclosure: I donated.)

Women make up just 20 percent of Congress, with women of color making up just 6 percent.

Nineteen states have no women representatives in the House.

Thirty-one states have no women representatives in the Senate.

In the entire history of the United States, only 51 women have served in the Senate, compared to 1,973 men, according to Senate statistics.

Women make up roughly 24 percent of state legislatures.

Throughout the country, in cities with a population of thirty thousand or more, women make up just 18 percent of mayors.

White men make up 31 percent of the population, and yet hold 65 percent of political offices, according to the *Washington Post*. White women make up 32 percent of the population and hold 25 percent of the offices, which, okay, seems close to something to shoot for: representation that matches, or nearly matches, societal makeup.

The story is, as you might imagine, worse for people of color. Nonwhite men make up 19 percent of the population and yet hold just 7 percent of the offices, while nonwhite women make up the same percentage of the population and hold an even lower number of offices, 4 percent.

What's it say to you and your kids when you read the paper or watch the news and see that nearly every position of power is occupied by a man, usually a white man? Even a casual observer of news can look at photos from the current White House and see who is seated at the tables and desks of power—and who is filming them, or asking questions, or providing aid, and even who is painted on the walls behind them.

Like many of the gross sexisms tackled in this book, it all adds up. We have a system that was created by certain people to exclude certain people, and, surprise, surprise, the system continues to exclude to this day—either through voter disenfranchisement or societal mores about who is most "qualified"—and yet we consider it "normal" or "just how it is" as opposed to something we can actively challenge, both in the voting booth and in how we discuss politics in our circles and with our children.

The repercussions are chilling.

DON'T TAKE IT from me. Here's what outside observers say about our society today.

The United Nations, which sent a three-person working group to explore gender inequality in America in 2015, found some pretty stark reminders that a country that has grappled with women's rights for generations still has a lot of work to do.

"The US, which is a leading State in formulating international human rights standards, is allowing its women to lag behind," the group reported.

From low representation in government to lower pay, hostile encounters when simply visiting health clinics, and gross stereotypes in our election process (how did "bitch" become a common election refrain?), the group discovered a sexist society worthy of some third world dictatorship, not the United States.

The group found women, especially poor women and women of color, profoundly lacking in basic rights—such as health care, maternity leave, and safety from domestic violence, especially gun violence.

"We acknowledge the United States' commitment to liberty, so well represented by the Statue of Liberty which symbolizes both womanhood and freedom. Nevertheless, in global context, US women do not take their rightful place as citizens of the world's leading economy, which has one of the highest rates of per capita income," the group reported. "In the US, women fall behind international standards as regards their public and political representation, their economic and social rights and their health and safety protections."

In other words, the United States is all talk and no action. We talk about life and liberty and freedom for all, but we have an entrenched government system that grossly underrepresents women, especially women of color.

> **We talk about life and liberty and freedom for all, but we have an entrenched government system that grossly underrepresents women, especially women of color.**

I HOPE BY now to have established that men have systematically kept women from office for hundreds of years and that, despite making up 51 percent of the population, women make up roughly 30 percent of government representation across all bodies and roughly 20 percent at the federal level.

It's really worth considering how many groundbreaking women in the political arena came to power in the few short generations since suffrage and just what our culture still demands of them to continue to break that ground. These cultural mythologies remain, very often in how dads and moms speak to their children about politics and who deserves to lead.

Jeannette Rankin was the first woman to win a congressional office a few years before white women were allowed to vote. She proved an early outlier. Most of the first women to hold elected office were appointed following the deaths of their husbands, in what was known as the widow's mandate. The Center for American Women in Politics counts forty-seven widows who followed their husbands into Congress, beginning in the 1920s and continuing to the present day.

These appointments were usually considered "safe"—the women largely played a caretaker's role while the menfolk fought it out for the permanent seat. These were also considered more socially acceptable political roles for women to play in the first generations following suffrage. After all, the women didn't ask to be appointed—heavens no, they weren't *ambitious*. (We'll get to that word soon enough.) They were simply fulfilling a temporary duty and viewed as stand-ins for their deceased husbands.

These traditions in our political and cultural storylines continued for generations, state to state, and have surely, along with so many subtle sexisms, influenced how we view women as politicians even today.

It's no coincidence that the first woman to win a major party's nomination for the presidency was also the wife of a former president. But just as male sponsorship has long been a necessity for American women in politics, so has putting ambitious women in their place, and she ultimately lost to an elderly white male with a long history of sexism, racism, and nearly two dozen charges of sexual assault.

What happens in a country with a history of language and laws designed to keep women from voting and running for office?

The 2016 election is a perfect case study of how people who support sexism can claim they are not, at the same time, sexist.

I DON'T THINK you'll be surprised to discover that this wildly feminist San Francisco stay-at-home dad is a huge Hillary Clinton fan.

Shocker, I know.

I donated to her efforts and worked on social media campaigns. I created the Dads For Hillary Facebook group. My wife and daughter attended a fundraiser at a fancy house across the Golden Gate Bridge and got to meet her, ask her a few questions, and even take a picture with her.

On election day, I brought my daughter, age ten at the time, into the voting booth with me so we could both "vote" for her at the same time, her hand resting on mine as we marked the ballot. Who knew when she would get another chance, I wondered.

On the night of the election, I have to admit we were excited. The vast majority of polls appeared to be in Clinton's favor, and, let's face it, her opponent said some pretty racist and sexist crap during the election—not to mention throughout his career.

We thought she had it in the bag and that America was about to elect its first woman as president.

Instead, we put our daughter to bed when the results remained unclear, and then woke her up with bad news: the man who admitted to sexually assaulting women—"grab 'em by the pussy"—had just won because . . .

When it came down to it, it was either him or a woman.

ONE OF MY favorite writers, Ana Marie Cox, says Donald Trump's presidency is an everyday trauma for many women.

It's really not difficult to imagine why, when even a cursory review of his views on women is shockingly disgusting. It's important to consider these for a moment, because we need to come to grips with what is acceptable in American society. Now, people who voted for him or urged you to "give him a chance" might not say or do these things themselves.

But history will note that in 2016, none of the following was a deal breaker:

"Look at that face! Would anyone vote for that? Can you imagine that, the face of the next president?"

"She's disgusting, both inside and out. I'd look her right in that fat, ugly face of hers and say . . . you're fired."

She's "unattractive both inside and out. I understand why her husband left her for a man."

She's "Miss Piggy."

She's a "dog and a liar," with the "face of a pig."

"Wonderful looking while on the ice but up close and personal, she could only be described as attractive if you like a woman with a bad complexion who is built like a linebacker."

"I really understand beauty. And I will tell you, she's not—I do own Miss Universe. I do own Miss USA. I mean I own a lot of different things. I do understand beauty, and she's not."

"I promise not to talk about your massive plastic surgeries that didn't work."

"Sadly, she's no longer a ten."

"You know, it doesn't really matter what [the media] write as long as you've got a young and beautiful piece of ass."

She's "a bimbo."

"Does she have a good body? No. Does she have a fat ass? Absolutely."

"You know, I don't want to sound too much like a chauvinist, but when I come home and dinner's not ready, I'll go through the roof, okay?"

"I did try and fuck her. She was married . . . I moved on her like a bitch. But I couldn't get there. And she was married. Then all of a sudden I see her, she's now got the big phony tits and everything. She's totally changed her look."

"Oh, it looks good." ("It" is a woman.)

"I better use some Tic Tacs just in case I start kissing her. You know, I'm automatically attracted to beautiful—I just start kissing them. It's like a magnet. Just kiss. I don't even wait. And when you're a star, they let you do it. You can do anything . . . grab 'em by the pussy."

I've lost friends and relatives over their support for him. It's just a "disagreement" or I'm being "too PC" or "too liberal"—I've heard it all.

I've also heard people, very liberal people, say he's not "normal."

I'd argue instead he's perfectly normal.

He is, indeed, the modern-day embodiment of how "good people" in America have always viewed women.

Oh, sure, his supporters, enablers, and collaborators might say they had "reasons" or someone else was "worse"—but the bottom line is this: when they went to the polls and ranked what was important to them, girls and women were at the bottom of their priority list. You simply didn't cast a ballot for a sexist asshole like that if you truly cared about the impact on girls and women, and it'd be silly to pretend that a country that looks the other way is also not a sexist hellscape for them.

But like I said before, we didn't magically luck into the first and only generation that subjugates women. We do it in law. We do it in language. We do it when we rank our priorities and put equal rights and common decency at the bottom.

In other words, it's perfectly normal. It's perfectly in line with the great sweep of American history. Dew-Steele points out the studies showing America won't reach equity in representation for a hundred years. So where does that leave us today? Right now? If we know men wrote laws and created customs to exclude others, and if we know equity won't be reached for another century, it's imperative to realize we're in the thick of it, and communities suffer because of it.

And though it's what passes for normal in America, it is, in no way, just. What role do *you* play in it all?

Do you tell your sons that language like that is not okay, but voting for him is? I honestly don't know how his supporters look their children in the eye. I guess no differently from how men in generations earlier argued in favor of segregation or slavery or native genocide and thought they were still "good" somehow.

I suppose my point is we can't yet say the field is level in politics when even the worst man among us is seen as the best option.

SO, WHAT CAN WE DO?

Like so many of these biases, one of the most important things we dads can do is talk about it. And then vote about it.

"The part the father plays is such a pivotal role," says Steele. "If a father says you should run for office, it resonates more than when a mother says it. The research really shows how pivotal that time of talking about politics is."

My cousin Trevor, a Coast Guard officer and father of a boy and girl, said something that really stuck with me about men's speech at home and what our kids see and hear.

> "If a father says you should run for office, it resonates more than when a mother says it."

"My kids know I'd be quick to engage someone talking shit about any one of the New England teams because they have seen me do it a million times," he said. "If they don't know how I would react to sexism, gender roles, and inequality, well that's on me. Additionally, if I haven't given them the words and tools to engage on their own, that's on me too."

I think of the father at home who brushes past what the president has said about women or excuse it away as "locker room talk." Think about that one for a second: America is okay with rape depending on where it is discussed. No joke. The message doesn't just disappear. It worms its way into the fabric of society, to the point that women of the #MeToo movement are considered liars and to the point where just 3 percent of rapists ever serve time in prison. It's no accident. America thinks women are lesser. And it's a lesson millions of parents passed on to their kids with this election. Basic human decency when it applies to women just isn't important, or perhaps not as important as other things.

When it comes to politics, one small, important way to cut down on inequality is to consider how we discuss who should run for office, who we consider qualified to lead.

With men, we consider it a cultural given that he would have ambition and drive to serve.

With women, studies have shown people express a "moral outrage" when women do the same.

Moral. Outrage.

"That's one of the signature parts of our training—that *ambition* is not a dirty word," Steele says. "It's really important that we teach our women and girls that ambition is okay, that it's okay to want to serve your community."

Indeed.

I THINK IT'S equally important that men call out men when we see sexist beliefs and mythologies rear their heads. Many women have written about how internalized misogyny has often led women to be their own worst enemies.

"I'd vote for a woman, but not that one" is one of my "favorites." I can't tell you how many people I witnessed saying they'd definitely vote for, say, Elizabeth Warren over Hillary Clinton any day of the week. But as soon as Clinton lost and Warren was perceived as a front-runner, these same assholes had a change of heart. Suddenly, any woman candidate was fine, just not Warren. Keep an ear out for that one in 2020. You'll hear it.

"Just not . . . that one."

Our expectations of who is allowed to serve are mirrored in a sordid and damaging expectation of the inverse: who is expected to stay at home. Indeed, they're tied together. Just as in work issues, dads in particular can do great good in this regard, in a way that doesn't just help their families but helps break down a damaging stereotype that keeps good leaders from serving.

I had the good fortune to hear Warren give a talk in San Francisco about her early years, how she married young, had kids, and returned to college, and then law school—only to encounter obstacle upon obstacle in trying to find childcare. (It's a standard stump speech she has been giving for a few years and can be found online.)

As she was telling the story of how her Aunt Bee ultimately came to live with her to help care for the kids as she sought to build her career, I couldn't help but wonder: you were married at the time, so where the fuck was their dad? I don't know the ins and outs of their relationship and won't get into it here, but certainly it's representative of a story that is too familiar today. The expectation is that women are the caregivers. That no matter what, childcare is up to them. That, when it comes right down to it, they belong elsewhere.

What does it say of our country that the first time an infant was brought to the floor of the Senate during a vote was when Illinois senator Tammy Duckworth did it a few weeks after giving birth while in office? Are you meaning to tell me that in the entire course of our history, literally no male senator had to deal with childcare?

"Hey, Grover. My deal is closing, can you take the kid for the morning?"

What does it say that the idea of using campaign funds for childcare wasn't adjudicated until more and more women started running for office?

What an incredible failing of our country—and of men—that this wasn't considered until women made it necessary.

In 2018.

Let me repeat for the audience in the back: if you only discuss childcare as a "women's issue," you're doing it wrong.

LOOK, I BELONG to an incredible group of actively engaged and involved and loving fathers who gather together each year—largely, it should be noted, without our children—to discuss the good and the bad and sometimes to just laugh or cry it out. I know the statistics on dads being more and more involved at home, especially dads of color. But I'd be remiss not to point out that the overwhelming cultural story is that moms are the caregivers, the expected nurturers and housekeepers, care providers for elderly parents, PTA bake sale sellers, and emotional laborers, and these narratives cannot be fully extracted from the results we then see in underrepresentation and unequal pay.

If the media and everyday stories we tell inform us that moms should do everything and that a man's role as dad is usually elsewhere, in business or in government, it can't then also be surprising to see these tropes play out, with damaging repercussions, outside the home.

As the primary, at-home caregiver, I've seen how it all works firsthand: moms giving other moms shit for not "doing it all" or slanting snide looks and remarking about them not being at school at one p.m. in the middle of a workday; moms judging outfits or cupcakes; dads acting like dopey dunces when it comes to caregiving—"Golly, how do I care for this child I actively tried to produce?"—moms complaining about not being able to "get away" because their adult spouse can't possibly manage a house for a few days; dads delighting in not being knowledgeable of their children's schedules. It's infuriating, because it feels like we're all trapped in shitty expectations and stories about who is "supposed" to do it instead of doing the shared, necessary labor adults simply need to do to manage.

Honestly, we also have to come to terms with the fact that a lot of this bullshit is white people problems personified, because the same structures that have kept women from high office have also undercut communities of color for generations, making it impossible for them to have all these intellectual debates about who should play which role when they're busy as hell working three shifts for percentages of the pay.

I can't overstate it: the ripple effects are damning. What we do and say in the home paves the way for how our broader society will one day treat our children.

The fix?

Talk about it. And think about it all when you vote.

"I don't vote for the woman candidate just because," Dew-Steele says. "We all want the best candidate possible."

But she urges voters to consider two things. One, all things being equal between candidates, vote for the woman; because, two, representation matters.

Representation does indeed matter. I'd argue that even if all things *weren't* equal, I'd still vote for the woman candidate. Lived experience in a country that treats you unequally is experience enough.

"The endgame is building this reflective democracy that looks like all of us," she says. "They're diverse in gender, in age, race, people with disabilities. It's about bringing people to the table making decisions who really understand what people go through every day."

—Chapter 16—

YOUR OPINION ON ABORTION IS INVALID

Let's be clear: in our everyday conversations and social media interactions to actual votes cast in legislatures, we put the basic human rights of girls and women on the table as if they warrant male debate, and we need to stop. Now.

W HEN WE, MEN, debate abortion, is the discussion alone a denial of fundamental rights?

I think so.

Now, are we the same men who gather in rooms to sign into law restrictions on what women can do with their bodies?

No.

But you can draw a line from one to the other, and though you might shake your fist at the absurdity of the latter situation, to be sure the everyday conversations and debates about who should enjoy bodily autonomy are equally as absurd.

They are, indeed, connected.

They add up.

They unite to weave a cultural tapestry still enamored with an inherited entitlement of men as the ultimate decision makers—even over other bodies—that enables them to doggedly undercut women's fundamental and everyday rights in every swath and segment of society—a rotten lineage of silence and gendered apartheid first spun in classical Greece and Rome.

Follow the thread.

"Speech will be the business of men," Telemachus tells us in *The Odyssey*, and not very much has changed.

"Nature intended women to be our slaves," Napoleon tells us, taking up the classical weave for modern times. "They are our property."

"You have to treat them like shit," said the future President Trump, as reported in a 1992 *New York Magazine* profile.

"Grab 'em by the pussy," the same man offers, caught on tape years later.

The point of it all is the gross inheritance of language we use to demean one sex while giving untold, seemingly "normal" power to the other. Whereas one swipe of a gilded pen does actual harm to women around the globe, to be sure, billions of everyday conversations pave the way for that act, painting the entire perverse thought process like it's a natural, perfectly respectable birthright of men—yet another arena for us to chime in, to play devil's advocate, to scream on the sidewalk, to shove our esteemed opinions into an argument that has clouded our nation in too many forms since the beginning and ultimately comes to this: Should women have bodily autonomy?

> **Whereas one swipe of a gilded pen does actual harm to women around the globe, to be sure, billions of everyday conversations pave the way for that act.**

GUYS, WE NEED to stop this. Let's not let our kids think it's okay to hold other people's rights in the balance.

But how do we get there?

Bear with me.

The threads of paternalistic entitlement run deep and necessitate exploration before we can reach a new avenue of debate—one that allows men to become tremendous allies and advocates for basic human rights while also eroding a cultural reality that paints a respectable patina on persistent second-class citizenship for a majority population.

To begin, we can agree on a few things, no matter your personal or political persuasion.

One is that America was created and founded by white guys. Our laws, our systems, our cultural mores were established by guys.

The second is that from the beginning women had few rights, and many millions of women were killed for their land, and many millions more were treated much like the land itself, as property—property to be worked, raped, seeded, and sold.

Still with me? Don't get in your feels just yet. No one is pointing fingers at you. Rather, we need to simply agree on our shared history.

Okay, good.

HERE'S THE RUB: to consider whether these foundational threads of oppression have ultimately been severed, and whether an entire body of citizens remains today second class and subject to the whims and dictates of the other, one must ask when true, lasting equality among the sexes and races was reached.

Surely, we've all heard that racist high school chum or sexist uncle beg off responsibility in the present for sins committed in the past, a mulish way of overlooking persistent inequities as if they are not indeed cultural progeny.

So I ask:

Was equality reached in the 1860s when slavery was abolished?

Or was it in the 1920s when white women got the vote?

The 1960s when women of color got the vote?

The 1970s when school busing became desegregated?

The 1980s and 1990s and 2000s when welfare and criminal laws unfairly targeted women and populations of color?

Or today, when women's reproductive health care is put to a vote in state after state?

Have we finally reached true equality among the sexes?

When women make up 51 percent of the population and roughly 20 percent of government representation—across every level of government, from federal houses to town mayors?

When white men make up 31 percent of the population and 65 percent of government representation?

When white women earn on average roughly 80 cents for every dollar a man makes, and black women earn only 70 cents, and Latinas earn roughly half?

When sports coverage of female athletes makes up 4 percent of major news coverage?

When women are outnumbered two to one as lead characters in movies and are very often portrayed as prizes for male characters?

When prestigious prizes in science and literature and mathematics consistently are awarded to men?

When more women are killed by their domestic partners than our soldiers in recent times of war? When women are in large numbers stalked, beaten, and abused—raped and regularly told their rapists deserve judicial mercy so as not to "ruin" their lives?

When states across the nation have enacted laws requiring women to have written permission from their husbands before receiving medical treatment? When women are forced into unnecessary, intrusive examinations before receiving the medical care they initially sought out? When a US Senate panel dedicated to reforming health care for the entire nation consists entirely of men?

Is *now* the promised land?

In Ireland last year, the entire country held a vote on whether women should be able to access reproductive health care.

"People will look back on this day and be shocked that we actually held a vote on whether or not women should have control over their own bodies," writer and badass activist Laura Bates said at the time. "It's 2018, how are we still 'debating' this?"

We always have. Men have considered since the beginning that all subjects are worthy of their knitted brows and a "well, actually." Men have always considered it our inherent right to debate, while also telling women to shut the fuck up about it, Penelope. Go knit.

It's in our cultural blood.

ALL OF THE above are examples of sexism that can be quantified, borne out by data and news reports. But threaded deeper into the tapestry of our culture is a sexism so pervasive that men, and tremendous portions of women, either ignore it or excuse it away as natural or normal, just part of "who we are" or "how it is."

To be sure, these microsexisms serve as bulwarks to injustice as equally as legislative chambers full of deluded, frightened men, and each seems to lay the groundwork for the other, creating a vicious cycle that perpetually finds us here: from birth to death in America, girls and women are reminded every day they are lesser and that it's perfectly reasonable for men to debate their bodies and worth whenever and wherever we please.

And do you know how we know?

Because girls and women tell us.

Every.

Damn.

Day.

Think of the schoolgirl who is told it's okay—an honor, really—for boys to hurt her to show affection.

The girl who is told her rambunctious awesomeness is cool and tomboyish, while the boy with weak aim is told his throw is girlish. Which is the ideal we celebrate?

Or the schoolgirls who are sold short shorts and tight shirts at every major retailer and then are told to go home from school for wearing short shorts and tight shirts because their bodies are a distraction to boys.

Or the young Latinas who are told sports are for boys.

Or the young black girls excused from school to go "fix" their hair by white women who pay black women to create the same hairstyles for their own damn daughters while on beach vacations.

Think of the older schoolgirls who are told science and math and technology aren't for them—they're sold glitter science kits while boys get genuine science.

The young women who find fewer scholarships for college.

The girls who get odd looks and legitimacy quizzes for suggesting they also like *Star Wars* or character role-playing or video games.

The women, young and old, who are told to smile for the pleasure and amusement of men and are then hounded for their phone numbers if they do or are called stuck-up bitches if they don't; the catcalls and whistles; the endless media barrage about ideal weight and look—not too heavy, not too skinny, but just right, the corporeal Goldilocks, whose health and worth are less important than her passing impact on, wait for it, dudes. You and me.

The women who aren't invited out to after-work drinks but are punished with lower pay and fewer opportunities for not being "one of the guys."

The men, including our own vice president, who refuse to dine or meet alone with women because . . . why? Men are constantly verging on rape depending on what she's wearing or women are just wanton sex temptresses, biding their time until they find themselves across the table at a business meeting? Think for a second about who plays the "victim" in each scenario—the innocent man befuddled by a woman—and who is the actual victim in each scenario—the woman who really just wants a raise or more opportunity from a bunch of overconfident white guys who will still be making more than her at the end of the day.

There are endless examples of microsexisms—you can find them in an instant online or around town or just by asking the girls and women in your life—but, to be sure, we bolster much larger ones in our shared stories, such as of the rich, racist white guy who was caught calling women nasty and bragging about sexually assaulting them and then was elected president of the United States. Or the Hollywood producer whose lasciviousness was covered for persistently by guys who knew—stars whose movies you enjoy—but who protected him anyway so as not to damage their own careers.

Yes, the data points are disparate and these are but a sample of them, but the pattern is readily apparent: a Western tradition that cut the template of exclusion early on. A country founded and created by men, nurtured in the oppression of many, remains perpetually in thrall to the same population.

And the total mindfuck of it all is how piteously aggrieved these men often feel, lamenting to the heavens about the sorry, outcast state of the white guy today—the white guy who has enough political power to elect a doddering old racist sexual predator while enjoying a media portrayal of being powerless or unrepresented, who literally controls every branch of federal power, the majority of state houses and governorships, and town mayor and council positions, who owns a cultural status that allows him to play every stripe of movie action hero no matter the race or nationality of the original character, and yet claim an outrageous "reverse sexism" when four women zap make-believe ghosts or when one finally, after two generations of storytelling, gets a turn at wielding the giant space stick to do mind battle with aliens.

Honestly.

What fresh hell, guys?

To be sure, I hear you. Men also face sexism—but it largely boils down to living each day in fear of being labeled the worst possible thing ever: feminine.

Seriously, guys, our fragile, fucked-up masculinity is going to do us all in.

ADD TOGETHER THE big sexisms with the small and here we are again—yet another moment in time when it almost *does* seem natural for two guys to sit down at a keyboard or across from one another at a coffee shop and have an earnest, reasoned debate about what women can do with their bodies.

> Seriously, guys, our fragile, fucked-up masculinity is going to do us all in.

After all, men are told all the time—in government representation, in media, in business, in sports, in movies, in books, in nearly every cultural mythology we pass down from one generation to the next—that their opinions and stories and weighty notions in every subject not only have merit but also must be heard, no matter the inherent harm it does for those listening to wonder whether the end of that debate will leave them wanting, lesser, unable in the land of the free to control their own bodies and destinies.

And, make no mistake, here's the rub: merely debating these rights causes harm.

If you don't think so, imagine yourself standing by as two strangers debate what *you* can do with *your* body—the horror show pain it must cause to wait, bootless, with your autonomy in the balance.

HOW DOES ONE whose worth is questioned every day argue her worth to the very people who deny it? And what sort of special asshole makes her?

We can't shake our fists at the outrageousness of all-male legislatures enacting laws against bodily autonomy but give a pass to Uncle Dave doing the same damn thing at the dinner table.

The fact is, we've become inured to the injury we cause because for centuries we've considered girls and women unequal and undeserving, their lives and standing forever up for discussion—in the legal systems we created and in the cultural norms we perpetuate.

We need to move beyond this point when bodily autonomy and worth and equality are notions up for debate.

But how?

THE GERM OF this idea was planted in a social media debate between two opposing forces: one group of men wanting to outlaw abortion and one group of men wanting to keep it available.

You've probably seen something like it. It starts with well-meaning science, perhaps bends toward religion, and ends with invective and social media blocking.

I remember witnessing, and partaking in, the discussion and coming to a realization: Am I participating in the same debates my forebears participated in hundreds of years ago, fifty years ago, yesterday, about which rights should be afforded "the weaker sex"?

And does merely participating in it eventually lead to the loss of human rights and bodily autonomy for women?

In other words, does a seemingly innocent argument among "good men" cause harm?

The answer is apparent. Men have inherited and maintain today collective permission to debate and declare who has rights; it's all perfectly acceptable—right, even.

But what are the results of these debates?

What happens next?

Here's the crux of it.

Should the group of men *against* abortion win this particular argument, more men are brought into the fold of believing that women should not have full control of their bodies.

Those men, now convinced, try to convince even *more* men of this, maybe yell at women outside health centers, write letters to their representatives, campaign for government officials who believe women should not control their own bodies, run for office themselves, and we wind up perpetually in the spot we are in now: groups of men deciding, through law, what women can and cannot do with their bodies.

But is it really any of their business?

Make no mistake: the other side of this argument is no less preposterous.

Should the group of men in *favor* of abortion rights win this argument, more men are brought into the fold of believing that women should have full control of their bodies.

Those men, now convinced, try to convince even *more* men of this, maybe support women outside health centers, write letters to their representatives, campaign for government officials who believe women should control their own bodies, run for office themselves, and we wind up perpetually in the spot we are in now: groups of men deciding, through law, what women can and cannot do with their bodies.

Although I happen to agree with this latter viewpoint, the question remains: Is it really any of *this* group's business either?

Nearly every argument I've seen against abortion deliberates the impacts on others—the men, the zygote, the baby, one's eternal soul, society—rather than the agency of the woman at the actual center of the debate.

And no wonder.

We still live in a patriarchal white supremacy in which it seems perfectly reasonable—nay, obligatory—for men to put a woman's health and well-being on the line in everyday social circles, and then for men in power to pass laws about it all.

Again, one paves the way for the other. We've been told since the beginning that it's all perfectly natural.

It's not.

We've merely thought we could because all along we always could.

SO, WHAT CAN WE DO?

Surely, groups opposed to abortion and female autonomy would rejoice if suddenly wide swaths of men disappeared from the debate.

We can't do that. Not now.

The sad realpolitik of the situation—though morally repugnant—is what it is: right now, as we speak, groups of male lawmakers are deciding on the rights of women, largely without any input from women, or sometimes even aided by women—elected Aunt Lydias who are no less complicit.

To confirm their "pro-life" stances, they've pushed legislation that would be the most regressive for women's health in a generation.

By proposing to cut funding for Planned Parenthood, they might make legal abortion less available, but they would also cut off necessary medical care for millions—from cancer screenings and birth control to maternity care and newborn care, a model of "pro-life" sentiments, to be sure.

And who largely suffers for it all.

You guessed it.

Women.

Overwhelmingly, women of color.

They are nearly always the last concern. Our collective village of children is growing up right now thinking we consider some of them lesser. To change this dynamic, we need a cultural shift in how men talk about abortion rights, about the reproductive health care our kids will require but may find absent by the time they need it.

WHILE I MAINTAIN that we one day need to reach a point when basic human rights are no longer subject to the whims and votes of some, when we no longer debate who has equal rights because even the mere consideration leaves those without them in a perpetual state of fear, when every "well, actually" typed on a screen or yelled over coffee no longer causes actual harm, we are simply not there yet.

But here's the thing: we'll never *get* there if we keep having the same arguments over and over, with no end in sight.

In short, men need to be actively, persistently, loudly engaged in the debate for full female autonomy. But we need to stop fighting a two-front battle on only one front; we need to stop accepting the initial framework of the discussion: that women's basic rights are even debatable in the first place.

It's an idea far, far too many of us think is our very birthright.

Men do it. Women do it. The idea of voting on who has rights is an American tradition, and we need to stop.

So, at least when it comes to us, men, dads, here's how we can be the best allies and advocates: by arguing two things at once every single time.

First, we need to assert that women alone should have control over their bodies, full stop. That's simply not debatable anymore, and if you're arguing against it, you're not just part of the problem, you're causing actual harm.

Second, to advance this cause, we also need to assert each time the sheer, mind-boggling absurdity of men arguing about what others can do with their bodies; we need to show base indignation at the idea of men's opinions carrying weight in this sphere. We need to teach this to our kids, intentionally, frequently.

IN SHORT, MEN need to be loud, vocal proponents of bodily integrity in the short term so that in the long term no one has to debate it anymore.

My daughter and I were talking about this on the way to school, and she raised the obvious dilemma: it'd be awesome if only women were allowed to discuss and debate and vote on these things. We came quickly to the same realization: Whether men or women, who is to say what medical care should be afforded to anyone?

Whose right is it to grant or deny bodily integrity?

We've all for far too long lived under the deluded notion that someone else, usually a man, can act in someone else's "best interest." But it's no less repugnant and horrifying and all-too-familiar a piece with the American tradition when a woman does it.

To be honest, I don't have the exact phrasing of the argument—one that offers unwavering support while also drawing to a close the idea that debating a woman's fundamental human rights is an acceptable everyday pastime, one that sticks up against outrageous attempts to deny basic humanity while constantly pointing out the absurdity that it's even a question.

In some instances, I've tried to be reasonable—offering full-throated support while drawing out my reasons for not engaging in an argument about whether women should have bodily autonomy—in ways far less wordy, I hope, than all of the above.

In other instances, I've laid out my case and then simply repeated: "Abortion on demand. No apologies. Fuck your beliefs."

Ultimately, no matter the exact phrasing, if we are ever going to reach that point of true, lasting equality, we need to wrestle with the competing idea that men are still largely in control of the legislative and cultural systems and feel entitled in everyday spheres of argument to bestow upon or deny rights to others—but that these realities won't change without vociferous defense of those without equal rights coupled with the acknowledgment of how preposterous and damaging it is for men to perpetually discuss who can have the same autonomy they enjoy.

Some days, this is all I got: "Abortion on demand. No apologies. Fuck your beliefs."

—Chapter 17—

DADDY'S GOT A GUN

*In seemingly innocuous and "funny" ways, boys and men perpetuate
broader societal notions that girls and women are property in need
of protecting, but you can help by no longer laughing it off.*

O ME A favor.

Put the book down.

Go on.

(My editor is probably having a heart attack right now. Bookmaking 101: Never tell people to stop reading the book.)

But put it down anyway and google this: Dads daughters dating rules.

Do an image search.

Unless my computer has been hacked by every Tim Allen TV-show-turned-T-shirt-maker, you'll likely see what I see: endless displays of T-shirts and posters and placards and prom photos threatening violence upon boys for having the audacity to date someone.

Someone who just happens to be your daughter.

Take a few steps back. What did you see overall? What's the overall image filling your brain?

Was it one T-shirt? One poster? One meme?

(Hopefully, you're back to the book by now . . .)

Because my bet is—like everything else we've covered in this book—it's not just one image or one T-shirt or one stupid prom shotgun-on-the-porch picture.

The idea of men "protecting" daughters through violence is everywhere. If you change one word in that Google search and type in: Dads Sons Dating Rules, you *still* get the same images about dating daughters, along with a few calling her a gold-digging stripper for good measure.

Guys, this is all incredibly horrible.

It's not funny.

It needs to stop.

Like, right now.

HOW MANY GUNS did you see?

Shovels?

How many T-shirts and cutesy, funny rules involved some real or perceived threat of violence?

"I'm going to do to you exactly what you do to her!"

Um, you're going to give your daughter's date a hickey in the backseat? *Awkward.*

Seriously, though, put yourself in the kids' shoes—the very shoes you once filled. You're going on a date. You're nervous. You're about to meet your date's parents. How sweaty are your palms? I remember being scared to death of meeting my future wife's parents, who ended up cooking us a nice chicken dinner and we talked for hours about politics. They are amazing.

Now think of your *own* son or daughter—filled with that same jingle-jangle of nerves, about to head out for a date or the prom or whatever.

Now think of some parent you don't really know threatening them.

With a gun.

Ha, ha, very funny, am I right?

SOME VERSION OF this violent bullshit creeps in at an early age. Practically the moment you tell someone you're having a baby daughter, some clown is going to say, "Watch out, daddy!"

Watch out for . . . *what?*

That your baby daughter will grow up and want to bag a dick or a clit every now and then?

Well, hate to burst your bubble, dude, but that's probably going to happen.

Whether you give your daughter a healthy appreciation for her own body, her desires, and her decision making is entirely up to you, however.

And what's the message boys are supposed to get from all this, anyway? "Talk to your date about consent"? "Communicate"? *Please.* The girl's desires or lack thereof aren't even part of the question. Dating under these dictates of aggression comes down to how much boys "can get away with" before dad arrives with a gun.

You're setting a horrible example.

Dropping these tired, unhealthy jokes, which turn daughters into objects—objects to be violated by a date and then protected with violence by men—is one way we can escape the effects.

Because here's the deal: People who actually study this shit? They say it's not so good. They say father-daughter relationships built around too much protectionism and "ownership" are actually *bad* for your kid and have real-world consequences. And you're only exacerbating a horrible part of rape culture that says boys can't really help it, that they need to be forcefully kept at bay with guns.

Come on, man.

> Dating under these dictates of aggression comes down to how much boys "can get away with" before dad arrives with a gun.

"I HAVE NEVER been a fan of the idea that the best way dads can protect their daughters is through physical force. It's always felt strange to me that a parent would want to threaten a potential partner. It also seemed to break the kind of bond of trust a parent builds up with their kids over the years," my buddy Mike Reynolds wrote in the *Huffington Post.*

That's from Mike's article "The Unrules to Dating My Daughters." You may have already read it. It was one of those posts that just blew up the internet, with thousands upon thousands of shares on social media.

Mike wrote to future dates of his daughter, "I trust that my partner and I raised our daughter to surround herself with good people. She's picked you as one of those people and your role is one of the most important pieces of her life puzzle. To me, that puts you in some pretty exceptional company."

That, to me, says it all.

As parents, we *do* want to protect our kids. It's our *job,* in fact. We set them on the right path and then hope for the best—hope that we've given them enough tools to deal with their independence.

So, do we protect our daughters by helping them find their own voice and letting them learn, with guidance along the way?

Or do we shunt them away to the convent of their room and barricade the door with a shotgun?

I talked to Mike about the responses he received after his article appeared.

"Every time I write about it, I get a healthy amount of positive feedback and also a lot of, 'That's how we do it around here (violent protectionism), and of course we're not serious,' kind of messages," he told me. "Both men and women have taken both sides."

Many, he says, have laughed it off as a joke kind of thing. You see this a lot when it comes up.

It's just a joke. Don't be so sensitive. Geez, people are too PC.

Deep down, Mike wonders whether the trope is a way for dads to connect in some way with their kids. He might be onto something, because society seems to have cut off many avenues for dads to connect—whether that means talking about changing bodies or discussing their own emotions.

"Many dads, when called on it," Mike continued, "will respond that, yeah, these kinds of jokes aren't funny. Too many people think that this is their best role for a dad to take up with their daughter. They don't think they can relate to shopping for bras or getting your period, so they try to fit themselves into a role. But a dad can help his daughter shop for bras and talk about her period. That's totally okay to do. Learn with them and experience life with them."

THE IDEA OF dads having one role as protector seems laughable to me, especially in an age of incredible demographic shifts. True, it was only a few decades—not centuries—ago when women couldn't buy property or have their own credit cards. Men could legally rape women until the 1990s if they were married to them. And to this day, sexual abuse survivors find themselves in prison for defending themselves against violent men, while boys who have been told all along that they are one absent father away from rape have gone on to do just that, and then have never gone to prison for it.

We're not in some made-for-1950s-TV version of America where dads are at work or on the commuter train, while mom is at home wearing pearls and vacuuming, ready to discuss periods and tampons as needed. Single dads, divorced dads, gay dads, widowed dads. Can you imagine if the only advice they offered to growing daughters came in the form of threats and guns?

"I looked up how to put in a tampon on YouTube," a divorced and remarried dad friend of mine told me over coffee. "What if she's at my house when she gets her period? I owe it to her not to freak out and panic and drop her off at Mom's house to deal. It's just not what dads do. It's just not real life."

No matter your opinion on the subject—whether you're for breaking out weapons to threaten boys or chatting it up about maxis and cramps or, I dunno, their hobbies and interests—psychologists say there's a right way and a wrong way to do it.

Science backs up the importance of dad-daughter relationships and how violence and threats of violence can do more harm than good. (Frankly, even a casual listener of Howard Stern gets a pretty good idea of the impact of "daddy issues.")

Jennifer Kromberg, a clinical psychologist from California, wrote in *Psychology Today* about the impact of father-daughter relationships and how we shape our kids in conscious and unconscious ways.

Kromberg cites a study that shows overprotective fathers actually turn out daughters with low self-esteem. And why not? The girls' thoughts, actions, very being, and body have always been protected under lock and key, or even under threat of violence—they've always been someone else's thing to protect.

> "I owe it to her not to freak out and panic and drop her off at Mom's house to deal. It's just not what dads do. It's just not real life."

THIS IS CRUCIAL. These stupid "jokes" about a dad defending his daughter's sexual purity don't exist in a vacuum—they exist in a society in which men have profound, everyday control over women's bodies.

This idea of girls and women being someone else's property is woven into our social fabric in ways that might seem "natural" on the face of it but that are, indeed, monumentally fucked up.

Consider this, dads. You've always been a Mr.

Since childhood, I'd wager, people have called you Mr. You put it on forms and business cards and probably don't for a second consider your relationship status when doing so.

But your daughter's name—her very identity—is linked to her relationship with men. She is called a Miss, Ms., or Mrs. depending on her marital status.

You might someday walk her down the aisle, "giving her away" to another man. She might change her name to fit his and take shit for it if she doesn't, or at the very least have to have a good explanation for it. You might see men you think are otherwise okay put their foot down for no other reason than "tradition" and demand the name change in a way they would think absurd if their future wives demanded it of them. Seriously, it's a big thing with some guys for no other reason than they really, really, really want to keep their name and identity and can't fathom that someone else might really, really, really want the same.

You might vote for male politicians who get together with other male politicians to decide what, exactly, she can do with her body. You might see guys on the sidewalk yelling at her, calling her a "slut," for seeking birth control from a health center. You might yourself engage in a debate with another man about what you think a woman can do with her body, about medical decisions she should be able to make with her own doctor.

You might, probably with good intentions, demand that girls or women deserve equal treatment, not because they are human beings and therefore deserving of it—but because they are . . . wait for it . . . "someone's daughter, wife, or mother."

Let me repeat that: someone's.

Would women deserve those things if they were not . . . *yours*?

You might be called "the man of the house," as a way to say you have ultimate authority over other adults. You might follow a faith that posits god "himself" has ordained it so.

You might attend a "purity ball" with her, forcing her to pledge her body to you until another man steps in and is blessed for male pleasure by the words of . . . wait for it . . . yet another man. (Ugh, please don't.)

You might see schools sending your daughter home for baring "too much skin," while your son can walk around freely in tank tops and shorts.

You might see books or movies or plays that erase her identity altogether and give her instead a title like "the zookeeper's wife" or "the pilot's wife." "The actor's wife."

You might see her considered a "prize" at the end of a movie, a trophy for the triumphant male hero. She might, indeed, one day be labeled a "trophy wife."

You might see her voice be labeled too shrill for public consumption, her face "too bitchy" for the subway, her age too old for work or other gigs, her body "too fat" for public viewing, her body too slim or muscular for attraction . . . as if all of this stuff is material.

You might see her abused, raped, beaten, threatened, or killed, and then blamed for it in a way that excuses a violent man's behavior.

What did she do? Why didn't she run? What was she wearing?

And that feels like the endgame. We live in a society in which men are by far the abusers, by far the rapers, by far the murderers, and we set the stage in language and mores to let them off the hook and blame their victims instead. How little time has passed in American history when men didn't even need an excuse at all. They could own women, beat them, rape them, kill them, lynch them, and face no penalties whatsoever because these weren't women—they were property.

> **It's the little things that add up to create a cultural system that oppresses girls and women. These little things are everywhere.**

These violent, disgusting "jokes" about men protecting their property didn't magically arise in the internet age. They're not new. They're the sordid fruit of generations not long removed that did more than brandish a gun for yucks. Although we might not actually pull the trigger anymore, the message remains the same: men consider girls and women property and threaten violence to "protect" them, as if it's a "dad's job."

And if some man is not around . . . well, boys pick up on the narrative too: *it's hunting season.* These tropes inform them that a girl's or a woman's agency is a laughing matter, the butt of a violent joke.

Like I said, it's the little things that add up to create a cultural system that oppresses girls and women. These little things are everywhere.

Now, TO BE fair, it's unclear whether these particular T-shirts and violent jokes themselves actually cause harm, Kromberg told me. There aren't really many studies of T-shirts and stupid internet memes. It's really more about the relationship between daughters and fathers and how these pieces of a horrible puzzle paint females as lesser. It's no stretch to imagine someone who considers pulling a gun on a child has an overprotective bent that can indeed be harmful.

"That's a hard one because the shape of the relationship is complex. I guess the short answer is: these alone can't make or break anything; I don't think any one thing can," Kromberg says. "The biggest thing to look at is the overall relational pattern over time—how he relates to her and all women (especially her mother), what overt and covert messages are communicated about how he feels and thinks about her, what his expectations are, what is acceptable in a relationship, what is not."

Don't for a second think your kids aren't savvy to the way you talk versus the way you walk, and the subtle and not-so-subtle ways patriarchy creeps in to keep her lesser—and the ways in which dads buy in to it.

My friend Jett really put it best, and I want to share her story here, because the idea of telling our daughters they're "strong and powerful" is just lip service when our actions undermine that idea.

"I was raised by a sexist father who told all his daughters that they could be and do anything they damn well pleased in a time when things like that weren't readily said by most dads. He made me believe it, made me never ashamed to be a girl," she said. "His behaviors toward my mother and other partners (and the occasional remark I heard waft in from the poker table) confused and angered me. So, be consistent in word and deed is my number one. And if you're not, own it immediately and vow to keep working at doing better."

THIS OBVIOUSLY APPLIES to how men raise boys as well.

If girls are told they are awesome and powerful, and then shown in words and deed that they are, in fact, hothouse flowers that require interminable, violent protection, boys are told that they are wild hellions a mere father's threat away from . . . what? Rape? Violence? When a man pulls the proverbial gun on a boy, he's not just sending a shitty message to his daughter, he's perpetuating the idea that boys can't control themselves, that they have only one violent, emotionless, sex-crazed role to fill—the same role they hear about in misogynist music and online porn, and see played out by your run-of-the-mill movie action hero.

When girls are sent home from school for showing shoulders, or are considered "trophies," or are questioned about why they were abused by men, what message is sent to boys other than one that continues generations of ownership?

None of this matches up with the sweet, loving, vulnerable boys we once were—the boys who had sweaty palms and nervous first kisses. It doesn't match up with the sweet, loving, vulnerable boys we know in real life. But for some reason we decide to laugh this stuff off all too often, think it's just a small thing instead of a broad stroke in a larger painting.

Here's my friend Kerry on how dads can do better in this regard: "It's not about being an ally to women but to change the rules that men are raised under. Men in all cultures are born into the world with such strict rules about everything they are supposed to do—don't cry, don't need hugs, love sports, do certain types of work, be the breadwinner, be tough, be strong and on and on. We got all excited about raising strong feminist girls but we forgot to bring men along on the ride."

SO, WHAT CAN WE DO?

As Kromberg says, modeling.

It's a big deal.

Your sons and daughters are going to be looking to you for lessons on how to treat men and women. If you say one thing—"girls are independent and awesome"—but then pack heat on the porch and threaten all their potential suitors, what lesson is going to take hold? Perhaps you've built a relationship with your daughter in which you both understand it's a joke. Great? But, remember, you're not the only one she's hearing these things from—think of just how many stupid T-shirts and posters you saw, how many movies reinforce the notion of a girl or woman in need of protection, what becomes of her very name in our society depending on her relationship with men.

It adds up.

"From my perspective, the role of a father plays a significant role in the development in the child's self-esteem," Kromberg says. "I believe early attachment patterns with all caregivers set a template early on for how the child learns to form later relationships. Because the father is (usually) the primary male caregiver, I believe a girl's interaction and attachment with her father shape the lens through which she will learn to view opposite-sex relationships."

Lee Reyes-Fournier, a friend of mine who has a doctorate in psychology and who has been a professional therapist for nearly three decades, says the role dads play is paramount, in word and deed, but that it is indeed a struggle, given society's expectations of men.

"Fathers are a child's first model of what a man is. A dad needs to model a willingness to listen, learn, and change," she says. "For some really weird reason, changing one's mind has become synonymous with weakness; as if there are cracks in the facade of manliness. Men who are vulnerable and open show their daughters and sons what true strength is. I think the coolest thing a dad can do is to change their mind and be open to other possibilities. In the discussion of gender, racism, and sex, a man can show that opinions can change and men will listen and support what is best for both daughters and sons."

A WEALTH OF research and study exists around dad's presence in his daughter's life—how he can affect self-esteem and risk-taking with drugs and sex, how he is seen as "perfect" because his absence (traditionally because of work) allows kids to build up a more idealized image of him and place his opinions higher than others' (yeah, that's a thing), and how, ultimately, his actions speak louder than words.

But it should be noted here that I'm talking about what I know: father-daughter relationships, simply because that's what I'm in the midst of.

I can't stress enough the idea that, yes, dads are important, but that doesn't mean others are not. Far too often the "family values" crowd puts forward the idea that dads are key . . . and others therefore are not. I ain't having it. Lesbian moms, single moms (thanks, Mom!), divorced moms, widowed moms—you name it—play an equal and yet different role in modeling good behavior and respect, and I am sick to death of politicians and other ass clowns bemoaning the idea of "absent fathers."

As a dad, I hope to speak to other dads about ways we can do better, not that other roles in our children's lives matter less.

If there was really one big important way for men, us dads, to change the world for the better through our daily actions, it's this: stop buying in to the notion of hegemonic heterosexual homosocial masculinity. Big phrase,

I know, but it boils down to this: stop being assholes to people we think are lesser or weak for the sake of a few yucks from our fellow guy friends. I've done it for sure. I carry tremendous shame to this day every time I recall slapping a boy's calf very hard for a few laughs in seventh-grade PE. In fact, if I were being honest, I'd argue that incident of buying in to performative masculine hegemony, fitting in and "being a man" through acts of violence on fellow boys, profoundly informs my worldview today that we desperately need to free our boys from a one-size-fits-all violent masculinity.

I frequently hear arguments about what it means to be a "real man," and I'd urge you to consider that masculinity exists on a spectrum and there's no "right" way to perform it. A real man, in other words, just doesn't really give a fuck and is completely over propping up violent cultural mores for a few yucks from friends . . . or for fear of violent retribution.

In the end, if the goal is to send forth into the world kids who feel good about themselves and who can participate in the world independently and positively, how we show them to behave and have healthy relationships may go further than any stupid T-shirt. But nodding and winking to a culture that constantly says girls are property that needs aggressive masculine protection has to stop.

"I believe many men laugh at these images because they think they are expected to," Reynolds says. "But they don't have to."

—Chapter 18—

HAVING "THE TALK"

For many parents, the talk about "the birds and the bees" is a one-time event, but it should be an ongoing conversation—that starts early.

I'LL ALWAYS REMEMBER the first time I had to give "The Talk," or explain "the birds and the bees," or whatever euphemism is popular nowadays. My wife—then girlfriend—and I decided to take my brother's young children to our local university's Picnic Day. Because UC Davis is an agricultural school, Picnic Day offers not just leisurely strolls and bag lunches but also some pretty heavy-duty animal fucking, all before a live studio audience.

Of course, we didn't realize this at the time.

We saw a bunch of horses, an arena, and a crowd, and thought, "Why not? Kids love horses, right? This is going to be great!"

So, we grabbed some seats in the bleachers and were soon treated to a young veterinarian-in-training jerking off a stallion into an enormous fake horse vagina sleeve, capturing the semen, and then using her entire arm to insert said semen into a mare. (It's cleaner that way, and more likely to work, apparently.)

Dana and I were all at once enthralled and anxious, wondering whether our young charges had any idea exactly what was going on. At first, it seemed as if we could say the stallion and mare were merely wrestling, with the humans acting as very attentive referees.

"Oh, look! They're playing! How cute. Okay, so let's go check out the duck exhibit."

No chance.

After a few minutes of "wrestling," the young vets intervened with big rubber sleeves, some lube, an enormous wooden wall to separate the horses and quickly got to work to finish the job manually.

"So . . ." one of the kids began, "what are they . . . doing? Exactly?"

We tried not to laugh.

Honestly, we were young—early twenties—and wholly unprepared. But we knew the gravity of the situation, so Dana and I kept it as scientific as possible. Making babies. Getting help from the doctors. Wait a few months and, *voilà,* a foal. Or something like that.

I had the fun task of calling my older brother later and saying something akin to, "We had a great time. They ate dinner. They also might have some questions about sex. Anyway, have a good night!"

click

As awkward as the moment was, it was an experience I would call on later with my own daughter. I kid you not, if you're feeling nervy about The Talk, the easiest way to broach the subject is a trip to the farm.

And, believe me, it's incredibly important to have The Talk—not just once, but a lot.

Because here's the deal: movies, magazines, clothes, the internet, video games, schoolmates, random adults, overheard conversations—they're all going to get together and teach your child about sex whether you like it or not.

Researchers have found that just as kids and teens emulate the smoking and drinking they see on TV or in movies, they can try to emulate the sex as well—even if they're not fully prepared or aware of any consequences.

A study published in *Psychological Science* surveyed nearly seven hundred top-grossing movies over a half century. The survey found that 84 percent of the films contained sexual content, including 68 percent of G-rated films and 82 percent of PG.

The study tracked more than twelve hundred kids ages twelve to fourteen through adolescence and found that the kids who watched more movies with sexual content had more sex earlier.

"Adolescents who are exposed to more sexual content in movies start having sex at younger ages, have more sexual partners, and are less likely to use condoms with casual sexual partners," said study author Ross O'Hara from Dartmouth College.

And that's just movies—not texts, internet images, magazine ads, secondhand information in the playground pipeline, random shit shouted on the sidewalk to young girls by pedophiliac men, conditioning by other girls or women who have bought in to it all.

Who do you want kids to get real, solid, healthy, useful information from?

You?

Or some Instagram celebrity, movie, porn site, or friends educated by all of the above?

"Kids suck all that up," says Laurie Berdahl, an ob-gyn who, together with her husband, Brian Johnson, a clinical psychologist, wrote *Warning Signs: How to Protect Your Kids from Becoming Victims or Perpetrators of Violence,* a book about rape culture in America. "They are learning how to behave by what they see."

Even seemingly innocuous things can have a big impact.

Let me give you an example. Lord, this is embarrassing. But also, hopefully, illuminating.

At a very young age, probably eight or so, I asked an older neighbor boy what, exactly, you call a woman's sex organs.

"It's called a bagina," he said.

Either he said it wrong or I misheard, but I spent far too long thinking that was the proper name and thought it was a travesty that dictionaries, encyclopedias, and entire *libraries* kept more detailed information from curious kids. No matter where I looked, I could find no information about the illicit "bagina."

I offer this only to explain that kids are, indeed, curious, especially about subjects adults might be queasy about—ooh, hidden knowledge!—but also to illustrate how easy it is for kids to be misinformed in profound ways, thanks to society, whether by stupid movies or neighborhood friends. In the end, I had a good laugh over a misspelled word, but what if I needed real, important information? About personal reproductive health or birth control?

Like a lot of kids, I'm not sure I would have felt confident going to my parents for real information and instead relied on a friend pool that was also educated on half-heard, random bits of complete and utter nonsense.

Not much has changed, I wager, considering how many adults still snicker and giggle about what should be seen as simple topics and just how many state and federal programs and churches want to teach "abstinence only" crap that, in the end, increases the risks involved with sex.

Like I said, someone is going to teach your kids about all this stuff. And, my god, if they don't consider you an open source for real information, they're going to learn some shit.

AS A GYNECOLOGIST, Berdahl began to notice more and more girls coming at younger and younger ages asking less about how their bodies function and more about how they look.

"They'd say, 'How sexy am I going to be?'" she said. "I blame it all on sexualization—girls are learning basically their value is entirely due to their sexual appearance and behavior, that they are not a whole person, but objects. It's a real sad phenomenon."

Peggy Orenstein, author of the hit book *Girls and Sex* (as well as *Cinderella Ate My Daughter,* an examination of princess culture), found something similar in her interviews with girls and women. Girls think of themselves essentially as pleasure vessels for boys, not their own desires, she discovered.

She noticed that kids weren't having sex—intercourse—at younger ages, or even more sex than earlier generations. No, the sexual landscape had changed in different ways. They were having different forms of sex—oral sex—earlier and more often, and very little of it was reciprocal. For girls, oral sex was almost like a way out of having intercourse rather than a pleasurable sexual experience between loving partners.

> "Girls are learning basically their value is entirely due to their sexual appearance and behavior, that they are not a whole person, but objects."

"It is considered to be less intimate than intercourse, and something that girls say repeatedly to me would be, 'It's no big deal,'" Orenstein told NPR.

BEYOND THE ACTUAL sexual acts and changing mores about sex, Orenstein explored the way sex education is different among the genders, whether in books or in classes at school, something I experienced recently with an elementary-school-age daughter. The boy's anatomy is detailed and orgasms are front and center—semen comes out of the penis and, soon, babies. Yay!

For girls, a sort of vague space "down there" was discussed with toddlers, and then later, all the internal anatomy and physiology was labeled and discussed—ovaries, uterus, menstruation, babies, unwanted pregnancies. But no clitoris, no labia, no attention paid to orgasms or pleasure.

Interestingly, I had just read Orenstein's book before I attended a "preview night" of sex ed at my daughter's school, so the idea of girls being "left behind" in the pleasure department was swirling in my mind. At the session, all the parents gathered around a poster sheet and were asked to draw in all the changes we went through during puberty.

Sure enough, the boys' drawing suddenly grew a bigger penis and dropped testicles—there was even a drawing of "nightly emissions"—while the girls' drawing had all the internal "bull's head" workings that had come up in Orenstein's studies: ovaries, uterus, eggs. But no clitoris.

It was really shocking to see the premise of her book play out before me. These lessons have been internalized for generations: sex is still very much about men's pleasure, not women's.

WE SEE IT in any internet porn, where the scenes usually end with a male orgasm—usually sprayed on a woman in some way. We see it in the very names given to the act of sex and the sex organs. Germaine Greer, in 1970, wrote in *The Female Eunuch,* "All the vulgar linguistic emphasis is placed on the poking elements: fucking, screwing, rooting, shagging are all acts performed upon the passive female; the names for the penis all tool names."

That hasn't changed in the past fifty years. In fact, any perusal of internet porn sites—the sites curious young boys and girls go to for illicit instruction in the things otherwise intelligent adults are afraid to tell them—shows it's gotten worse. It's no longer implied violence, but actual violence.

I immediately think, Okay, if two consenting adults want to get together and clearly communicate what's consensual and pleasurable for them, great! No, seriously, great. Communicating should be just as much a part of sex as the acts themselves, and finding someone to engage in loving, pleasurable, consensual sex should be an aim our kids strive for. (Thankfully, my daughter's sex ed teachers hit a home run with this part as well as with consent.)

But we'd be kidding ourselves if we think these lessons are being passed on to young internet porn consumers, who are learning, much as Greer noted half a century ago and Orenstein tells us today, that the through-thread for generations is that girls and women are passive pleasure vessels for men—not a shocking revelation in a country founded on sexual slavery and where it continues to this day.

Consider, for a moment, the "incel" community, which gained notoriety after a man who called himself "involuntarily celibate" ran his van into crowds of people in Toronto in 2018. Like mass shooters before him, he thought he "deserved" sex with women and took his anger out on them because he was a "good guy" who couldn't attract a mate. The killings brought to light the incel community, an online bastion of . . . I truly don't have the right words to describe it, because *horrible* is not bad enough . . . men who want to have a literal, state-sponsored system of sexual enslavement of women for male pleasure.

> **We hold women in such low esteem, and male pleasure in such high esteem, that it's reasonably acceptable to discuss sexual enslavement in public, in newspapers, as if it's worthy of consideration.**

It may seem crazy and disgusting, but it's also easily accessible online. Hell, not long afterward, the *New York Times* wrote an article about a man, a so-called intellectual, who intimated in some weird way that the "incels" might be onto something.

Check the narrative on that for a second: we hold women in such low esteem, and male pleasure in such high esteem, that it's reasonably acceptable to discuss sexual enslavement in public, in newspapers, as if it's worthy of consideration. The idea that this is all an intellectual discussion worth having cannot be unlinked from other debates we think are socially acceptable, such as voting on the health-care choices of women.

Women are forever on the bargaining table.

We do this from the beginning.

We teach boys to be little "gentlemen" and fill their heads with notions of "scoring" and "screwing," but with precious little discussion of consent or female pleasure. It shouldn't be a surprise that we also enroll our girls in self-defense classes to fight them off.

And it's all just sort of a "normal" thing we do.

IT'S BEEN THIS fucked for ages. We're merely passing it on.

I recall that John Stuart Mill, who wrote *The Subjection of Women* in 1869, argued that society does its best to keep its unequal structures out of view from children. But they learn. They learn quickly. They see the dots we hide and connect them.

"Such people are little aware, when a boy is differently brought up, how early the notion of his inherent superiority to a girl arises in his mind; how it grows with his growth and strengthens with his strength; how it is inoculated by one school boy upon another; how early the youth thinks himself superior to his mother, owing her perhaps forbearance, but no real respect; and how sublime and sultan-like a sense of superiority he feels, above all, the woman whom he honors by admitting her to a partnership of his life."

Just ponder, for a moment, how many men and women in your life—either through "traditionalism" or religious edict—consider the man the "king of the house," the ruler, the one to be followed by helpmeets.

If this is the culture we raise our children in, where men are the perceived "rulers," it shouldn't be surprising to suggest that the subjugation in the bedroom follows them into the boardroom.

John Stuart Mill may seem like an ancient, and Germaine Greer wrote her piece fifty years ago now. But it's not as if this cultural subjugation vanished in the meantime.

It was still legal for married men to rape their wives in 1992. Men raising children now, like me, like you perhaps, grew up with so-called reasoned debates about this as the undertone of their own formative years.

Can men legally rape women? Hmm, let's discuss! We go now to our panel of experts . . .

Well, surely, things have changed since the 1990s, right?

Just last year, in 2018, Delaware became the first state to ban child marriage with no exceptions. Given that some 90 percent of these so-called marriages involved adult men and girls under eighteen, I'm going to go ahead and say this is child molestation with a stamp of government approval—because, again, male pleasure takes precedence over female rights.

What I'm saying is that, in the end, there's no avoiding it. Sex infuses our culture, and the paradigm perpetuated for generations—from schoolboy to schoolboy and now from iPhone to iPhone—is that sex is usually for male pleasure, or at the least indulges the male gaze if not his out-and-out power.

Simply by walking the grocery store aisles where they can pick up sex tips to please your man, watching the World Series amid erection pill commercials, and listening to stories about the "bagina" on the schoolyard, kids are exposed to what seems like an interminable barrage of sex messages with this construct at the fore.

And adults are generally itchy about having The Talk to help them filter out the BS. We're inundated with sexual messages from every angle, and yet impossibly ashamed about it at the same time.

Come on, dudes. Recognize it. Get over it. Talk about it. You got this.

Like I said, someone is going to teach our kids about this stuff. Who's it going to be?

SO, WHAT CAN WE DO?

"What we can do is talk to kids about those images and try to challenge the exaggerated notions of sex they see every day," says Common Sense Media, an organization that rates and tracks the age appropriateness of children's media. "We can help our kids develop a normal, healthy perspective about sex."

Common Sense Media recommends not letting elementary-school-age kids watch media containing sexual messages—which, let's face it, is difficult given that the vast majority of G- and PG-rated movies include sexual situations. Still, it's a good goal. It also recommends setting filters on internet searches.

As kids grow older, Common Sense advises parents to find teachable moments to discuss sex and media and not to be afraid to "share your values" in discussing sex.

I can relate. As my daughter has grown, we've had what probably amounts to an ongoing, unending The Talk. At first, it was pretty simple stuff. How are babies made? This came up a lot after trips to the farm where she rides horses. One day, there's a mare, and the next, a foal beside her. It's going to come up.

In fact, I remember a fellow parent asking how we had segued into the conversation, and I fully endorsed the idea of heading to a farm if possible. The conversation just seems to pop up there. By the time my daughter hit eleven, we were having detailed discussions about artificial insemination, including a whole-family online scavenger hunt to find frozen sperm samples from a famous show horse. Fun times, I know. But probably not inconsistent with the early American farm experience.

And if you can't find a farm but are still looking for a good "in" to having The Talk, one that seems less forced and more natural, flip on just about any sports program. Within minutes a Viagra commercial will air, and you'll have a good starting point. (How many commercials have you seen during a ballgame about female pleasure, by the way?)

"It's not 'the talk,' it's a series of small talks over a long period of time," Buzz Bishop told me. He's a father of two boys and the author of the Dad Camp website.

He's a big proponent of talking it out—everything—from early ages using appropriate language as the kids grow.

"I'm not shy about talking to my kids about heavy issues. I use age-appropriate language and scenarios to lay the foundation for a greater understanding," he writes. "All of the conversations leading them down a path of acceptance, consent, respect, and empathy."

When it comes to sex and consent and how to interact with partners, he puts it all out there.

"'The Talk' is not one big event you have with your children and then you're done with it. It's small conversations solving minor issues every day that teaches your kids how to treat each other," he says.

IT'S NOT ALWAYS easy, obviously. There are just as many tricky subjects and conversations as there are people to have them. Still, my fellow dads and family health experts agree that the best advice is more talk—even if it's awkward at first.

"I'm a weird mix of liberal and conservative handling of sex and culture," says my friend Tshaka Armstrong, dad to sons and a daughter as well as a tech writer and founder of a nonprofit dedicated to teaching digital-age skills to kids. "We've definitely talked about sex in the context of marriage, but been honest with them about not making it to marriage. We've always talked to all of them about what I believe is the most important thing and that is personal responsibility and consequences. If you have sex, there's always the potential someone can get pregnant and being young, that will slow you from achieving your dreams."

He's tried to talk about how the media images his kids see on TV or on-line don't always match up with reality—something he thinks kids need to learn early.

"I've made it a point to talk to them about media and how the purpose of media is to grab attention and so boundaries are often pushed to do so," he says. "What you see on TV or on Facebook or Instagram doesn't work in real life."

It goes to having lots of talks—some big, some small—to pass on your values and ideals as opposed to clamming up out of shyness and embarrass-ment and letting the rest of society do it for you.

"We have continued to talk about these things from the time our kids could talk," says dad Mike Reynolds, a proud "feminist father."

"We talk about consent by using examples like them saying no to bed-time kisses or wanting to hug relatives when they leave our house, etcet-era," he told me. "We have talked about menstruation because my partner menstruates and there's nothing to hide about it. We use proper terminology for body parts. My kids know a fetus grows in a uterus, that many female-identified bodies have a uterus. That families have many different makeups etcetera."

I'd offer that for early-age kids, start young by simply naming the parts correctly. The penis. The vulva. Breasts. All of it. Take the squeamishness out of it early, because (1) that's what they're called, and (2) it's probably a good idea for kids to know what to call their parts because they'll have to visit doctors someday soon and explain what's hurting or they'll have to have an intimate talk with their sex partner about what feels good and what doesn't, what's okay and what's not.

Human sexuality professor Emily Nagoski, author of *Come as You Are*, says it best. No one points at his forehead and calls it his throat, or his ear and calls it his eye. Ludicrous, right? But how often do we hear "down there" for women referring to a vagina? Rather than naming the specific parts, it's all sort of an amorphous canal. (I'm guilty of this, too, much the same way I catch myself saying, "Hey, guys!" to a mixed group and centering heterosex-ual sex in this discussion.)

So, pick your spots. You don't have to make every day a Sex Talk 101 course, but you can weave into your everyday language the idea that bod-ies are natural things everyone has, and that sex is a natural, loving event adults partake in with good, constant communication. (Also, read Nagoski's book. Like, right now. I guarantee you'll be amazed at the cultural mythologies we've built around hymens versus the reality of them, and you'll probably also come away a more passionate, considerate lover yourself. Winning!)

LISTEN, GUYS. HARD truth here.

We need to talk about consent more, about telling our boys it's not okay to harass a girl—or vice versa—until she "gives in."

We need to tell our kids it's their responsibility to accept no for an answer—not because we're "good guys" but because we're decent fucking human beings.

We perpetuate a host of problems—not just around sex but also around abuse and violence and sexual assault—when we buy in to and pass on these notions that boys and men just have to "try harder."

Or that sexual assault is excusable if the perpetrators are young, teens too innocent to be held accountable—something we all remember hearing in 2018 during the confirmation process for Supreme Court nominee Brett Kavanaugh. That notion is really no different from your friends and relatives excusing away the president grabbing women "by the pussy" because there are other, more important things to consider. In these horrible arguments, I hear far too often that those men were shaped by a "different culture," a different time when that type of thing was acceptable—glorified in romantic teen movies, even.

But get this. And let's pay attention and be aware of it. Those older men were indeed raised in a different time, when sexual assault served as a socially acceptable punchline. But make no mistake, our children are being raised in a moment when sexual assault is excused away for political convenience or accepted as "just boys being boys."

This is the horrifying, dangerous culture our children are being raised in, and it is incumbent on us to do our part to weave the ideas of consent and communication into our personal interactions with our children and fellow parents.

Our kids are going to hear endless messages that boys just need to "try harder" from uncountable songs, movies, politicians, friends, the internet— you name it. It's not disconnected from the broader whole, from the stories we pick up everywhere: women exist for our pleasure. We need to be more aware of these tropes and talk with our boys about them. I'm just as complicit. You don't grow up in the white supremacist patriarchy without the atomized pieces of it landing on you.

And we, all of us, need to model good behavior and make sure our guy buds are doing the same.

Bottom line: the boys in our lives, the men, they should feel just as uncomfortable laughing about rape or other violence against women around *us* as they might be around girls and women, and if they're not, that's on us; we need to take a hard look inward at why we think that's okay.

Truly, we need to call ourselves on that the moment we hear it, because it's not okay. It's not funny. It's part of an endless, horrible, historical narrative that reminds us ceaselessly that girls and women are somehow possessions, subject to violence and control.

It's a lot to take in, all of it. Sex is, to be sure, hard to talk about. It's exalted and glorified in every facet of society, and yet almost unspeakable for some reason. Weird, right?

I LEAVE YOU with a reminder of grace. My good friend Graham, also a stay-at-home dad, says it best. He struggles with exact wording and phrasing and all of it—you'll not always have the correct thing to say either, and that's okay—but mostly he strives to be the go-to resource, the safe harbor where factual information can be had with no judgment. In a world where the sex messages and power constructs seem almost beyond repair, this is a great goal that could do great good for the future. Keep the lines open. Like I said, you got this.

YOU'RE ON THE RIGHT PATH. KEEP GOING.

There are many, many great resources to help guide you on your journey as you try to raise empowered children, and I want to leave you with some that have inspired me. As they say, the internet is free.

WE OWE OUR children—our daughters *and* our sons—freedom. We owe them freedom from the limitations we grew up with, and from the narratives we perpetuate, and from the expectations that surround them—that surround us all.

We owe them the gift of seeing these atmospheric droplets of everyday bias, first off, and then disrupting them, together. We owe them the freedom to decide their fates, their happiness, their futures, without something as absurd as cultural notions or fear of ridicule or violence coming together to guide their lives like so many invisible hands, pushing them this way or that.

That's the thing we share, no matter our religious creed, our political bent, our gender, sex, sexual orientation, or abilities—that we want, all of us, the best for our children, the freedom to make of their lives what they will.

A fair shot in a fair game.

In a nutshell, that's this book, and I hope it has, in at least one way—that would be enough—helped you discover the forces we consider "normal" but that are otherwise endangering the dignity of our children.

We owe our children— our daughters *and* our sons— freedom.

Quick story. In the first chapter, we discussed clothes and colors and how we have a socially acceptable notion today to dress boys in roomy blue clothes emblazoned with wild, violent predators and to dress girls in pink tight-fitting clothes bearing appearance-laden, flowery messages.

And it's all so normal and everyday and just how it all . . . is. It's simply what the people . . . want.

But clothes change. Styles change. Think of what you yourself wore growing up, perhaps in the 1970s or 1980s or 1990s. Does it much resemble what you think is "cool" today? What you're wearing right now?

Do me a favor. Pick up your phone. Go to your computer.

Google "FDR baby."

What do you see?

An image of what you might at first glance consider "a girl on a horse" perhaps? A curly-haired girl posing for a photo in a pretty white dress and a big flowery hat?

That's our thirty-second president, Franklin Roosevelt.

You can do the same for Hemingway and all manner of rich white boys who were raised in that era. (Whether it had some impact on Hemingway's absurd toxic masculinity and suicide later, who knows.) But he, they, weren't alone. It was merely the style at the time, for myriad reasons. A little later, as people began to wear mass-produced clothing, pink was considered the "boy" color and blue used to be a "girl" color.

How many friends or online commenters have you heard recently being "outraged" that a boy would wear a dress for playtime or—*gasp!*—wear pink?

It seems absurd when you know the history, doesn't it? The evolution and change of styles?

It makes you wonder what the arguments will be in three more generations on whatever incarnation social media takes: "Boys wear green and girls wear bananas and that's just the way it is!"

This is all I'm asking: for you to see the quiet, seemingly disconnected storylines at work around you, today, right now. See how our collective stories are told and who they are normalizing and who they are "othering."

Times change, and our customs, our mores, our traditions, no matter which generation you find yourself in, seem on their face "natural" and "normal" simply because they form the shared reality we are experiencing at the moment. They may be normalized. But that doesn't mean they are always just.

Like I said earlier, if we know our history of endless subjugation, we can't also believe we somehow magically lucked into the one generation without it.

We'll always be in transition, in evolution. Things we think are perfectly normal and socially acceptable today will be looked upon as no less absurd than we right now view past inequities. Readers twenty-five years hence might think it absurd we ever denied the dignity of our trans sisters and brothers, although debates about their rights and freedom are horrifyingly commonplace today, the same as were debates about Native American genocide, slavery, women's suffrage, civil rights, equal rights, gay rights only a few years ago or women's bodily integrity is today.

> If we know our history of endless subjugation, we can't also believe we somehow magically lucked into the one generation without it.

"When you are in the middle of a story it isn't a story at all, but only a confusion; a dark roaring, a blindness, a wreckage of shattered glass and splintered wood; like a house in a whirlwind, or else a boat crushed by the icebergs or swept over the rapids, and all aboard powerless to stop it," Margaret Atwood tells us in *Alias Grace*. "It's only afterwards that it becomes anything like a story at all."

I offer the brief discussion about clothes and style because it's so easy to see the outcome of the evolution, not the evolution itself—the freakish cave thing with less hair and a bigger head that nevertheless changes everything afterward.

Our children are struggling through these evolving narratives today that are all at once different and achingly similar to the ones we grew up with.

Let's help them see.

Let's give our boys the freedom to reach their full emotional potential, to express themselves in ways that friends and family may disapprove of but that will ultimately give them the dignity of finding their whole selves.

Let's give our girls the freedom to break the strings that for far too long and in far too many ways have lashed them to certain roles, robbing them of the ability to reach their full potential—but also to allow them the same sense of peace and dignity and autonomy that we, men, have enjoyed by ourselves for so long.

I think of Susan Faludi again, writing in the 1990s about the backlash to gains women made following the second wave of feminism—and now here we are again, nearly forty years later, with things having improved a bit, but the arguments still all too familiar, as if we never fully realize that we're always in the transition. I'm not so sure we'll ever stop being merely in perpetual transition, until we see and excise the expectations that would have us collectively weigh dignity as if it's acceptable to toss it on the scales, as if it's okay to label some humans as undeserving.

Feminism's agenda asks not to make women choose between public justice and private happiness, Faludi writes. "It asks that women be free to define themselves instead of having their identity defined for them time and again by their culture and their men. The fact that these are still such incendiary notions should tell us that American women have a way to go before they enter the promised land of equality."

When will that statement stop ringing true, and what will you do to help all our children reach the promised land?

WE LIVE IN incredible times, when the entire library of human knowledge is available at our fingertips.

For those interested in continuing on this journey, I list below the resources that have shaped my views and, I argue, made me a better human.

I hope you enjoy them, too.

Podcasts

Despite being very slow to adopt this medium, I am finding now that I like podcasts the best, probably because I can do all my household cleaning with a good show ringing in my ears. And, oh boy. Are there some really quality shows. I tend more toward the well-researched ones rather than just a couple people yammering on and telling jokes. These are some of my favorites.

Code Switch. Less about parenting and more about how our society talks about race and gender.

Feminist Frequency Radio. Anita Sarkeesian, Ebony Adams, and Carolyn Petit break down the tropes behind our latest pop culture influences.

The Guilty Feminist. You will laugh, you will cry, you will cheer, you will stare down the hypocrisies we all face, and you'll call yourself a proud feminist at the end of it all. Debra Francis White needs a Nobel in podcasting, stat.

The Modern Dads Podcast. My buddies Matt and Lance (and Josh) started this, and I'm partial because they have me on every now and then. It's a fun, well-done podcast that looks at the shifting roles and expectations of the modern dad. Love it.

New Books on Gender Studies. More professorial than funny, it explores hot-topic books of the day with simple, in-depth interviews with experts. Always informative.

Pod Save the People. Brittany Packnett is the best part of the week.

Rad Parenting. Fun, witty, told from the point of view of experts who are also parents. It's sort of like listening to good friends who happen to know a shit ton of good stuff about raising kids today.

Slate's Represent. An excellent take on pop culture and how gender and race intertwine in many discussions.

Stuff Mom Never Told You. If this book you're holding has a big failing, it's that it fails to accomplish what this podcast does week in and week out: tackle a subject with humor and history and research-backed analysis. It is truly an entertaining podcast, an informative show, and a public service.

Anything by **Vox media,** which does an amazing job of breaking down the latest research into easily digestible bites.

Books

I read a lot. A ton. Often, I do it in my comfy chair in the living room. But, as with podcasts, I'm finding more value in audiobooks because I can do things around the house and still get some quality, fun information. These books helped inform this book in some way and provided resources for our family to deal with difficult subjects while raising a daughter.

All the Single Ladies by Rebecca Traister. An examination of single women in America and the amazing social changes that have sprung from shifting demographics.

The Blessing of a Skinned Knee and its follow-up for older kids, *The Blessing of a B Minus* by Wendy Mogel. They've basically become our family bibles for lightening the fuck up in an age of high expectations. I think these are a must for parents.

Cinderella Ate My Daughter and *Girls and Sex* by Peggy Orenstein. One is an examination of princess culture, and the other is how we are teaching some pretty antiquated sex education lessons when the actual landscape of kids and sex has shifted dramatically in a short amount of time, and keeps shifting thanks to lessons in porn from the internet. Both well worth it.

Come as You Are by Emily Nagoski. Come for the wild myths about the hymen, stay for the science-backed research on female pleasure, consent, and, of course, the gas pedal and the brake pedal. Trust me, dudes. You want to know all this. Share it with the kids.

Everyday Sexism by Laura Bates. If you buy no other books when you decide to have children, buy this one. It should be required reading for every man alive.

The Parents' Phrase Book by Whit Honea. I just find myself thumbing through it for advice to tackle tricky conversations, from sex to death to friend problems.

Queen Bees and Wannabes by Rosalind Wiseman. There's a reason I quote her a lot in this book. This one is a great look at girl friendships and what parents can do to help foster good ones.

Online

Bitch Media. Essential pop culture website for feminist ideas.

Black Girl Dangerous. Its mission is to amplify the voices of queer and trans people of color.

Feminist Frequency. In videos, podcasts, and stories, host Anita Sarkeesian, along with Ebony Adams and Carolyn Petit, recounts the seemingly endless ways the tech industry, and specifically the video game industry, is profoundly misogynistic—just profoundly and absurdly and dangerously misogynistic.

Jezebel.com. I confess. I'm biased. I used to write a regular column for this pop culture feminist site and still follow it for great breaking news coverage of issues relating to serious antiwoman bullshit.

The Representation Project. Makes films and continually highlights the ways cultural stereotypes seek to keep boys and girls in archaic roles.

Seejane.org. The Geena Davis Institute on Gender in Media tracks the portrayals of girls and women on film and works to reach more equality in those portrayals.

Target Women by Sarah Haskins. She made these episodes years ago, before moving on to movies, but they are still available online. Wonderful, informative, biting—these short videos break down the bullshit that consumer culture throws at us every day. Watch with the kids.

Movies

The Mask You Live In. By the documentarian Jennifer Siebel Newsom, it highlights the many ways boys and men are kept in a box of toxic masculinity. Consider this and *Miss Representation*, a fun, horrifying 101 class in how your boys and girls are raised by society.

Miss Representation. Cannot possibly recommend this one more. It highlights the sexisms that absolutely bombard girls and women, and boys and men, in our daily media.

13th. This documentary, directed by Ava DuVernay, traces how the sad lineage of slavery is alive and well today, an absolute must for viewing.

Hashtags

I have blind spots. Many. Far too many to count. Writing a book informs you of them fast, and for leaving out the struggles of far too many of our brothers and sisters, I am sorry.

If you don't read any of the books or listen to any of the podcasts or watch any of the movies, I implore you to do this:

Go on Twitter. Type in these hashtags and then . . . just listen.

Don't engage. Don't comment.

Just . . . listen.

Here's the deal. The #MeToo movement seemingly exploded in 2017, but its roots go deep—stretching back nearly to the very founding of social media.

For as long as we've had the collective ability to broadcast our every thought instantly to millions, women have been trying to tell us about the pervasiveness of rape culture.

It's everywhere.

If you think #MeToo is a surprise, you haven't been listening.

So, please, if nothing else, set aside an hour or two and take a stroll through some or all of these hashtags and just absorb. It'll change your life. And you in turn will change your children and your circles—for the better.

Twitter was founded in 2006.

In 2008, the **#fem2** hashtag emerged to purposefully raise more women's voices.

In 2010, **#mooreandme** called out men for endlessly giving sexual assailants the benefit of the doubt over legions of survivors in response to a statement by filmmaker Michael Moore.

In 2012, **#everydaysexism** exploded around the globe, offering an intimate portrait of the common objectification, abuse, and harassment girls and women face every single day in every possible situation.

Also in 2012, **#girlslikeus** called attention to transgender support and experiences; **#flushrushnow** dragged the radio host for calling a woman a "slut" because she was asking that reproductive health care be covered by insurance; and who can forget **#bindersfullofwomen** in response to a statement from presidential candidate Mitt Romney?

In 2013, **#notyourasiansidekick** called out sexist stereotypes of Asian Americans; **#blackgirlmagic** called out stereotypes of black girls and women and amplified their successes instead; **#solidarityisforwhitewomen** shined a light on the continuing problems of white feminism only seeing issues when they impact white women; and **#masculunitysofragile** called out the childlike fragility and anger of men who fear anything remotely labeled as feminine.

2014: **#whyistayed** highlighted the trauma and complications abuse survivors faced; **#youoksis** called out sexual street harassment or catcalling; **#rapecultureiswhen** sounds just as familiar today as it did then, because survivors of assault are always put under the gun first; and how can we forget **#yesallwomen,** which spotlighted the everyday harassment and abuse, yes, all women face.

2015: **#shoutyourabortion** reminded the world that women should have the say over their own bodies; **#hispanicgirlsunited** spotlighted the cultural roots of trends that are glorified for white celebrities and mocked for Hispanic women; and **#ilooklikeanengineer** called attention to the fact that, yes, women can do science.

2016: Following quickly on the idea that women can engineer, **#likealadydoc** reminded the world that women can be doctors as well; **#thingslongerthanbrockturnersrapesentence** shined a glaring spotlight on the fact that just 3 percent of rapists face prison time because we wouldn't want to "ruin" a rapist's life; **#nowomanever** called out, who could have guessed, everyday harassment and abuse women face; and how can we possibly overlook **#nastywoman,** which reminded everyone of the sexism of the president.

2017: **#shepersisted** heralded the start of a momentous year by showcasing how women are often silenced, even powerful senators; and here we are with **#metoo** in response to the decades of abuse that continues in every field and segment of society.

I'm finishing up this writing in 2018 because that's how this publishing process goes.

Have the hashtags stopped between then and now, when you're reading this? Or are there new ones, new everyday voices urging us to see atomized storylines and help stamp them out?

I'm guessing we all still have a lot of work to do.

Let's get to it.

MIKE ADAMICK is a stay-at-home dad. It's the best gig he's ever had. He's also a former journalist who has been writing about gender bias in childhood for more than a decade for such outlets as *Jezebel,* NPR, the *New York Times,* and the *San Francisco Chronicle.* When he's not busy writing or parenting, he likes to run, watch the Portland Thorns and Liverpool soccer clubs, and build stuff with his daughter. Mike and his wife, Dana, and daughter, Emmeline, live in San Francisco.